HERE'S TO SUCCESS!

SUCCESS!

Michael Korda

BALLANTINE BOOKS • NEW YORK

For James H. Silberman
—in gratitude for his enthusiasm

For Richard E. Snyder
—in friendship

And in memory of
Sir Alexander Korda
1893–1956

Copyright © 1977 by Success Research Corporation

The author wishes to thank the following sources for permission to quote material for this book:

The Association for Humanistic Psychology: Selections from "Levels of Existence: An Open System Theory of Values" by Dr. Clare Graves. Reprinted from *The Journal of Humanistic Psychology*. Copyright © 1970.

McKinsey and Company: Selections from "Profit Decline Shows Rise in Top Executive Pay" by George H. Foote. Reprinted from *The McKinsey Quarterly*. Copyright © 1976.

Matsushita Electric Industrial Company, Ltd.: for Selections from Matsushita Electric Corporate Advertisement. Copyright © 1976.

Schocken Books Inc.: *The Way of Response* by Martin Buber. Copyright © 1966. The Society of Authors on behalf of the Bernard Shaw Estate.

Ziff-Davis Publishing Co.: Selections from "Competition—The Star-Spangled Scramble" by Linden L. Nelson and Spencer Kagen. Reprinted from *Psychology Today*. Copyright © 1972.

Ziff-Davis Publishing Co.: Selections from "The Machiavellians Among Us" by Richard Christie. Reprinted from *Psychology Today*. Copyright © 1970.

Library of Congress Catalog Card Number: 77-5980

ISBN 0-345-31055-1

This edition published by arrangement with
Random House, Inc.

Manufactured in the United States of America

First Ballantine Books Edition: August 1978
Second Printing: November 1982

CONTENTS

Part 1: SUCCESS!

Part 2: How To Succeed

Part 3: The Meaning of Success

All the virtues and all the joys of living
are contained in one word—success.

Anatole de Laforge

PART 1

Success!

The Way to Success

The common idea that success spoils people by making them vain, egotistic, and self-complacent is erroneous; on the contrary it makes them, for the most part, humble, tolerant, and kind. Failure makes people bitter and cruel.

—W. Somerset Maugham

Anyone can be successful, and everybody wants to be. It is at once the most compelling and least complicated of ambitions. Much has been written in condemnation of "the American bitch-goddess,"[1] but I take the view that success is fulfillment, and that most people would rather succeed than fail—if only they knew how! So this book is intended to show you how to become a success. In it, we will meet a number of successful people, learn how they succeeded, and examine some of the rules—and the dangers—of success.

I won't pretend that you can succeed in business—or at anything else—without really trying. The truth is that you usually do have to try if you want to get ahead, but perhaps not quite as hard as you think. In any case, most people don't *mind* working hard to achieve success—their problem is that they work damned hard and never get anywhere. Though hard work is certainly an ingredient of success, it is not the only ingredient. If you're going to work at all, and most of us have to, you might just as well become rich, famous and successful in the process. The people who succeed do not as a rule work all that much harder than the people who fail, and in some cases very much less hard—they have simply mastered the rules of success.

You can too. Far from requiring great sacrifices, success comes most quickly to those who enjoy the process. To succeed, you have to learn to follow your natural instincts and appetites, to convince yourself, first of all, *that what you want is O.K.*

You should start out by not feeling guilty about what is a perfectly natural and healthy ambition. You have a right to succeed, and as you will see in reading this book, your chances of succeeding are probably just as good as anyone else's, and almost certainly better than you think they are. Before you read any further, stop and tell yourself:

- It's O.K. to be greedy.
- It's O.K. to be ambitious.
- It's O.K. to look out for Number One.
- It's O.K. to have a good time.
- It's O.K. to be Machiavellian (if you can get away with it).
- It's O.K. to recognize that honesty is not always the best policy (provided you don't go around saying so).
- It's O.K. to be a winner.
- And it's *always* O.K. to be rich.

A word of caution: people will tell you that success can't buy you happiness. This is true enough, but success is the next best thing to happiness, and if you can't be happy as a success, it's very unlikely that you would find a deeper, truer happiness in failure.

Defining Success

Others may ask how you define success. This is more difficult. Success is relative; not everybody wants to put together a four-billion-dollar conglomerate, or become President of the United States, or win the Nobel Peace Prize. It is usually a mistake to begin with such grandiose ambitions, which tend to degenerate into lazy daydreams. The best way to succeed is to begin with a reasonably realistic goal and attain it, rather than aiming at something so far beyond your reach that you are bound to fail. It's also important to make a habit of succeeding, and the easiest way to start is to succeed at something, however small, every day, gradually increasing the level of your ambitions and achievements like a runner in training, who begins with short distances and works up to Olympic levels.

Try to think of success as a journey, an adventure, not a specific destination. Your goals may change during the course of that journey, and your original ambitions may be superseded by different, larger ones. Success will certainly bring you the material things you want, and a good, healthy appetite for the comforts and luxuries of life is an excellent goad to success, but basically you'll know you have reached your goal when you have gone that one step further, in wealth, fame or achievement, than you ever dreamed was possible.

How you become a success is, of course, your business. Morality has very little to do with success. I do not personally think it is necessary to be dishonest, brutal or unethical in order to succeed, but a great many dishonest, brutal and unethical people in fact do succeed. You'd better be prepared for the fact that success is seldom won without some tough infighting along the way. A lot depends on your profession, of course. There is a great deal of difference between setting out to become a success in a Mafia family and trying to become vice president of a bank, but the differences simply consist of contrasting social customs and of what is the appropriate way to get ahead in a given profession or business. Whether you're hoping to take over a numbers game or an executive desk, you have to make the right moves for your circumstances. In the former example, you might have to kill someone; in the latter, you might only have to find ways of making your rivals look foolish or inefficient. In either case, you have to accept the rules of the game and play to win, or find some other game. This is a book about success, after all, not morality. The field you go into is your choice, but whatever it is, you're better off at the top of it than at the bottom.

Your Success Potential

You may feel that success is something that only happens to other people. Rest assured, it can happen to *you*. It's simple enough to analyze your success potential:

- Are you ambitious?
- Are you willing to work hard when you have to?
- Are you willing to put your interests first?
- Are you willing to take risks?
- Do you sincerely want to be rich?
- Have you got the guts to accept change?

If you can answer Yes to these questions, even with reservations, you have just as much motivation to succeed as any of the people you will meet in this book, and just as much of a chance to make it. It takes very little talent to succeed in most cases, but it is vitally important to use whatever you've got to the maximum degree, and not to overlook the slightest weapon in your armory. Never write off a talent or skill, however small: it may come in handy someday. There is a story that when the old Lord Rothschild, the head of the great banking family's English branch, was asked the secret of his success, he replied, "Sooner or later, in every man's life on the Stock Exchange, there comes a time when the turn of fortune rests on his ability to speak Yiddish." Your ethnic roots, your half-forgotten school lessons, your skill at sports, your hobbies, fantasies and interests—all these may seem unimportant in daily life. They may even be things you would go out of your way to conceal. But they form part of that special human being who is you. Each one of them, however obscure, may prove to be useful one day.

Invariably, we know far more than we think we know. We have simply decided that a large part of our accumulated knowledge is either useless or counterproductive. Successful people tap these reserves of knowledge, and consider nothing useless. And what they know well, they concentrate on and put to use.

Start today. Make an inventory of your skills and the things that you know how to do well. They provide the springboard for your success. Even the ability to add and subtract correctly is an asset, since half the businesses in the country are run by people who can do neither. Learn to think of your talents and skills as precious commodities, however limited they may seem. If you don't value them, you can hardly expect other people to.

The Success Profile

"You only have one life to live; you may as well live it as a success," said my friend Laurence, looking out from the back seat of his chauffeur-driven Cadillac limousine, silver-gray with a black top, TV set and radiophone, at people huddled in the rain around bus stops. Nor is he wrong. Success cannot insulate you from the major emotional and physical dangers of life, but it is generally more comfortable than failure. Almost everybody wants to succeed, but most people are held back by the fear that they haven't got what it takes. Such fears are unrealistic. Don't forget: *Desire, determination* and a *good sense of timing* are the common denominators of success, of far more importance than any other factors.

Not that there *aren't* other factors . . .

- FAMILY BACKGROUND

It helps to have been born in that quarter of the nation's families headed by someone with a college degree.

Success comes easily to those lucky few who are in fact the boss's son, and those who have been sired by the head of a corporation have a remarkably good statistical chance of succeeding him even today. The emotional problems of inheriting success, however, are great enough to have spawned an organization called "S. O. B. International," which attempts to provide career and family guidance to the disturbed "sons of bosses." [2]

- GEOGRAPHICAL FACTOR

It is slightly better to have been born in the Midwestern United States. Forty percent of the country's top five hundred executives were born there, although it accounts for less than 27 percent of the total population. California provides an increasingly large statistical percentage of successful people, and the so-called "Sunshine Belt" is not far behind.[3] The successful person has usually attended college, but has not done any postgraduate studies. He or she takes three weeks of vacation a year, and works between 45 and 64 hours a week, the success median being 54 hours. Over 50 percent of successful people are the children of upper-middle-class and -income business executives.

- JOB PREFERENCE

It is astonishingly better to stick with one company than to change jobs. Nearly 40 percent of top executives stuck with their original company, and over 80 percent of them attribute their success to "long experi-

CHANGES IN CHIEF EXECUTIVE COMPENSATION, PROFITS
AND SALES *

Percentage increase (decrease)

Industry	Compensation	Profits	Sales
Household appliances	13.7	37.4	(1.1)
Food products	13.1	15.5	10.7
Soaps and cosmetics	12.6	11.1	15.7
Apparel	12.4	9.8	5.0
Meat products	11.6	(17.2)	0.8
Machinery and equipment	10.3	10.6	11.7
Retail food chains	9.1	246.1a	8.8
Alcoholic beverages	8.7	(15.0)	6.7
Tobacco	8.3	13.7	31.2
Pharmaceutical	7.9	8.4	11.5
Electrical and electronic equipment	7.8	(0.4)	2.6
Instruments & scientific equipment	7.7	6.5	6.2
Retail trade	7.7	25.5	9.4
Life insurance companies	7.0	b	7.0c
Commercial banks	6.9	12.4d	3.1e
Office machines	6.1	9.2	12.5
Diversified companies	5.8	(11.1)	3.8
Aircraft and parts	5.8	(3.2)	8.0
All industries	5.3	(10.5)f	5.5f
Motor vehicles and equipment	5.1	(1.1)	7.4
Petroleum	4.8	(24.4)	6.4
Building products	4.6	(0.9)	(1.5)
Utilities, electric and gas	4.1	12.0	17.9
Paper and allied products	3.7	(19.3)	(3.6)
Railroad transportation	2.9	(20.7)	0.5
Chemicals	0.9	(9.5)	4.0
Fabricated metal products	(1.4)	(13.5)	(1.1)
Iron and steel	(4.0)	(33.9)	(11.7)
Air transportation	(4.3)	(134.8)	4.5
Rubber and plastic products	(6.2)	(11.7)	2.3
Textiles	(7.1)	(59.8)	(8.0)
Nonferrous metals	(7.8)	(52.8)	(19.8)

* The McKinsey Quarterly, Autumn 1976.
a When Great Atlantic and Pacific Tea is excluded from this industry group, profits show only a 39.9 percent increase
b Data not comparable
c Percentage increase in insurance in force
d Percentage increase in income before security transactions
e Percentage increase in total deposits
f Averages in these columns exclude the banking and insurance industries

ence in their present company," and strongly feel that "loyalty counts."

Your choice of the profession in which to succeed depends a great deal on what you want to do and on what your qualifications are. It may be interesting to note from the chart below that certain industries reward success better than others. It is more important to note that *the pay of major executives tends to rise even when profits decrease*. Here is an analysis by industry:

● Religious Preference

Although Episcopalians represent a very small percentage of the national population, they represent over 20 percent of the nation's successful executives, with Presbyterians, Congregationalists, Methodists and Jews just behind. Baptists and Roman Catholics are underrepresented in percentage terms among the success élite, as are people who have majored in the humanities, the social sciences, education and the physical sciences.

● Upbringing

It is an advantage to have been born in a small, nonauthoritarian family, in which your mother's education was roughly equivalent to your father's, and to have been the firstborn child. "Intelligence," it has been determined, "declines with family size; the fewer children in your family, the smarter you are likely to be . . . Intelligence also declines with birth order [and] the fewer older brothers or sisters you have, the brighter you are likely to be." [4]

● Age

However it's acquired, success seems to be occurring earlier in life than it used to. Thirty-five to forty-four is now the period at which a person starts to be a success or probably is never going to be. The bulk of successful people fall into the forty-five to fifty-nine

age group, and maximum earnings power is commonly
reached at fifty.

Evaluating Your Own Success Profile

The fact that you *don't* fit into this profile need not
prevent you from succeeding. As we shall see, many
successful people don't fit into these statistical general-
ities at all. But it is helpful to recognize that there *is* a
success background and type, and that the odds
against you are slightly higher if yours doesn't match.
This means you will have to work harder and develop
your faculties more fully if you're going to win. (Of
course, you can always turn yourself into an Episcopa-
lian, Midwestern first-born son of upper-middle-
income parents—a transformation which a great many
people have already attempted, some with considerable success—by simply changing your name.)

The basic attributes of success are not, of course,
statistical, but psychological. Clare Graves, Professor
of Psychology at Union College, has developed a
structure of "value systems," which neatly categorizes
the different levels at which most people work. They
look like this:

"A SYSTEM OF WORK VALUES

To understand and cope with the differences in
values among workers, a framework is helpful. The
following structure of value systems has been useful
to our research and to practical studies. It assumes
that human beings exist at different psychological
levels and that these levels find expression in the
values the individuals give to many aspects of life,
including work.

System 1—Reactive. At this level of existence values
are absent. It characterizes infants and individuals
with serious brain deterioration, and therefore is not
likely to be applicable to employees.

System 2—Tribalistic. At this stage the individual derives his values from another (his chieftain), such as his father or his boss. He values highly routine work, friendly autocratic supervision and a compatible work group (tribe).

System 3—Egocentric. This describes rugged individuals who are usually tough and aggressive. They are likely to take any job so long as they get the money they want. They need and respect a boss who is tough—that is, who controls his employees closely.

System 4—Conformist. The employee at this level exhibits the rather traditional traits of loyalty, hard work and attentiveness to duty. He prefers to work in a place where structure, policy and procedure are clearly defined, and where supervision is consistent.

System 5—Manipulative. Materialism, activity, goals, achievement and advancement are valued by the employee at this level. He likes work that lets him "wheel and deal," and a boss who understands company politics.

System 6—Sociocentric. People count more than situations for employees with sociocentric values. Harmony in the work group, friendly supervision, and equality for mankind are important to them.

System 7—Existential. The individual at this level likes work that allows for freedom and creativity, and a job with open structure. Money and advancement are less important than challenge and an opportunity to learn and grow." *

It ought to be obvious to you that these different "values" also represent the different *qualities* needed

* Clare Graves, "Levels of Existence: an Open System Theory of Values," *Journal of Humanistic Psychology,* Fall 1970, by permission.

for success, except for number one. It is necessary to have a *tribalistic* respect for the organization in which you work, but it must be balanced by a degree of *egocentricity,* for after all, you have to look out for yourself. An element of conformity is usually called for, but the *existential* ability to handle creativity and freedom is equally important. You can go a long way by being *manipulative,* but unless you have *sociocentric* ability to care for your fellow employees or subordinates, you are not likely to reach the upper levels of management, or stay there.

If you examine these seven "value systems" you will quickly be able to categorize many of the people you know. Most of your fellow workers are essentially tribalistic or conformist. And who does not have, within his or her organization, an egocentric or a manipulative personality on the prowl? Note that certain of these characteristics are passive while others are positive, implying action:

PASSIVE	ACTIVE
(2) TRIBALISTIC $\longleftrightarrow$	(3) EGOCENTRIC
(4) CONFORMIST $\longleftrightarrow$	(7) EXISTENTIAL
(5) SOCIOCENTRIC $\longleftrightarrow$	(6) MANIPULATIVE

You will also note that these values have been paired as *opposites.* To achieve success, you must effectively learn how to combine opposite values in the required "mix" for a given situation. The *passive* qualities, on the left, are those you must display to survive in any organization, and are essentially self-protective, serving to disguise or modify your adherence to those more *active* values on the right. Thus, an egocentric act (reaching out for a portion of somebody else's responsibility or territory) ought to be preceded or covered by a display of tribalistic loyalty (indicating that you are only doing it for the good of the company). Similarly, a manipulative move (persuading your boss that his or her career will be furthered by giving you a better title) must be accompanied by a sociocentric gesture (going out of your way to teach the ropes to a new employee who might eventually pose a threat to you).

Remember these points in building your career:

(1) Although your company may require a certain degree of conformity (most do), have you been conforming so much (i.e., ignoring your existential quotient) that you have simply faded into the woodwork?

(2) Are you such a company man/woman (i.e., tribalistic) that you are assumed to be devoid of egocentric ambitions?

(3) Leaders are positive and active (that is, egocentric, existential and manipulative), but also know how to pay their dues in terms of tribalism, conformism and sociocentricity. This is to say that your personal ambition, however strong, must always appear to others in the guise of loyalty to your company, your department and your colleagues.

In short, once you have analyzed the basic components of the success-oriented personality, you can begin to assess your success strengths and weaknesses, and build the proper "mix" of values for your particular work situation. You must understand that some people are born with a fortunate personality that combines the necessary values naturally. These are the people who seem to succeed effortlessly, assuming they pick the right kind of job.

Once you have assessed your own basic values, you may find that you are the proverbial square peg in a round hole. If, for example, you are by nature *tribalistic, conformist* and *sociocentric,* you might do well in an organization like IBM, which sets a premium on group work, team spirit and conformity, while you might be hopelessly handicapped at the same job in a corporation which favors *egocentric, existential* and *manipulative* behavior, that is, cutthroat office politics.

If you *don't* want to change jobs, but feel your success values are unsuited to the place you work, start changing them—fast. Remember that the passive values can be used to screen and conceal the active ones, and that this concealment serves a useful social and business function, since a display of naked ambition is likely to frighten your inferiors and irritate if not antagonize your superiors.

PLAY FOR NUMBER ONE

The fastest way to succeed is to look as if you're playing by other people's rules, while quietly playing by your own.

Loyalty is vital for success, but by no means simple to demonstrate. Nobody *expects* you to be 100 percent loyal at heart, but it is one of those values that must be publicly displayed if you're going to get ahead. You have to show loyalty to your subordinates (even if you don't feel it), loyalty to your superiors (even if you're trying to unseat them) and loyalty to the organization (which is the ultimate justification for doing whatever you want to do). Displays of loyalty win respect, and the more you espouse the passive qualities, the more likely you are to succeed with active ones. Any overt hint of disloyalty will eventually hinder your chances of succeeding. Nobody minds ruthless, egocentric careerism and self-interest, provided they are suitably screened. If you can undermine your boss and replace him, fine, do so, *but never express anything but respect and loyalty for him while you're doing it*. If you're caught out at it, justify your actions by claiming that you had the greater good of the company, or department, at heart. An ounce of hypocrisy is worth a pound of ambition.

The Responsibility Factor

Second only to loyalty is the ability to take on responsibility. Success on any major scale *requires* you to accept responsibility. You have to assume all the problems, difficulties and doubts of other people, and to reflect back your capacity for decision-making and action, and for enduring without visible signs of worry or panic. "Grace under pressure," as John F. Kennedy was so fond of saying, is indeed a definition of success, whether it's on the battlefield or in the office. In the final analysis, the one quality that all successful people have (and which is the most difficult one of all to learn or fake) is the ability to take on responsibility.

It is easy to be responsible for things you control and are sure of; but to be successful you must make yourself responsible for the blunders of the people who work for you as well. Responsibility requires a highly developed ego and a good deal of courage, but it is ultimately the one test you cannot afford to fail. You must be willing to accept *personal* responsibility, for the success of your assignments, for the actions of the people who work for you and for the goals you have accepted or been given.

Lion or Fox?

Some people—the lucky ones—thrive on responsibility. Successful people are easily divided, in fact, into two groups, the lions and the foxes, a distinction cleverly made by Michael Maccoby in *The Gamesman.*[5] The lions are natural leaders, responsible, powerful, aggressive and courageous, and confidently at ease in the ways of their group. The foxes are cunning, sly, quick and usually rather poor at group thinking, though they may have to feign a respect for the group. At the very highest levels, men sometimes combine the virtues of the lion and the fox to some degree. For convenience, one can examine the characters of recent Presidents in this light:

Franklin D. Roosevelt: A lion in his courage and his powerful ambition, he was also cunning, sly and secretive—all foxlike traits—and the combination made him a formidable President . . .

Harry S. Truman: A lion, Truman was eager to accept responsibility (as indicated in his famous phrase "The buck stops here"), courageous enough to openly fire General Douglas MacArthur (a more foxlike man would have avoided a confrontation) and after a lifetime in Congress, at ease in the give-and-take of a group . . .

Dwight D. Eisenhower: Another lion, Eisenhower was a natural leader, very conscious of his responsibility and in no way awed or frightened by it . . .

John F. Kennedy: A lion in the making, he nonetheless had certain foxlike characteristics of cunning, caution and fear of groups . . . (Robert Kennedy was a man with all the characteristics of a fox who turned himself into a lion when he came out against the Vietnam war, and finally determined to run for the Presidency.)

Lyndon B. Johnson: A fox who failed to turn himself into a lion. Although it was his life's ambition to be a lion, cunning, caution and the desire to evade responsibility prevented his emergence as a true lion. He nevertheless pretended to be one to the very end . . .

Richard Nixon: All fox, Nixon was hardly even able to put on a show of lion-like qualities . . .

Gerald Ford: A lion, not a very bright or strong one, perhaps, but a lion all the same, rather reminiscent of Bert Lahr's performance as a lion in *The Wizard of Oz* . . .

The lions are *natural* responsibility takers; the foxes attempt to achieve success without taking on any more responsibility than they have to. The lions move directly, the foxes indirectly. The lions take stands, the foxes make compromises. Ultimately the ambition of every fox is to become a lion, and the secret of every successful person is to combine both qualities in *the right proportions*.

Lion or fox, you will sooner or later have to accept responsibility if you're going to be a success. If you're a born lion, it's no problem: you crave responsibility and aren't afraid of it. Your only fear is that you won't get enough, that you may have to share it or have it circumscribed. When you get a promotion, you look for the maximum amount of autonomy and try to enlarge the area of your responsibilities.

Most people avoid responsibility (thereby restricting themselves to menial jobs), or approach a new and more important position by attempting to limit their area of responsibility and spread the decision-making process among as many people as possible. If your first question on getting a promotion is "Who do I go to for a final decision?" you need training in being a lion. Your aim should be to take on as much responsibility as you can handle—you will quickly find out for yourself what the limits are when you run into conflict with your colleagues.

"Nothing Succeeds Like Excess"

Sometimes, instead of waiting for responsibility to be delegated to you, you can simply seize it—except in the most arteriosclerotic and hierarchical of organizations, like the civil service. In one large company I know, there was a strict rule that only a corporate vice-president could sign certain forms such as vouchers for checks, contract authorizations and personnel changes. When a friend of mine went to work there, he observed that his fellow executives scrupulously observed this protocol, and decided to ignore it himself. He signed everything he wanted to sign, with the final touch of a rubber stamp that read "authorized." He was not surprised to find that nobody noticed or objected to his assumption of what had hitherto been a zealously protected special responsibility. Everybody assumed that my friend had been given some special authorization to do so. His fellow executives were soon *bringing* him things to sign for them, though they were equal to him in status, title and authority, and before long he was being discussed in higher management as a young man to be watched and groomed for leadership.

"Nothing succeeds like excess," he says now, having achieved the vice-presidency himself. "You've always got to work on the assumption that you have a right to do anything you want to, and act on it. Never ask, because the chances are that somebody will say no. If you want an expense account, don't *ask* for one, go out and spend, then put the vouchers through. Always act directly."

A Mini-Course in Self-Esteem

If taking on responsibility is hard for you, then you will have to train yourself to do so. The best way is to give yourself a daily course in self-esteem. It is no good saying, as people are taught to do in EST seminars, "I am nothing." In order to be responsible—and successful—you must believe you are something—in fact, that you are *terrific!*

Make a list of your positive qualities and concentrate on them. Forget the negative ones. Write down whatever seems to you a positive quality that might apply to your career. For example:

- Loyalty
- Willingness to work hard
- Honesty
- Diligence

Write this list on a piece of paper and carry it with

you. Refer to it whenever you're in doubt, or whenever other people seem, somehow, to have more going for them than you do. Remember: *They don't!* You are unique, and you have your own values.

Your Ego is O.K.

Think about these qualities, remember them, forget the negative ones (which might be, for example, lack of ambition, fear of responsibility, too much respect for other people's feelings), and tell yourself that your positive qualities are surely worthwhile, and can be put to better use. Don't worry about the values you *don't* have. Concentrate on the ones you *do* have, and put them to work for you. Don't be afraid to develop a healthy ego! Use the qualities you already have to give you the self-confidence that will enable you to reach for responsibility—and success.

Remember: *the person who takes the responsibility usually gets the credit and the reward.*

Much of what looks like mere ego and self-aggrandizement in successful people is in fact a genuine desire for responsibility being carried forward to larger and larger arenas. Such people thrive on responsibility, particularly at the upper levels of management, because they have convinced themselves that they are just better equipped than most people to make decisions. What may seem to be raw ambition is not always that simple: successful people genuinely *want* to take on larger responsibilities and genuinely enjoy making decisions for other people, and experience a real need to enlarge their capacity for responsibility to the maximum degree.

To achieve this you must be convinced of your own worth. You need self-respect to be truly responsible—not egomania, which is a form of self-delusion in which you persuade yourself that you are *better* than other people—but a solid respect for your own special qualities and competences, without reference to those of others.

It is fear of *yourself* that holds you back from assuming responsibility, not fear of others. It is the fear that the child in you is still stronger than the adult you have become. The child wants to be protected, guided, forgiven and loved, and willingly or unwillingly accepts the fact that other, older people are responsible for major areas of his life. Even as an adult, you can easily seek out surrogate parents, older siblings or teachers, and attempt to make *them* responsible for yourself, as your parents once were. But it is an illusion in adults, and a self-limiting one.

Remember: *Responsibility is the keystone to success and self-realization, and the only way to become autonomous.*

You are Already a Responsible Person

It may be helpful to record every day the responsibilities you have taken on, and the ones you have avoided and are afraid of. Analyze them carefully. Why are you afraid of them? Is it the sensible fear that you may be taking on responsibility for something you don't understand or aren't equipped to handle, or simply the fear of being exposed, even though it's in an area where you are perfectly competent and knowledgeable?

Write down the things you are *involuntarily* responsible for. Consider this list. You may already be responsible for

- supporting your family;
- your children's welfare and behavior until they reach twenty-one;
- obeying laws you may never have heard of;
- paying taxes;
- damage you may do quite accidentally;

- things you may say (libel, defamation and slander);
- things you may not say (failure to warn somebody of an impending danger can render you liable).

The list of your responsibilities is endless, and yet you fulfill them, like most of us, without too much thought or trouble. So why worry about taking on a little additional responsibility at work, particularly when it pays off in terms of success like nothing else can? Remember this rule: *There is no way to succeed without exposing yourself to risk.*

LAURENCE W. PRINCE: PORTRAIT OF A LEADER

"Don't talk to me about our glorious leader, goddammit! I'm your glorious leader now!"
—Laurence W. Prince

Laurence W. Prince exemplifies the principles of leadership and career building to an extraordinary degree. Enormously ambitious, at thirty-five he has reached the top by taking over the presidency of a major motion picture corporation.

Larry, as he was then known, came into the movie business almost by accident. He had always presumed that he would go into his father's business. But when he came out of the Navy his father gave him a hundred dollars and told him, "I'd much rather have a son than a partner." Larry, who had been looking forward to settling into a comfortable job in the family business, soon found himself standing on Sixth Avenue with a friend wondering what to do. The friend was on his way to a job interview in the promotion department of a major movie company. Larry went along with him and took the interview too. He got the job, and his friend didn't.

"I just realized," he said, looking back, "that I had to have that job. I didn't know anything about movies, but I didn't figure that mattered. You can always learn about a business once you're *in* it."

Larry, in those days, was hardly a commanding presence or an instant leader. But he had physical vitality, enormous energy and an undiluted capacity for hard work and factual information. From the very beginning, he asked questions, and kept asking them until he had the answers that satisfied him. He was astonished to find that the corporation was run on assumptions rather than facts, from the top to the bottom. Forty years of habit had persuaded the management that the movies *ought* to make money, and if they didn't, then it was somebody else's fault.

The management was controlled by the elderly president and chairman of the board and majority stockholder, who ruled by the policy of divide and conquer. The major executives were given enormous privileges and encouraged to stay within their mutually hostile empires. It was a $200,000,000-a-year business run with no one in charge, and with no clearly defined structure of responsibility. The head of the West Coast television production never talked to the head of the movie production, though they were in the same building in North Hollywood, and even went to the trouble of having the doorways between the two departments sealed up with brick and plaster. Neither of them reported to anybody but the chairman of the board himself, and he no longer had either the time or the energy to control their activities. The promotion and advertising department was run as an independent fiefdom, preparing plans for movies that had already been canceled and scheduling millions of dollars of advertising without any information from the people who were in fact making the product, or failing to.

Larry quickly realized that the major problem of the corporation was not stupidity or venality—business can survive that—but the simple fact that nobody was responsible for anything, and that even those few executives who *wanted* to do a good job could find no one to encourage or lead them. In short, there was no leadership.

Since the corporation's policy was to avoid change at all costs, and to prevent questions from being asked, even the most minor attempt to promote efficiency and sensible management was likely to mark one out as a troublemaker. Larry therefore very sensibly played on the essential laziness of his superiors. Energetic, intelligent and adaptable, he fought for the promotion department at every possible opportunity, convincing his department head that here was a new, loyal recruit to his faction in the corporation's internecine wars.

Larry also relished responsibility. He gradually made himself so useful, simply by knowing more about the department than anyone else, that people began to bring him their problems, which he energetically solved. Soon he became the department head's assistant.

In this company there was a long tradition of after-hours drinking. Whereas others had gone along to conform to the habits of the department head (who had created not a few alcoholics in his time), Larry put these sessions to good use. He got to know his colleagues, and developed a small group of discontented activists who looked to him as their leader and spokesman. At the same time, he maintained a cordial relationship with his superiors, deliberately going out of his way not to frighten them.

Soon he had established what amounted to an alternative system of management, which, somewhat embarrassingly, *worked*. Despite lack of incentive or direction from the top, the department was operating efficiently. And the more efficient it became, the more evident it was that its own boss was a hopeless nonentity.

As for Larry, he was well aware of the fact that everybody above him, including the chairman, wanted to see him fail. His success, even on a minor scale in one department, threatened a change, and any change could only lead to disaster for a group of senior executives who had been systematically ignoring the corporation's best interests for twenty years.

"That was when I grew up fast," he said. "When I realized that people don't *want* you to succeed. It's a paradox. When you're in school everybody orients you to succeed—your parents, your teachers, everybody. But once you're out in the real world, you have to learn self-motivation, because your success threatens everyone. Your father wants you to do well, sure. But *better* than he has? Not necessarily. Your wife wants the charge accounts and the vacations in Acapulco, or whatever, but she also wants you home more. Your kids want to see more of you. And in most companies, your ambition gets in the way of other people. Every time I did something new and good, I stirred up real hate. So what I did was to pick out the people who had potential and to show that I was willing to fight for them. After all, they had nothing to lose. I used my position to go out into other departments and meet the people who were bright and ambitious there. I let my boss think that I was acquiring information for him to use against his rivals. And in a sense I was, but in the process I picked out the people who wanted to work and had something going for them. And I went to meetings. Christ, did I go to meetings! Dull meetings, pointless meetings—if there was a meeting, I found a reason to go—until I'd met just about everybody in the company. Unless you're some kind of genius, you can't make it alone, and you can't make it against everyone. God knows, it's easier if your superiors are for you, but that's not often the case, and it wasn't for me. So what you do is to create your own backers and supporters, however far down the line they are. *They* have to want to see you succeed as much as *you* want to!"

Larry was disdainful of titles: proximity to power interested him more. Thus, when he could have taken a vice presidency, he chose instead to become assistant to the president, a task which had hitherto been menial. Using his influence he was able to get vice presidencies and raises for some of those who were "on his side," even though this put them temporarily ahead of him in the hierarchy. Looking back on that, he says, "You don't get to be president of a company by faithfully going up through every promotion. Life is too short for that, and anyway it doesn't work that way. You get there by leapfrogging, by keeping your eye on the ultimate goal."

By the time Larry had spent a year as the president's assistant (a year of humiliation, hard work and tension, for the president still resented his success), he was ready. All that was needed was a crisis to give him the position he wanted. The crisis was in the making. The company had plunged more than $20 million into a movie which was running far behind schedule and far over budget. As director succeeded director, and as the star's illnesses and misadventures filled the press, the bankers took stock and decided to insure their investment. Bad management is tolerated so long as it provides a profit and doesn't need to borrow too much money. But when it has to go, hat in hand, to look for cash, it is doomed.

Larry had the essential quality for success: a sense of timing. Although there had been previous crises, he had ignored them, simply because he wasn't in a position to take advantage of them. Now he was. Wisely, he consulted with his friends and obtained a consensus. As the meetings dragged on with the bankers, he allowed the management of the company to prove its incompetence. Then, taking aside one of the younger financial men, he told him the time had come for change.

"He knew it, they knew it, I knew it," he said. "But nobody had spoken the words, and the first one who does gets credit for it. I knew the first instinct of the bankers would be to bring in new management to clean house, and the important thing was to let them find out for themselves how bad things were. If I had told them, they would have thought me disloyal. Then I knew I had to suggest that there was an *existing* alternative, that they didn't have to go outside. It's the moment of truth, and you have to seize it and go for broke, and I did."

Larry moved quickly, a move made easier by the facts that he had supporters in the company and that he had no real title or management position. He was therefore not implicated in the disasters that had brought the company down or stuck in its hierarchy. In moments of corporate crisis, those who have imposing corporate titles are almost automatically excluded from consideration—promoting them is difficult because they have usually reached their present positions by balancing off against other executives, and therefore have too many commitments and debts to just those people who will either resent their advancement or are, very likely, the cause of the problem in the first place. The total picture shows that Larry's view of success was a generous and a responsible one. He wanted it for himself, of course, but he also saw it as linked to the success of other people, and to the ultimate test of the company's success.

Now the motion picture company is the heart of a growing conglomerate, and Larry has not only "turned it around," but is clearly on his way up even further. A Lockheed Jetstar II waits for him when he needs to fly to the Coast, and a limousine is at his disposal twenty-four hours a day. Money is a meaningless concept, so much so that he never carries any, which is the ultimate mark of success. What could he buy, after all? His secretary places a pack of cigarettes on his desk every morning next to his coffee. The newspapers are ready in the back seat of the limousine that picks him up. After lunching in his private dining room, where a French chef prepares low-calorie foods, he can exercise in his own squash court. Wherever he goes, the bill never appears: it is sent on to his office, with the appropriate tip added—he doesn't even have to *sign* any more, let alone pay.

"You have to want success more than anything else," he says, "and you have to begin right where you are. You can't say, Well, I'd be a success in some other job. I never wanted to be in the movie business —in fact, I never even *thought* about it. But once I was in it, I decided I could succeed at this just as well as at anything else. You don't win at Vegas by switching from table to table trying to find one you can win at. You sit down and play. To succeed, you have to sit down and play, right where you are, right *now*.

"And the most important thing is to know when you're being offered a chance, and take it. People get chances thrown at them every day, and don't even notice it's happening. Your boss is out and the president calls. You take the call, and show him that you can answer questions he has about the department. Or, for instance, there's a lot of statistical drudge work to be done, and nobody wants to do it. You take it over, and in the process you learn something about cash flow, or pensions, or hiring practices, or whatever. You go to a sales convention, and instead of screwing around and drinking, you listen to people, and find out what makes the salesmen tick, what motivates *them*. Success is just an accelerated learning process, a form of growth. You learn from everything, even the moments of failure, but you *stay in the game*, you never give up."

An assistant comes into the huge white office, with its tapestries by Jan Yoors glowing in primary colors against the walls, the Empire table desk with a Call-Director Speakerphone on the red-leather top, the spectacular view of the skyline beyond the park. Larry takes a piece of paper from the man's hand, examines it, leans back in the traditional success recline, and says, "Jim, it's terrific, really exciting, but I don't know . . . I don't think it's the best you can do with this. I think you're holding back on yourself . . . Go back and think about it and see if you can find what's wrong." He hands the piece of paper back with a grin, holding it between thumb and forefinger as if it were contaminated.

"I learned that, too," he says as the door closes behind Jim. "Keep people on their toes; don't overpraise. Most people can do better than they *think* they can, and the better they are, the more you have to keep them on the ball. It's hard for some people to learn, *but you can always do better!* When I'm satisfied—100 percent satisfied—that I'm doing the best I can do, it'll be time for me to get the hell out and let someone else take over."

Larry moves to the window and looks at the view. It is well past seven at night, and the huge buildings are all lit up—thousands and thousands of windows, more than anyone could even begin to count. The buildings themselves are dazzling monuments to success: the Seagram building, a tribute to Bronfman, who built up a vast empire starting as a liquor distributor; the Revlon building, Revson's grandiose tribute to himself; the G&W building, placed by Charles Bluhdorn to rise above the park, the towering symbol of one man's epic and single-handed creation of a four-billion-dollar-a-year conglomerate; the CBS building, the powerful monument to Paley's drive to succeed (known in the industry as "Black Rock" both because of its granite exterior and its reputation as a place where executives shoot it out with each other for promotion); and the Olympic Tower, which Onassis placed to loom over St. Patrick's Cathedral and Rockefeller Center, the last, daring achievement of an adventurer who not only won the American princess but seized the most expensive site on Fifth Avenue to immortalize his success.

Larry looks out at the blaze of lights. One day he too will have *his* building. Why not? It is not money that interests him—he has always known he could earn money. It is success, growth, achievement, a mark to be measured by. Already he is taking an interest in architecture—expensive architectural books and magazines are scattered on his coffee table, the huge tapestries on his walls are a new departure for a man whose office was only recently decorated with posters and photographs of his own children. "I love to look at this view," he says. "It's beautiful at this time of night."

With a sigh, Larry brushes back his blond hair, which is just beginning to turn gray. He picks up a brief case full of file folders and puts a stack of them on his desk. "Now, get the hell out of here," he says with a cheerful grin, a man about to return to what he enjoys, "I've got to get back to work."

How to Be a Leader

Larry was a first-class candidate for success because along with his foxlike attributes, he is, of course, a lion, a natural responsibility seeker. His story contains many valuable lessons, not the least of which is that it is sometimes much easier to succeed in a badly run, failing company than to take the safer step of going to work for a successful organization. Beyond this, Larry exemplifies the importance of leadership as a success quality. You can learn from his example:

- *Ask* questions. Leadership is often a matter of self-motivation. Don't wait for your boss to take the initiative. You will often find yourself in situations where *no one* wants you to succeed.
- *Listen* to other people's problems. There's nothing a born leader likes more than hearing about the problems of his colleagues and subordinates. This will help you understand their motivations and how you can link their own ambitions with your personal goals.
- *Deliver* what you promise. Very few people succeed without allies, and to have allies you must have something to offer them. If, like Larry, you can make people believe that their own careers are dependent on you, you will have multiplied your success potential.

Beating the Organization

Note that Larry succeeded in a company that was on the verge of failure. Companies in crisis are frequently good places to succeed, because there is a great deal of chaos and a real need for new talent, which an ambitious, clever person can put to good use. If you want to get ahead fast, pick a company that is in trouble, but which has a product or service that ought to be profitable if there were new management. Big successful companies are a safe choice for the unambitious, but doubtful for the success-minded. Small, family-owned companies are just as bad, since the ambitions of a newcomer are almost certain to conflict with the interests of the ownership family.

Unfortunately, it is usually just those qualities that lead to success that are most distrusted in American corporate life, which still sets too high a value on conformity. Very few organizations are designed to fulfill *your* success needs; most of them, in fact, seem to be designed to deliberately thwart them. This being the case, remember: You can never go through an obstacle, you can only go around it, climb over it or turn it to your advantage:

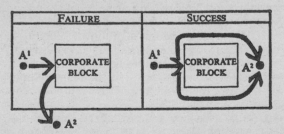

Hitting your head against a stone wall is a waste of time and energy, a fact which surprisingly few people ever learn. There is just as little reason to believe (as so many young people do) that any organization is likely to set up a clearly defined, step-by-step path toward success for its employees. On the contrary, the organization is far more likely to block your success in every possible way, both because those who have already succeeded need you coming up behind them like a hole in the head, and because there is an implicit corporate belief in the survival of those with the most patience and ability to conform. As a result, the path to organizational success is usually more in the nature of an obstacle course, designed to eliminate the maximum number of people and discourage all but the most determined. There is no easy ascent up the ladder of success—the way is more likely to be through a maze or a battlefield:

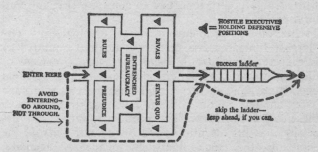

Note that entering the maze can consume a tremendous amount of time, and that your chances of emerging at the other end intact are slim. Also note that once you have emerged unscathed (more or less) on the other side, the climb up the success ladder begins —if you can make it through the maze at the lower and middle levels of any corporation, you are very likely to find the further ascent very much easier. It is more of an escalator than a ladder, in fact. Once the long, bitter struggle of making it through the first phase of your career is over, your promotion in this kind of organization is sure, although *slow,* and may well carry you inexorably up the levels of middle management to the point where your interest in the company (and its interest in you) peters out, and you remain static while waiting for retirement or a seat on the management committee (the two are often synonymous).

The key to success in a large corporation or organization of this kind is the ability to *outflank the obstacles,* as Larry did. Successful people know how to *retreat,* examine an obstacle and find a way around it, even in the most conformist organizations—*especially* there, in fact. They try to find a place for themselves in which their job function, position and responsibility are difficult to define, seeking out the jobs that bridge the divisions between departments. If nobody can find the right place to put you on the organization chart, you're ahead of the game. The more people there are who assume you're reporting to someone else, the better for you.

One of the problems of large organizations (by "large," I mean more than five hundred employees) is that very few people have a realistic overview of the organization itself. To some extent, management encourages this, on the grounds that most people have quite enough to do without involving themselves in these larger problems. The president himself, by necessity, has his attention fixed on matters *outside* the company—the stockholders, the regulatory agencies, the press, the unions, the outside directors, the banks, etc.—and the senior executives are usually division or department heads, who may be actively discouraged from getting involved in matters outside their immediate area of responsibility, or simply reluctant to tread on their colleagues' toes by showing too much intramural curiosity. Consequently, the only person who really knows the organization thoroughly may be the executive vice-president, and since he is usually concerned with corporate administration and finance, he may have no idea of the operations involved.

In many companies, whole departments and divisions have continued to function for years at the edges of the organization, in almost complete isolation from the rest of the company. In one case, when a major communications company was purchased by a conglomerate after protracted negotiations, it was discovered that the company owned at least two operations that nobody but the president and the executive vice-president had ever heard about—and both of *them* had forgotten their existence until an auditor for the acquiring conglomerate discovered them in the recesses of the balance sheet. One was an operation manufacturing plastic wrappings and cartons for a product the company no longer made; the other was a shipping and warehousing service that seemed to have no function at all.

The surest way of avoiding the obstacle course of slow promotion in a large organization is to become the one key person who has a clear picture of the whole. You may be earning only $15,000 a year as a very junior executive trainee, but if you have a real knowledge of the company's overall activities and how they're related, you will know more than most of the senior executives earning over $50,000, many of whom will have become imprisoned in their departments and blind to anything beyond. In such a position you, like Larry, will eventually meet your opportunity. Of course, you must also know how to seize it.

RAY KROC:
NEVER SAY NO TO OPPORTUNITY!

Other things help: Hard work, the ability to seize the right moment, courage, the willingness to learn from failure, the belief in success as the American dream, as one's right and obligation—these are the common denominators of successful people. Look at Ray Kroc, who built a single California hamburger stand into a personal fortune of $500 million, and made McDonald's a world-wide success story. His Grumman jet cost $4.5 million and seats 17, his 72-foot yacht is anchored near a magnificent house (with

a doorbell that plays "You Deserve a Break Today"),
his private railway car, "McDonald's Special," has the
famous Golden Arches painted on it.[6]

Kroc, however, is living proof that you don't have
to fit into the Success Profile (discussed earlier in this
chapter) to become a success. In the first place, he
was a high school dropout. He then went on to sell
Florida real estate and eventually became a salesman
for Lily-Tulip paper cups. It was in this capacity that
in 1954 he discovered a successful hamburger stand
in San Bernardino, California, which was clearing a
remarkable $75,000 a year under the management of
Mac and Richard McDonald. Since the McDonald
brothers were able to produce forty-eight milkshakes
at one time, it was natural that they would provoke the curiosity of a paper-cup salesmen. But Kroc
was so struck by what he saw that he offered the
brothers $500,000 for their business, including their
secret recipe and the rights to their sign, a pair of
golden arches. It was Kroc's vision on the road to
Damascus, and he seized it, even though it meant going into hock for nearly $3 million. At the time he
was fifty-two years old.

Fifty-two years old! A high school dropout! A man
going into a business he knew little or nothing about!
Kroc is proof that for a man with courage and vision
it is never too late to succeed.

There are other lessons to be learned from his startling career. In the first place, he set out to make himself rich by enriching others. He sought out aggressive
franchisees and developed a remarkable capacity for
leadership and communicating his enthusiasm. He is
as proud of the number of millionaires he has helped
to make as he is of his own fortune.

His capacity for detail, passed down like Holy Writ
to each member of his organization, is in itself a major
element of Kroc's success. "There is a science to making a hamburger," he says. What he really means is
that there is a science to selling $3 billion worth of
them, so many in fact that McDonald's buys more

than one percent of all the beef in the United States. Kroc limited the serving of the complete Big Mac to a closely timed 50 seconds, decreed the exact weight of the patty (1.8 ounces), the diameter of the bun (3 ¼ inches) and the number of minutes they could be kept before being discarded for a fresh batch (7). His leadership consisted of more than the single promise that he would make his people rich; he drove them to meet his own standards of perfection and to dedicate themselves to his own vision of growth and success. "I have had the satisfaction of seeing McDonald's become an American tradition," he says. "Such a dream could only be realized in America." [7]

Like Larry, who entered the movie business by accident, Kroc found his foothold on the mountain by chance, though later in life, and he determined to start out then and there, on a sunny California afternoon, to reach for success. If he could at fifty-two, when most men are thinking of retiring, so can you.

For Ray Kroc, *timing* was of crucial importance, as it was for Larry. To succeed you have to be awake and aware, ready to seize the opportunity when it comes up, ready to follow your hunch.

CURTIS CARLSON: THE MAN OF THE GOLDEN STRINGS

Curtis LeRoy Carlson transformed himself from a soap salesman into a multimillionaire by paying a secretary ten dollars to let him study the contract for a small trading-stamp company that had fascinated him as he made his rounds peddling soap. He drew up his own incorporation papers because he couldn't afford an attorney, and created the Gold Bond Stamp Company. He then pyramided this into a business empire with over 8,000 employees that does over half a billion dollars of business a year, and includes "hotels, property development companies, business incentive firms, food retailing, catalogue showrooms and real estate." Never one to pass up an idea that will make profits, he replaced "name acts" in his hotels with strolling violinists, thus saving the cost of hiring entertainers while continuing to provide a show. Besides, as he says, "with the strings we can keep on serving." [8]

Carlson believes above all in *momentum,* one of the key factors in success. Once you're moving upward, you have to *keep* moving, you can't pause. Seizing the moment, as we have seen with Ray Kroc, is important, but as we have seen with Larry, momentum is equally important. Carlson not only believes in momentum, but manages to define it pretty well. "It isn't just the money itself. You keep score with the money you make, but you've got to get a thrill out of doing something that works. A business that isn't growing is a no-good business." [9]

One way to keep momentum going is to have constantly greater goals. Carlson makes a habit of keeping a piece of paper in his pocket with a business goal written on it. When he has achieved it, he throws it away and writes out another. His new goal, annual sales of $1 billion, is important enough to have been put up on a huge sideboard in the corporate dining room in Plymouth, Minnesota, where his executives can see it every day. "It simplifies the petty day-by-day things of everybody if they have a target, and they know they'll be an executive of a lot bigger company if they meet their objectives." [10]

In the meantime Carlson motivates his senior executives by giving each of them a new Cadillac every year, all the cars the same color (presumably to avoid jealousy or the complications of taste). In 1976, the Cadillacs were smoke gray. "One of the biggest prides I've got is my executive group driving Cadillacs and living in nice homes," he says, nicely combining motivation and leadership. One suspects, however, that Carlson's *real* pride lies in having built up a monument so big that it answers, finally, his own passionate need to succeed.

ROBERT SYON:
CURIOSITY PAYS DIVIDENDS

Robert Syon began his spectacular rise to success in a large insurance office where he was taught to file papers into different-colored folders for storage in a vast filing system that filled a building roughly the size of the Lakehurst Blimp Hangar. For several days he worked silently at this menial task, along with dozens of others. Then one day he asked his supervisor just what the papers were and why they had to be filed this way. "I don't know," the supervisor replied, "and you don't need to know either. Just do it."

That seemed an inadequate answer to Syon, and he continued to ask around. In the process, he not only found out, but attracted enough attention to become promoted to supervisor himself. While still continuing to ask questions, he began to make certain judgments of his own about the efficiency of the operation. He worked hard, but above all he learned. Now his office is on the thirty-second floor of a new building on the Avenue of the Americas in New York, a minute's walk away from his own private dining room, one of the many privileges reserved to him as the president of one of the largest insurance companies in the United States. Syon is still asking questions and still forming judgments, and makes his assistants a little nervous by walking around the building asking people what they are doing. If they don't know, their supervisor is in for a pointed memo from the president himself. "Everybody wants to keep me up here," he says, waving around the huge office which is now his, with the Noguchi marble free-form desk, the conversation pit, the vast sculptured metal mural that faces him, the view out over Rockefeller Center. "But I'm still curious. I think it's an element of naïveté in my character, and that element is an important part of what got me here. I want to know *why*. When we switched to computers, I not only asked questions, I went and took the same computer programmer course we were giving our employees, and when I realized they weren't asking enough questions, I had a Q. & A. seminar built into the course. I think we pay too much attention to hard work, as if that were the answer to everything. It's a reversion to our puritan heritage; we have to believe that the man who works hardest gets ahead, and we explain everything in those terms because it answers a moral need.

"Well, God knows I've worked hard all my life, and I think hard work is the glue that binds the package in anyone's career. But curiosity—asking questions—is one of those things we never think about much. I've asked some stupid questions in my time, and I've sometimes been embarrassed, but I don't regret a single one. And I think that when you're no longer curious about people, things, processes, systems, you're burnt out as a manager. I have to make judgments about a company that has offices all over the country, thousands of employees, a technological system for information retrieval that wasn't even thought of when I came into the business. What someone else may see as a simple mechanical improvement that any fool can understand very often thrills me, gets me really charged up. Hell, I can't sit here like a goddamn Buddha and drag the judgments out of myself by looking at my navel. I have to ask, I have to be curious, I have to retain a capacity for wonder and excitement."

J. PAUL LYET:
HOW TO BE LUCKY

In the traditional American success story, luck has always played a significant role. Horatio Alger, who is generally thought to have proselytized for hard work, early rising and moral purity, in fact made luck the determining factor in his success stories. Ragged Dick, the bootblack, rescues a rich man's daughter who has carelessly fallen off a ferryboat; Phil the Fiddler is himself rescued from a snowdrift by a wealthy physician who adopts him. The lesson of Alger's tales is that you must be worthy of your luck when it unexpectedly appears. To a remarkable degree, people do indeed make their own luck, in the sense that hard work, knowledge and ambition place them at the right time and place for luck to strike them.

J. Paul Lyet, chief executive of Sperry Rand Corporation, ascribes his success to "sheer luck." But he puts his success in perspective by adding, "The rewards come if you have worked hard. If your objective is to get your head above the pack and be seen, one way is to work like hell." [11]

A poor boy from a rundown neighborhood of North Philadelphia known as Brewerytown, Lyet was motivated by a burning ambition to get ahead; he puts it simply: "I wanted not to be poor." In pursuit of success, he worked by day and studied at the University of Pennsylvania's Wharton Evening School of Accounts and Finance. After being a suitcase wrapper, a rent collector and a real estate broker, rising by gradual steps to a salary of $18 a week, he decided to go into accounting, because it was "a class thing." Soon he was assigned to audit corporations. One of his superiors remarked, "I never met anybody who had the eagerness to learn that he did." [12]

Like Syon, he asked questions, weighed the answers, and learned the details of every company he audited. Even though he was only an expert in a narrow field, he was already training himself to become a generalist by asking questions and making judgments about things outside his field.

For all his success as an auditor, Lyet was still only making $120 a week. When he received "a nice note from the management" in lieu of the raise he expected, he very sensibly decided to accept an offer from New Holland, a manufacturer of farm implements, to become their controller. New Holland grew rapidly. When it was acquired by Sperry, the purchasing man-

agement soon found that Lyet was one of the hidden
assets. He knew the business and had all the answers.
He was, in the words of one observer, "always prepared."

Once again, Lyet took advantage of the classical
moment at which success can come quickly. When a
company is merged or bought, the new owners are
looking for someone who can tell them what the business they have just purchased really consists of. They
are naturally not inclined to trust the company's own
top management, whose decision to sell out is likely
to be a recognition of defeat. Also, the acquirer wants
to find people who will be loyal to *him*, rather than to
the old ownership. It is the moment when the wings of
success often brush hard-working people at the second
level of management. Careers can be made or destroyed at this critical point in a company's life. Lyet's
was made. Sperry took notice of him.

When Sperry itself was acquired by Remington
Rand, Lyet was once again one of the management
assets. He was soon assigned to master the rapidly
accumulating problems of the company's Univac division as part of a task force of company talent. Once
again, Lyet did well, proving that one of the quickest
routes to success is to plunge into a high-visibility,
high-risk task when it's offered.

Lyet was on the fast track, and soon became the
hand-picked selection to run Sperry Rand. But even
when he had almost reached his goal, he was put
through the ordeal of making a presentation to a hostile group of senior executives, including the chief
executives of the company, who, in Lyet's words, "cut
me down right at the ankles." It was a test, the final,
deadly examination to see if Lyet had the guts to be
chief executive himself, to see how he measured up
as a leader. What does Lyet's story say about success?

● Luck can often mean simply taking advantage of
a situation at the right moment. It is possible to
"make" your luck by being always prepared.

• To the man who wants to succeed, a crisis (such as Sperry's problems with Univac) is the best opportunity of all. It is difficult to become a hero when things are going well, but when things are going to hell you can hope to make some impact on people who would never notice you under more normal conditions.

• All life is a series of tests. (*Never* forget this!)

This is not unusual. In any corporation, large or small, your promotion is generally preceded and accompanied by a series of tests. You may not even be aware of it, but every time you attend a meeting, make a presentation or dictate a memo, it will be judged, and each judgment will affect your overall chance to rise further. You may be the most efficient and hard-working executive in the company, but if your first speech is a dismal, tongue-tied disaster, it will count against you. You have failed to deliver in an area that's important to the company and to you as a senior executive, and your pretensions to success are just that much less credible. For anybody who wants to be a success in business, every day is opening night, and there are no dress rehearsals to make it easier.

WILLIAM H. DONALDSON:
HOW TO CHANGE CAREERS IN MIDSTREAM

Granted that most people reach success by getting into one place and staying there, a certain ability to leapfrog from one career to another is not always a disadvantage. Any ambitious person should be courageous enough to switch to a new game if the one he or she is playing is no longer productive or satisfying. Sticking with the company should be a voluntary decision on your part, because you think it's best for you; fear and inertia should not keep you from trying something new. Despite the fact that he was a scholarship student from a poor family, Donaldson made Skull and Bones at Yale, then graduated to take Wall Street by storm, make a fortune and marry a debutante. He then left Donaldson, Lufkin & Jenrette, Inc., which he had started with a borrowed $20,000, to work for Henry Kissinger at the State Department as Under Secretary of State, and later for Governor Carey of New York. At forty-four, he accepted Yale's offer to head the newly created Graduate School of Management and Organization.[13]

What is striking about Donaldson's career is the way in which he methodically fulfilled his goals, one after the other. First he made his fortune; then he went into government service; finally, with the maximum of prestige, he took on a new career as an educator. It is a perfect example of success planning.

INNOVATORS

Given the fantastic wealth and diversity of this country, why should it be necessary to stick to the beaten career path? America loves a new idea. After all, how many successful lawyers, bankers, doctors and conglomerators does a country need? Success can come to those willing to follow what may seem like a wild hunch.

• *Paul DeDomenico* made his mark in macadamia nuts, of all things, an item which would not jump to most people's minds as a springboard to success. DeDomenico had already done well in the family business, which included a number of West Coast food industries, such as Ghirardelli Chocolate and Golden Grain. The young DeDomenico created something of a sensation in the family by introducing Rice-A-Roni and taking the corporation boldly into convenience foods.

DeDomenico is a man with a super-salesman's personality. On a trip to Hawaii he bought out a faltering macadamia nut producer for less than a million dollars, and proceeded to revolutionize the business. His macadamia nut chocolate bars were followed by onion-flavored macadamias, hickory-smoked macadamias, macadamia-coconut brittle and a macadamia-Granola candy bar. A total of fifty new products were based on this intractable Australian "bush nut," which was originally introduced to Hawaii as a decorative plant. DeDomenico expects to exceed $4 million a year in sales, and given his dynamic drive, he will certainly go far beyond this. Already, he is talking of the macadamia replacing the pineapple and sugar cane as Hawaii's staple cash crop, and no doubt his inventive spirit will not stop with onion-flavored macadamias. In a recent interview, he summed up his attitude toward change by remembering his mother's deathbed opposition to the changes he had made at Golden Grain. "She never wanted us to make Rice-A-Roni," he said, "and its success didn't change her mind. When she seemed near death, she sat up in bed and yelled: 'Maka da mac! Forgetta da rice!' " [14]

• *Philip Marshall Hecht* is another innovator. He "turned $60 into $60,000 in just four years of buying and selling comic books." [15] According to *Success,* a magazine devoted to the stories of those who have succeeded in a bewildering and bizarre number of noncorporate ways, Philip started his comic-book business at the age of twelve, against the wishes of his mother. She merely saw in them "a fire hazard," and wanted him to become an accountant. (A lesson here: parents and other loving relatives are not likely to share your belief in the success potential of your idea, and will usually recommend a safe course.) Philip is already staging his own conventions, and has expanded into "Howdy Doody china plates and cups, Babe Ruth underwear and Shirley Temple materials."

• *Harry Friedenberg,* a tax accountant, is one of the leading merchandisers of Star Trek memorabilia, and makes as much as $1,000 a day at Star Trek conventions, while conducting a thriving mail-order business in Trekkie goods in his spare time. Well, why not? The fact that you're a middle-aged tax accountant does not necessarily mean that you can't succeed in something a little more flamboyant than accountancy. The kind of open mind that allowed Friedenberg to see an opportunity in Trekism is a valuable asset to anyone.

In my own circle of friends, I know an art director who has made a fortune as a cooking expert, a journalist who has become a success with a chain of gift shops, a counterculture rock singer who became a millionaire in the poster business, a successful businessman who made a fortune buying up the leases of Chinese restaurants in his spare time, a novelist who has become one of the country's most successful rare book dealers, a fashion model who opened up a safari tour agency, a show jumper who parleyed an interest in motorcycles into one of the biggest courier and delivery services in New York, and a banker who turned his wife's interest in crafts into a major jewelry business. Look at Amy Green, who turned her experience at *Glamour* magazine into a chain of cosmetic shops where women are advised how to use make-up.

Stories like these show that innovation can be a shortcut to success. Sometimes the more unlikely an idea is, the better its chances are. The *sudden* leap to wealth and success that is at the very heart of the American Dream seldom comes through the normal channels, however safely they may lead you upward. If you think you're on to something new that will work —gamble on your hunch! There's nothing wrong with becoming rich.

Get Rich to Get Ahead

In fact, it is *always* better to be rich.

Whatever career you choose, it is likely that there will come a time in your rise to success when your further progress will depend on whether you have money, or access to someone who will lend it to you. It may be that your freedom to strike out on some new path is only possible if you can finance yourself and your family during the experiment. Or it may be that you will find yourself in the kind of corporate struggle where your survival in the game depends on cash. Even in corporate life, ambitious managers take the time and trouble to use what little capital they have to make money of their own. No matter what you do, it is better to have money behind you. With money as with health, tomorrow is too late.

Look at Clay S. Felker, an authentic genius of American journalism. When he founded *New York* magazine, he became one of the most powerful men in New York communications. He set out to build an empire, and by 1976, he had succeeded, having added the *Village Voice* and *New West* in California to his company. Felker was—and still is—dynamic, ambitious, a man who relished his own power and sought out those even more powerful than himself. His talent as a publisher and editor had carried him a long way. But he had neglected to make his fortune in the process, supposing, like a great many people with meteoric careers, that spending it was the equivalent of having it.

When Felker bought the *Voice,* he traded 400,000 shares of *New York* magazine stock for Carter Burden's shares in the *Voice,* without pausing to reflect that Burden, a rich young socialite with political ambitions, thus became the largest stockholder in *New York* magazine. Felker, a man of imperious nature, soon found himself in conflict with the board of directors, and became aware that his own share of the company was not large enough to give him the final word. After disclosing this state of affairs, together with his ambitions, to Rupert Murdoch, the Australian newspaper magnate, Felker was startled to hear that Murdoch had managed to buy Carter Burden's shares. Murdoch thus took over the company from Felker instead of helping him to keep it.

Felker, after a much-publicized struggle, remarked that his "only mistake was not being born rich." But this is not the whole story. He simply hadn't realized soon enough the necessity of being rich, and despite his admiration for power, had underestimated the cynicism of those who *are* rich. At a crucial moment in his game he neither had the money to put on the table, nor ready access to those who might have put it up for him on conditions he could accept. He was therefore out of the game.

In major and minor ways, the same can happen to anyone. Just because you have chosen a profession in which money is a secondary consideration (and this is true of most jobs, since only bankers, financiers, stockbrokers and traders are directly involved in the acquisition of money itself as a commodity), do not suppose that money in and of itself will not at some point become the factor upon which your entire career hinges.

FRED SILVERMAN: PORTRAIT OF A WINNER

Fred Silverman, the programming executive of ABC who was lured away from CBS at the age of thirty-eight with a salary of $250,000 a year, stock options and a paid-up life insurance policy of $750,000, works hard. Often putting in a thirteen-hour day, he drives his subordinates hard. But it is above all his own willingness to make decisions quickly, to take on responsibility and to get what he wants that have made Silverman a success.

A man who doesn't like small talk and who goes straight for the jugular of every problem, Silverman has the essential ability to close a deal. This is a vital quality. Almost anybody can negotiate and discuss a deal, large or small. But the money and success always go to the person who can get the deal *signed,* and rightly so.

In the automobile business, large car agencies have specialized salesmen known as "closers," who are the stars of the sales force. They seldom bother with showing the customer a car, or extolling its virtues. Their job is to move in when the other salesmen have brought the customer almost to the point of purchase. The closer then takes the customer into his office, and it is his job to see the customer doesn't leave without buying the car. It takes energy, determination and a single-minded drive to bring people to the point where they are willing to stop talking and actually sign something, and Fred Silverman is just such a specialist, on a larger and more brilliant scale.

One of his favorite tactics is to bring a recalcitrant producer or agent in, and tell him, "Before you leave this room, we'll have a deal." [16] Almost always, he gets the deal signed, in part because he has the inner fire of a man who wants to win, in part because he knows how to make the instant compromise that clinches the deal. Silverman understands the mechanics of deal-making—the fact that most people would rather sign than write off as worthless the hours of negotiation and thought that have preceded the "closing." Everyone usually wants to come out with a positive achievement, even if they don't get exactly the terms they wanted. And when Silverman drags people into his office in the middle of the day, especially if they're busy executives whose time is worth a lot of money, there is a built-in desire to make the deal and get back to work. As one observer of Fred Silverman's style says, "If you want to make a deal, get the other guys into *your* office, and keep them there, until they begin to feel 'My God, let's get this thing done and out of the way.' Very often, you can get people to sign by suggesting both sides are so far apart that the meeting ought to be postponed for a week. For guys with heavy schedules, that's a frightening thought. They start thinking of what they've got on their calendars for the next week, and suddenly the deal doesn't look so bad after all."

Silverman's career illustrates two important points:

- concentrate on what is important, instead of letting yourself get bogged down in routine;
- always go for the jugular.

If you want to succeed, you have to develop a real passion for winning. People who don't care, don't get there.

FRANK BORMAN:
PORTRAIT OF A PERFECTIONIST

If Fred Silverman exemplifies the value of a driving will to win, astronaut Frank Borman, the president of Eastern Airlines, is the very prototype of the man who can accept nothing less than perfection. "I'm success-oriented," [17] Borman says, with commendable understatement, considering he's a man who has not only circumnavigated the moon but become the head of one of the country's largest airlines. Borman is intent, hard-driving and reputedly somewhat humorless, but in every respect the modern corporate manager. As a military man, Borman does not have the businessman's traditional fear of Washington, and is remarkably free of the knee-jerk reaction to government involvement that characterized an earlier generation of managers. He recognizes that if you're entitled to, or can make yourself entitled to, a government handout, you might as well take it. The same practical approach marks his management of Eastern. He gets into his office at 7:30 A.M. and makes his presence felt. He is, in fact, a master of that invaluable executive talent which consists of appearing to be everywhere at once. His eye, like God's, is on the sparrow, and it has proved sufficient to revitalize a company.

Although you can't literally look over all your subordinates' shoulders, by maintaining a high visibility and keeping up random contact with them, you can achieve virtually the same effect of being everywhere at once. A great way to keep people on the ball is by asking them about something they would naturally assume you haven't even heard about, thus staying one jump ahead of them. Occasionally check other people's figures, for example, instead of simply looking at the bottom line. Very often you will find a small mathematical error, and thus acquire a reputation for attention to detail. Spend the time to look at everything that crosses your desk, and send it back indicating that you've read it, if possible with a comment, a correction or an expression of your opinion. It helps to develop a distinctive style, and the worse your handwriting is and the more cryptic your style, the better, since it will then be necessary for your subordinates to decipher what you've written, and ponder about what you really meant.

You can't be a success in any ivory tower: Frank Borman has even been known to load baggage on Eastern's flights!

WILLIAM HEWITT: NOT A COMPANY MAN

The usual criticism of ambitious people is that they become part of their company—"company men" in the old, and sexist phrase. But if you want to get to the top, you have to turn the company around so that it fulfills *your* dreams.

When William Hewitt took over Deere Company, a respectable Midwestern manufacturer of farm machinery, it was the start of an extraordinary success story. Deere's sales grew from $300 million in 1955 to nearly $3 billion in 1975. The company had been basically successful and satisfied with things as they were, but Hewitt couldn't conceive of himself as running anything less than a hugely successful major corporation. Therefore he gradually turned Deere into the realization of his vision, until its ambitions matched his own. In storybook fashion, he got his start by marrying the boss's daughter. (His future father-in-law went to the trouble of having him checked out by private detectives before giving his consent!) He was smart enough to take advantage of the special position the marriage offered him, without feeling guilty about it or using it as an excuse to do nothing. When luck or fortune comes along, the successful man takes it gratefully, without pretending that he'd have been better off without it. With energy, charm, grace and an eye on the ball, Hewitt steered what had hitherto been a prospering but dowdy company toward the kind of size and performance that seemed to him appropriate for something he was associated with.

Highly ambitious himself, he was not stopped by the fact that management was complacent, and had comparatively modest goals. Hewitt knew that his own growth would be determined by the company's growth.

As one observer says of Hewitt, "He made us realize just how good we were. We knew we could make it in Moline, but we didn't know we could make it in New York. Bill showed us we could." [18]

Showing people what they can do is an important component of success. Hewitt changed a management which was happy with things as they were into one that could only be satisfied by making things bigger and better—simply because he himself could contemplate nothing less as a life goal.

Remember: the *company's* growth is vital to *yours*.

JIM STONE:
A MAN WHO WASN'T AFRAID TO ASK

Jim Stone always insists that you have to ask for what you *want*. This sounds easy, but the truth is that we seldom do anything of the kind. We ask for what we think we can get, or ought to have, not for what we want. If you want a raise, a title, a promotion, *ask* for it. The worst that can happen is that you'll be told No. But a surprising amount of the time those who ask for something get it, if not now, then at the next opportunity. Never limit yourself to what you think is reasonable or possible. You have to learn that your ambitions and desires may seem more unreasonable to you than they do to other people.

Jim had always wanted to produce a movie, and believed that this was an unlikely dream, which was certainly true. A modestly successful lawyer, he had no reason to believe that he would ever succeed in the movie business, or even get a crack at it. However, when Fate sat him next to the owner of a large movie studio at a political luncheon in New York, he brought up a movie property that had caught his attention. To his surprise he found that the man was willing to listen. A lesser person than Jim might have brought the idea up timidly, and the encounter would have come to nothing. Jim, perceiving that there was interest, actually sold his luncheon partner the idea, then almost as an afterthought, said that he wanted to be the executive producer on the project. The movie magnate did not laugh or protest. "Have you ever produced a movie before?" he asked. Jim modestly acknowledged that he had not, but added that he saw no reason why he could not.

"Why not?" said the great man. "Why not? God knows, half the producers in Hollywood don't know what they're doing, and we can always get you enough people who know the business to help out. Anyway, you'll learn more quickly at the top than coming up through the ranks, which is a lot of bullshit, frankly. The way to learn how to produce a movie is to produce one. If it's a success, you're a successful producer. Even if it fails, you'll probably have met enough people in the business to make sure somebody will stake you to another try. My boy, if we make a deal on the story, you can consider yourself a producer."

Three years and two movies later, Jim was living in Bel Air, driving a Mercedes-Benz 450 SLC, and dressed head to foot in tailored buckskins, with embroidered beads and gold chains. The pale-faced lawyer in a ready-made suit had become a Hollywood personality, and has decided that what he wants next is to run a major studio for a while. And why not? At the crucial moment, he had the intelligence and courage to ask for his wildest dreams, his farthest-flung fantasies, to ask, in short, for something so absurd and unlikely that most people would have been reluctant to confess it to their wives or psychotherapists. He got what he asked for.

And so can you.

The Rewards of Success

When a fellow says it ain't the money but the principle of the thing, it's the money.
— Artemus Ward

As executive talent gets more sophisticated about compensation, the price of retaining the successful will increase. The most perceptive executives already recognize that it takes larger and larger sums of money to motivate.
— David J. McLaughlin
The Executive Money Map

THE MONEY GAME

Too Much Is Not Enough

The statement "Nothing succeeds like success" is so true that it requires some further analysis. We are so committed to the principle of rewarding success lavishly that a sizable industry has developed whose only purpose is to invent new and more elaborate schemes of compensation for that 5 percent of the nation's wage earners whose success can no longer be rewarded with a mere raise. Not that money isn't considered important, both for its own sake and as the ultimate index of performance and status. A recent survey indicated that the chief executives of the nation's 581 largest publicly held corporations received an average of $228,000 in salary, an impressive figure even in an age of inflation and high taxes. In 1975, a year of recession and economic difficulty, Meshulim Riklis, chairman of the Rapid-American Corporation, received $915,866; Harold S. Geneen, chairman of the International Telephone and Telegraph Corporation earned $776,085, Charles Bluhdorn, chairman of Gulf & Western Industries was paid $588,560; Michel C. Bergerac received a five-year contract to run Revlon at $325,000 a year, plus a lump-sum bonus of $1,500,000 merely "for reporting to work"; and David J. Mahoney got a ten-year contract with an annual salary of $400,000, a bonus that could add as much as 125 percent to that figure and a company-paid insurance policy of $4,375,000.[1]

Companies which will fight to the death to "hold the line" on secretaries' salaries and make endless difficulties about giving a $15,000-a-year employee a $1,000 raise will cheerfully pay substantial fortunes for a high-level executive front runner. Success is a commodity, and a very much rarer one than gold; if you have it, or appear to, you can strike almost any bargain you please. It is the key that opens up all the benefits of the reward system—money, "perks," fame, possessions, security, freedom of choice, privilege.

These vast sums of money are a kind of ritual sacrifice of free enterprise, designed first of all to prove a corporation's solvency and confidence by showing that it can afford to pay anything for the right people; and secondly, to appease the gods of profit, as the ancient Greeks once threw bread and wine into the sea to ensure a safe voyage. Huge salaries represent a pious sacrifice, as well as a totemic symbol, as if the more we pay the senior executives of a corporation, the greater will be its profits. And who knows? Perhaps it's so. Napoleon is said to have believed that the most valuable quality a general could have was luck, and that troops always fought better for a "lucky" commander. The same is true for executives: a person with an aura of success and a reputation for being lucky can do wonders for the morale of an organization simply by his presence, and his six-figure salary inspires confidence. One of the reasons that the six- or seven-digit salaries usually go to outsiders (When did you last hear of anybody who was promoted from within to a salary like this?) is that the people who qualify for this kind of job are seldom selling their skills or their specific knowledge of a business; they have learned how to merchandise themselves, and what they are selling is their reputation for success.

A good steady rise through the ranks is certainly valuable, but the big stakes are only won by the sudden burst of success that puts you decisively in the lead, a magic point at which you become "a success," and are transformed into a different kind of person. Reaching this point triggers off the reward system of our society, like hitting the right combination on a slot machine.

What to Ask for—and How to Do It

The system of rewards is so sophisticated that many otherwise intelligent people are bewildered by it, and make the great mistake of asking for less money than they could get. It is always best to ask for far more than you think you deserve, and surprising how often this figure will be taken as a basis for negotiation or even be accepted as fair. It is just human nature to prefer someone who thinks highly of himself to one who seems to lack confidence.

Despite the proliferation of benefits available to the high achiever in a corporation, nothing can replace money as a reward. Company cars, a new set of office furniture, the right to fly first-class on domestic airline flights—all these are nice things to have, but they must never be accepted as *substitutes* for money; they have to be part of the money package. Besides, it isn't *just* money: the more money you can get for yourself, the more fringe benefits will be attached. Below a certain level, usually $50,000 to $100,000, fringe benefits are rigorously withheld. Above that level they are given with a lavish hand, since they are considered to be obligatory trappings of success.

Despite the arguments that money no longer means anything, the examples of people like Barbara Walters ($1,000,000 a year), Robert Redford ($2,000,000 for three weeks' work) or Tom Seaver ($230,000 a year)[2] should be enough to convince anyone that money is still a desirable goal. And for good reasons: fringe benefits are what the company chooses to give you; with money you can buy whatever you want. In addition, while the company could take back fringe benefits at any time, money is yours to keep.

The Executive Shopping List:
Get What You Want

Almost as important as earning money is saving it: not saving it yourself, which is both difficult and unlikely in this era's economic climate, but structuring your life so that the corporation saves you money. It is a simple proposition: the more of your basic necessities the corporation pays for, the less you have to spend of the money they pay you. Many otherwise intelligent people fail to grasp this essential truth, which is the very heart of our rewards system.

In extreme cases, a successful executive's salary, however large, is hardly more than the equivalent of pocket money. It is possible to live in a corporate apartment, drive (or better yet, be driven in) a company car, eat most meals on an expense account, combine enough business with a vacation to make what one executive calls "a workation," and have the corporation pay for financial planning, medical expenses, life and disability insurance, and almost anything else you can think of or invent.

Always remember:

- Money comes first. After you've got the money you want, you can ask about the perks and benefits —and the more money you get, the more of them you'll be entitled to.
- Greed pays off. If you're any good at all, you're probably worth much more than you're asking.
- Corporations believe in capitalism, and are not likely to be shocked by your desire for a higher salary.
- Whatever you ask for, you may be sure that someone in your organization has already asked for it, or already gotten it.
- The purpose of business is to produce profit, so don't be ashamed to make a profit for yourself.
- The benefits worth having are those that save you money, not those that merely consist of display and status.
- Don't worry about what other people are getting. Get what you want for yourself; if someone else gets more (or less) what do you care?

Success As Insurance

Some people get one shot at success, but very few get two. It is therefore vital to make your success pay off for you right away. Organizations are full of people who reached some level of achievement, then failed to exploit it. Success gives you leverage, but only if you act fast. Nothing is as boring as last year's success (or yesterday's, in some high-pressure businesses), and half the reason why successful people surround themselves with all the trappings of success is that these things serve as a monument and a reminder that they have succeeded.

We have, all of us, the need to hold on to success, to institutionalize it. Of course, there is a need for constant reaffirmation of success by your actual daily performance; but the large office, the handsome furniture, the two windows, the attentive secretaries with their IBM Correctotype Selectrics and their cheerful smiles, give you at least some visible proof that you have reached a plateau. People have a tendency to forget *how* you succeeded, or what you succeeded at. You may even begin to wonder yourself. But the benefits you receive and the handsome office you inhabit continue to make it clear that you are still counted "a success."

Business novels and movies are always full of powerful executives whose careers suddenly fail, sending them on a dramatic downward trajectory. Of course, this does happen in real life, but not all that often. On the whole, successful people retain their advantages long after they have ceased to be functioning at top capacity; it takes singular ineptitude to lose the rewards of success once they've been won. Younger and more ambitious men or women may drive you from the inner circles of power, you may find yourself reduced to trivial tasks and meaningless meetings, but it is very unlikely that your salary will be reduced, your benefits curtailed and your office partitioned off.

It is, of course, possible to be ejected from the system, that is, fired, but if you can avoid that, you are likely to retain for decades your benefits and privileges. After all, those above you don't want to see *their* rewards taken away from them, and those below you want to feel that they too will enjoy what they've earned when their time comes, so both your subordinates and your superiors form a kind of mutual protection society in your favor.

BEYOND THE FRINGE: THE PERQUISITES OF SUCCESS

In a survey of "executive perquisites," it was revealed that no less than 4.4 percent of the companies surveyed provided yachts for the personal use of corporate officers and chief executives, a rather surprising statistic.[3] Of course, the question of who uses the yacht is a burning issue in such companies. In many cases, the yacht is maintained for the exclusive use of the president or the chairman of the board, but it is thought more tactful to pretend that it's available to any senior executive who requests it. The problem is that everybody knows you're not supposed to ask, and that you'd be frowned upon if you did. This is quite a common phenomenon, and extends well beyond yachts, for instance, to limousines.

Luxury perks like yachts are generally speaking more for prestige and show than for any practical convenience. A few companies, for example, maintain private railroad cars, which can be attached to any scheduled Amtrak train and towed behind at $1.35 a mile (the Canadian railroads are less expensive).

The range of executive perks is breath-taking. Some glimpses of life at the top are offered in such usually mundane documents as draft tax legislation. A recent attempt to put some order into the IRS regulations on "fringe benefits" reveals such items as an executive who used the company jet to take his wife on a shopping trip and see a play in another city (this, by the way, was judged to be a taxable addition to his income, whereas another executive was permitted to take his secretary on the company private plane without its being judged to constitute taxable compensation, despite what the report tactfully refers to as "the incidental personal pleasure involved"), private parking spaces reserved for executives in an urban underground garage, a full-time private bodyguard for the head of a multinational corporation *and* his family, a corporation which gives a monthly cocktail party for its senior personnel, and a company president who not only takes his secretary on trips with him, but her mother as well.[4] One financial corporation sends its executives to an "Outward Bound" camp to learn survival techniques in the wilderness, while another provides senior executives who commute with a luxurious corporate apartment for nights when they are working late.

Boeing's new "Executaire" helicopter is advertised in *Fortune* with the typical promise that it provides the comfort to which a senior executive is entitled. The advertisement reads: *"You* are the reason Boeing created the Executaire. You are demanding of certain creature comforts. You want a helicopter with air conditioning . . . and a distinguished custom interior . . . The Executaire will carry five big men and their luggage—and even their golf clubs—from, say, New York to Washington in less than two hours . . ."

The top of the line in perks these days is, revealingly enough, in the area of security. Several firms now specialize in providing chief executives with armed bodyguards, a service which can cost as much as $3,000 a week for what one security specialist describes as "the kind of protection in which your bodyguard will throw himself in front of you and take the bullet himself, if necessary." For $1,000 a week a trained armed bodyguard will protect the successful entrepreneur from assassination, threats and kidnaping, but will stop short of the supreme sacrifice.

Expensive as they are, the popularity of these services is on the increase.

Many successful executives, who may already have a jet, a helicopter and a yacht, now feel they are entitled to the same kind of security as senior government officials. At least, this is the opinion of the president of a large security and private investigation firm that deals exclusively in corporate accounts.

His cheerful and spacious offices on Park Avenue are nothing like those of Philip Marlowe or Sam Spade. High above the Four Seasons restaurant, they are provided with thick carpeting, muted telephones and pretty secretaries. "Listen," he told me, "these guys read that the government spends $500,000 a year protecting the Secretary of the Treasury, for God's sake! Who's going to assassinate the Secretary of the Treasury? Who even knows his *name?* It's not as if he needs crowd protection—nobody even wants to shake his hand. But he gets full Secret Service protection, and in an age of anxiety, that's the real status. People read about executives being kidnaped, and they want protection. Why not? They've got everything else. And we have a full range of services, not just bodyguards. We do a weekly sweep of your offices to search for bugs and wiretaps, we check out employees and associates when we're asked to, we investigate crank calls and hate mail, and we provide a discreet private investigation service to deal with personal problems. It's expensive, but with a package deal we can provide a chief executive with a real feeling of security twenty-four hours a day."

So pervasive is this need for security at the top that Bob Bondurant, a successful racing car driver, has set up a Corporate Chauffeur Driving Course at his School of High Performance Driving in Sears Point, California. There he teaches "stunt driving, high-speed pursuit and how to turn the pursuer into the pursued." Several large corporations, including United States Steel, Bechtel, Alcoa and the major oil companies, have sent their executive chauffeurs to learn the secrets of "anti-terrorist driving." Why not? One Alcoa executive was quoted as saying, in justification of the expense, "These chauffeurs are carrying around valuable cargo." And there is no better way to prove that an executive is, in fact, "valuable cargo" than guarding him.[5]

At least one large Western oil company has managed to combine two functions into one by sending the "anti-terrorist"-trained president's chauffeur to a combat pistol course in Arizona. Students are taught how to defend the successful executive in a firefight or a kidnaping attempt, with much emphasis on multiple targets ("Always shoot from left to right") and the use of the Colt .45 automatic pistol. Special instruction is given to cope with the possibility of running into a "no-win" situation, and students practice surrender techniques as carefully as they do marksmanship.

Applications for pistol licenses for corporate personnel zoomed everywhere when terrorist groups began kidnaping businessmen in South America, and at least one East Coast arms distributor has reported a healthy corporate interest in such sophisticated weaponry as the Israeli "Uzi" submachine gun (the same model that is carried by Secret Service bodyguards) and a neat new device called the Tasar that can be kept inconspicuously on top of the reception desk. It shoots an electrified barb into an unwelcome visitor, "temporarily" paralyzing him.

Privacy—the Ultimate Perk

Most of these perks have one thing in common: they tend to insulate the successful executive from other people, to smooth and protect his passage through the world. It is not so much that the privileges are significant in themselves, but rather that the true test of success is the degree to which one can isolate oneself from others. In most cases, a corporate jet is no more efficient than a commercial airplane—in fact, they are usually slower and more cramped. The advantage is that the executive is not exposed to people who do not know how important he is.

In New York City, corporate executives use their limousines to make a trip of ten blocks. They could walk the distance in ten minutes, or make it on the subway in five, whereas the limo may take half an hour. But in the limo you retain your image as an important person, while on the street or subway you are just like everybody else.

The same is true for private dining rooms, private toilets, corporate helicopters and executive offices. The more difficult access to the executive is made, the more he can carry his success with him, like a snail's shell. Nothing is more distressing to someone pampered by success than being exposed to people ignorant of his status. I well remember a famous motion picture producer who was caught in Chicago's O'Hare airport because of a blizzard. When he was told that there were no taxis to get back to town—by now the drifts of snow were two feet high and the wind like something out of the Antarctic—he shouted to the dispatcher, "Don't you realize that I'm a very important man?" Although it did him no good, it is typical of the need to avoid being treated like an ordinary person. This may sound silly, but keep in mind that success is mainly a psychological phenomenon. Anything that shakes your self-confidence is to be avoided at all costs. Once you have become successful, it is better to stick with people who *know* you're successful. And privacy and exclusivity are useful tools for this purpose.

Determining Perks

Of course, some perks are more worth having than others. Corporations have a way of rewarding executives for reaching a high level within the hierarchy, which is to say for being good at office politics and lucky in the promotion game. Unless, let us say, the executive vice-presidency is "worth" $100,000 a year, plus bonus, fringe benefits and stock options, the logical conclusion is that the office of executive vice-president is extremely overrated, and probably ought to be removed from the table of organization. But if it were abolished, half the other titles might be questioned, and the whole structure would collapse. In order to make a hierarchy meaningful, the various levels must have a built-in value. Most corporations are much better at paying off for promotion than they are at rewarding achievement, if only because achievement is out of the ordinary and hard to assess.

What is more, a corporation is a world apart. Ultimately, the board of directors is responsible to the shareholders. This responsibility may be taken seriously or not (usually not), but the corporation's real concern is its own survival and growth, and its basic

loyalty is to its own people, not the shareholders.
Anybody who reads corporate reports knows how
much they conceal, not so much in the reporting of
finances, which is to some extent controlled by law
and custom, as in the cheery and optimistic analyses
of the corporation's activities and goals. It is a little as
if children were allowed to write their own report
cards, describing what they'd accomplished at school
during the year, predicting their future goals and explaining that their failures were somebody else's fault.

The board of directors is rather like a ship's crew,
and the shareholders like the passengers. If you haven't
battened down the hatches during storms, dealt with
navigational crises and lived with knowledge that the
ship's timbers are rotten and the captain a hopeless
drunk, you can't expect to share the confidences of the
crew. The "shareholders" are on board for the voyage,
and risk going down just as much as the crew, but nobody is likely to tell them that the captain has a low
opinion of his officers and his engines, when he's sober.

.   One of the consequences of this corporate isolation
is that salaries for senior executives are seldom linked
to any rational scale of achievement. The compensation for a given position is likely to be based very simply on what the previous incumbent was paid, plus the
amount it would take to ensure that a new incumbent
will stay for a resonable period of time. What is more,
all schemes for creating incentives inevitably become
institutionalized. These are then replaced with yet another incentive scheme, which in turn will become accepted as part of "normal" compensation. It may seem
like a good idea to give senior executives a bonus when
the company has had a good year but the bonus will
eventually become normal, even in a bad year, and be
treated as part of the regular compensation scheme.

Stock options will then be provided as an incentive,
a way of rewarding executives for contributing toward
the rise in value of the company's shares. In theory, if
the stock doesn't rise, the executives haven't done their
jobs, and therefore shouldn't expect to profit by their

options. In practice, if the stock declines and the options remain, as they say, "under water," then the options are deemed to have failed as a means of compensation. Something else will be tried, perhaps free stock based on long term-growth in earnings per share, a special bonus based on profits above a certain figure or a large increase in salaries to make up for the failure of the additional compensation schemes.

Most of these incentive schemes actually have nothing to do with incentive and have long since become as institutionalized as the executive washroom or the corporate dining facility. Many of them have long since proved unworkable or unrewarding, and survive only because nobody has bothered to eliminate them.

In case you're wondering what to ask for next time you're entitled to a substantial increase in compensation, you might consider the following perks listed in a recent management survey.[6]

- Nine percent of the companies surveyed provided free personal legal counseling for executives.
- Fourteen percent provided free personal financial counseling and tax advice.
- Twelve percent granted executive low-cost loans.
- A whopping 65 percent paid for their executives' memberships in country clubs, tennis clubs, health clubs and what are genteelly described as "supper clubs."
- One company pays its executives a double salary while they are on vacation and another pays them an extra hundred dollars a day for each day of vacation as an incentive to take time off.
- Five companies actually reported paying for their executives' vacation expenses.
- Three companies provided their chief executives with domestic staff (butler, maid, gardener, cook, etc.) and 3 percent gave educational grants for the children of senior executives.
- Eleven percent of the companies listed in one survey actually buy the previous home of a new

executive to save him the trouble of trying to sell it in a depressed market.

• Fifty-one percent of the companies provide a "favorable" mortgage rate for new or relocated executives.

• Sixteen percent make up the difference between the old and the new mortgage rate when the new one is higher; Executives have asked and received special consideration for the moving of a boat or a horse, and in one case the company agreed to buy the executive's old furniture at his own valuation.[7]

Greed Is Good for You

Success gives you the right to be greedy. When qualified stock options were the rage, corporations handed them out to successful executives with a lavish hand. But only the greedy ones arranged to have the corporation make them a low-interest loan in order to exercise their options. In extreme cases, the corporation not only lent the money to exercise the option, but actually reimbursed an executive for unanticipated tax increases resulting from exercising his option.

It is just as well to face it squarely: *the successful get rich, and the unsuccessful get poorer*. It is not for nothing that when the House Ways and Means Committee was debating tax cuts it swiftly approved $165 million worth of tax rebates "to wealthy investors who had sizeable capital losses . . . in the stock market," while arranging matters so that the only group which did *not* benefit from the projected cuts was "low-income families with children." [8] Not surprisingly, a report from the U. S. Senate indicates that 53 percent of the benefits from federal tax loopholes go to the 14.6 percent of taxpayers who make more than $20,000 a year, and that seven persons with incomes in excess of $1,000,000 a year paid no federal income tax at all.[9] Under the circumstances, it makes sense to get what you can.

THE HEDONISM FACTOR

It helps to be strongly motivated to improve your life style.

The simple ambition to live better is a potent factor in succeeding. Generally, those people who have a definite vision of what they want to become are the ones who eventually succeed.

What you have now has to be intolerable compared to what you want. The more you see the future in concrete terms of material gain, the easier it is to get there. A vague desire to succeed in some way, which is what most of us have, can never equal the success-oriented person's firm determination to move on to a clearly defined goal, to which he or she is totally committed.

In our culture, the puritan ethic accounts for much of the drive to succeed. Oddly enough, it is easier for most people to aim for success out of a kind of moral obligation to adhere to the values of our culture than out of a need for personal gratification. But the impulse toward hedonism needs to be cultivated as well; in fact, those who seek enjoyment often succeed faster than those who approach success as an exercise in self-sacrifice.

A great deal of nonsense is written about the quality of life today, with the underlying premise that society is crumbling while the "haves" waste our resources and pollute the atmosphere in search of frivolous pleasures. There is, of course, some truth to this. Personal success does not absolve us of our responsibility as members of the larger society, and ought not to separate us from a reasonable interest in the fate of others.

Still, we owe it to ourselves to enjoy life. The recent attacks on upward mobility seem to me unjustified. Why shouldn't we want to live better, drive a better car, eat caviar, enjoy ourselves as much as we can in the time we have left to us? The pursuit of happiness is a basic right, and the new puritanism has tended to substitute social issues for the old Calvinist belief in God's dislike of pleasure.

My uncle the late Sir Alexander Korda, the motion picture producer, was a pleasure-seeking leviathan whose wake stretched from continent to continent. He always used to contend that the only rational approach to success is to covet the good things in life, and to learn early on just exactly what it is you covet. It was the desire to own a pair of butter-colored boots and a gold-topped cane that goaded him on to succeed.

"I had a vision," he used to say, "of what I wanted to be, and it came from seeing a man walk across the square of Kesckemet, in Hungary, when I was a small boy. You have to understand, it was a small Hungarian village—dusty, dull, provincial—where the only conversation was about the price of peaches, for it was the home of Hungary's famous peach brandy. One day, as I left school, I saw a carriage stop, and out of it came a man dressed in a beautiful suit, with a homburg hat, and a cane and a pair of narrow shiny yellow boots, on top of which he wore spats, which I had never seen before. I have no idea who he was—probably some kind of government inspector or a local landowner's relative from the gay life of Budapest; who knows or cares? But I had never seen such a pair of boots. You have to understand, in Kesckemet everybody's boots were ugly. The peasants had big heavy boots, like those of Russian soldiers, or went barefoot; the gentry wore slightly less ugly boots, with thick laces up to the ankle; and children wore the ugliest boots of all. This man's boots were soft and supple and shiny, and I suddenly knew that my life would not be complete until I owned a similar pair. To get them I knew I would have to leave Kesckemet, and my family and my friends, and go out into the great world myself and become a success. And I was very sad, because I knew that I would eventually do it, and at the same time very happy because I knew I would succeed.

"And so it has always been, you see. First the boots, then the beautiful women—which is the most expensive luxury of all—and the chauffeur-driven Rolls-Royce, and the collection of art, and the good wine and food, and the cigars. I always knew what I wanted and had a clear vision of it in my mind. I could say: 'I am going to do this, because I want that.' People say that luxury and comfort and money are bad for the soul. I don't believe it. Nothing is better for the soul than having what you want, and anybody who can become rich and comfortable and doesn't is a damned fool."

My uncle's advice is sound. One of the best ways to ensure success is to develop expensive tastes, or marry someone who has them. The range of options open to those who succeed is so large as to encompass almost everything: yachts, art, clothes, jewelry, travel—all these can be yours.

SUCCESS IS THE BEST MEDICINE

The conventional view is that the demands of achievement lead to ulcers, hypertension, heart attacks, impotence and early death. We constantly hear of people who have "worked themselves to death" or "worried themselves to death." But anybody familiar with life at the top soon observes that a remarkably large percentage of high achievers are fit, healthy and active.

Statistics bear this out. A study by the Metropolitan Life Insurance Company reveals that successful executives as a group enjoy longer life and better health than the average American. Their mortality rate is only 63 percent of that of the total white, adult, male population. The presidents of *Fortune*'s top five hundred corporations did even better. Their rate was only 5 percent of the average mortality, indicating that big-time success is not only rewarded with money, but also with longevity and good health.[10]

In another study of mortality rates among eminent

and successful men, business leaders and scientists proved to have lower mortality rates than the average. They lived longer than successful lawyers, judges, journalists and writers. The highest mortality rate, oddly enough, was that of correspondents and journalists, whose death rate was twice that of the businessmen and politicians whose actions they were reporting, and exceeded by almost a third the average death rate of adult Americans. Clearly, a person who wants to live a long, healthy life ought to think twice about being a journalist, or for that matter a writer of any kind. Business success, on the other hand lengthens life. In the words of one survey:

"This favorable longevity [of top executives] is believed to reflect in large measure the physical and emotional fitness of business executives for positions of responsibility; many of those who attain high status are able to cope with and even thrive on stressful situations by harnessing tensions for productive use . . . It may well be that work satisfaction together with public recognition of accomplishments is an important determinant of health and longevity." [11]

In almost every health area, there is a direct correlation between success and longevity. Diabetes, for example, drops off sharply as income rises, as do most other major medical conditions. To some extent, this is doubtless because of the nature of health care in the United States. The rich and the successful take better care of themselves because they can afford to do so. Health care is also a built-in perk for successful people. More than 76 percent of major corporations provide their "key" executives with free medical examinations, in many cases compulsory. As people rise up the ladder of success, their medical coverage increases, so that they are fully protected against medical problems that would financially destroy the average family, and might, therefore, be ignored until it is too late to cure them. Still, it seems likely that success tends to keep you healthy.

It Pays to Be Thin

Companies are increasingly health-conscious. There is a natural tendency to weed out those who are likely to fail for health reasons before they are put in positions of great responsibility or given expensive training. Interestingly, it pays to be thin. A survey of 15,000 successful executives showed conclusively that on the average, fat executives receive less pay than thin ones. One headhunter remarked that, "Fat people pay a penalty of $1,000 a pound." Fat people are less likely to advance as quickly or as high as thin persons. In a survey taken of people who earned between $25,000 and $45,000 a year, only 9 percent were more than ten pounds overweight. What is more, many companies, in looking for people to fill important jobs, request that applicants be "thin," a circumstance which has led at least one executive-placement expert to complain that "the overweight have become America's largest, least protected minority group." [12]

I would not go so far as to argue that thin people always get ahead faster than fat people. But in fact successful people do tend to be thin, perhaps because corporations feel that a lean, hard look in a man or woman symbolizes a lean, hard mind. Fatness is often seen as a sign of self-indulgence. A person who wants to be successful might just as well start by getting into shape—it pays off in money as well as health.

Success As a New Lease on Life

Failure is one of the least recognized health hazards. There is a tremendous benefit to using all your resources and a great relaxation simply in winning what you have set out to achieve. A colleague of mine, who remained stagnant in his job, suffered from asthma to the point where he was almost unable to function. Then one day, he changed jobs and took on new and more challenging responsibilities. Most of his friends had warned him against making this radical move. His health would break under the strain, they told him. Nothing of the kind happened. As he rose to meet the new demands on him, his asthma vanished, his energy increased, he became a vigorous man. It was not illness that had held him back. Inertia and caution had locked him into a physical problem which gave him an excuse to underachieve. His body responded automatically to the stimulus of a new job, with the chance to put his natural energies, his intelligence, his "germ of greatness" to work. He was cured.

It's a common phenomenon. Don Brooker, a young advertising executive who felt that he was getting nowhere in his organization, was constantly troubled with physical problems. Every day he would complain of sleeplessness, constipation, hay fever, nausea and the inability to digest anything more solid than cottage cheese (which he hated). No sooner was he promoted than his complaints stopped. He began to exercise, he found he could sleep without taking pills, and his energy increased. It was no longer necessary for his subordinates to wait in terror for the outcome of his daily attempt to move his bowels, a ritual which had hitherto taken a good hour of the morning. Stalemated in his job and his ambitions, Don had closed in on himself, become sluggish; released to move upward, he regained his physical momentum.

The last time I saw Don, he was jogging around the reservoir in New York's Central Park at seven in the morning, on his way to play a game of tennis before going to the office. He looked fit and totally relaxed.

"Success," he told me, "gives you a new lease on life. Of course you have new demands on your time and energy, but you feel your potential is being used, and it's very natural that there's a physical effect. You also get a chance to reshape your life—that's part of the fun of succeeding. I thought I would have less time if I was successful, but in fact I have more. To do my new job, I've had to plan out my day intelligently, instead of going to the office and putting in as long a day as possible just to prove I'm working. Now I can build into my day the kinds of activities that keep me going. I plan for two games of squash a week, I work in a couple of mornings of jogging and tennis, and I don't let myself become stagnant. It's like being reborn!"

Sex and Success

Success is a rebirth in many ways. Significantly, successful people often report more intense sexual activity in their lives. This doubtless comes partly from the fact that success itself is a kind of aphrodisiac. People are attracted to success—it is after all more exciting than failure. The ability to control and shape things in one's career inevitably suggests a sexual ability as well, though this may be deceptive. Women are attracted to successful men (and not just because they have more money), and in a liberated society men are increasingly attracted to successful women.

One entrepreneur, who rose from obscurity to sudden fame and wealth, underwent a radical transformation of his personal life at the same time. He left his wife, his children, and his $250,000 house in Armonk to go and live with a top woman banking executive, who is as busy and as ambitious as he is. "Look," he said, "it's not just your usual turning-forty love affair. There's more to it than that. My wife and I got along fine, but I couldn't begin to tell her what I was doing in my day. She was happy enough that I was successful, sure, but she loved me just as much when I wasn't, and she couldn't really share the excitement of it.

"I met Susan during a merger negotiation, and I *admired* her. I mean that. She's beautiful and charming, and all those good things, but I didn't just look at her and say, 'Hey, there's a great body,' which is what I'd always done before. I mean to say, I've been to bed with a lot of women since I've been married, but it's always been for the sex, pure and simple. But this time, I was looking at someone who was just as smart and tough as I am, maybe more so, and who understood what I do. I can learn a lot from Susan, as a matter of fact. And we really turn each other on in other ways than sex, which is a teriffic feeling. I don't feel threatened by her success, either. I admire it, and it makes her more exciting. So we're both busy. O.K. But even if we have fewer hours together than most people do, they're good hours. I know she's not sitting at home waiting for me to come home, with nothing but time on her hands, and *she* knows that when I come home we'll have something to talk about and exchange."

Success builds up self-esteem and self-confidence and opens up wider horizons; it stimulates what amounts to a process of rejuvenation. It would be remarkable if this did not lead to higher sexual expectations. It does not, of course, always follow that these expectations are met. Several analysts report that the incidence of impotence among successful men who suddenly fling themselves into a new and more ambitious sexual life is remarkably high. After all, ability to perform in one new area does not *necessarily* mean ability to perform in others.

A marriage which has endured ten years of benign stagnation may crack when the husband succeeds. He may come to expect the kind of adulation at home that he gets at work, and expect his success to be reflected in his sexual life. But to his wife he is still the same man. His new office and responsibilities do not alter his physical person and are unlikely to change the habits of a marriage of years. It is not surprising, therefore, that a great many people are embittered by success, disappointed that it does not magically transform their domestic lives as it has their working lives. This is not to suggest that divorce need necessarily accompany success, though if it does, then it is a painful process that must be gone through realistically.

The momentum of success should rather be used to

improve marriage—to improve the totality of life. When you succeed, you finally have an opportunity to make those changes in your personal life that will give you satisfaction. It is the time to take stock, to go on a vacation, to pay more attention to your family, to ask your wife what *she* wants to do, to make the same kind of basic changes in your personal life that you have had to make in your working life. Success implies and demands change, and anyone who has been dynamic in one area and attempts to remain static in another is bound to run into serious trouble.

Success should be a kind of liberation, extending to all aspects of life; and in the realm of sex, success has great potential as a source of attraction—as one person put it, it's "the ultimate turn-on."

PART 2

How To Succeed

3

Success Techniques

Happy is he who is born cruel, for if not he
will have to school himself in cruelty.

—John Fischer

> A leader is best
> when people barely know he exists.
> Not so good
> when people obey and acclaim him.
> Worse when they despise him.
> But of a good leader
> who talks little
> when his work is done
> his aim fulfilled
> they will say:
> "We did it ourselves."
>
> —Lao-Tse

ENERGY:
THE NUMBER-ONE QUALITY

The first rule of success, and the one that supersedes
all others, is to have energy.

It is important to know how to concentrate it, how
to husband it, how to focus it on important things instead of frittering it away on trivia. But first you have
to have it. And a surprising number of people don't.

Working long hours, taking a slavish interest in detail, worrying about office politics—these may or may not be necessary sacrifices, but they don't indicate energy. In fact, by doing all these things you may merely be draining away whatever energy you have.

Energy is a positive quality—a desire to get things done, and done the right way. It's an active quality—an urgent need to move from one point to another, to rise to a specific goal, to advance to a new position, to accomplish a given job. Energy is never static.

It's a pleasurable quality; as in exercise, those who have energy enjoy using it and are excited when it's put to the test.

Your Energy Potential

Some people are born with energy. They're lucky. They work hard at school and in sports, they take on extracurricular activities, they put their heart and soul into everything they do, and invariably succeed. Most of us don't. We may work hard enough when we have to, or even when we want to. But it's uphill work, like that of poor Sisyphus pushing his rock to the top of the mountain, only to have it roll back down again. For many people, work seems like just that—an unremitting and exhausting struggle to do something, which will only need to be repeated as soon as it's over.

Such people have no sense of accomplishment. They view their work as an endless stretch of drudgery, a far horizon that can never be reached. Under the circumstances, it is hardly surprising that their energy level is low. Perhaps the best way to develop energy is this: *Split up your day into the smallest possible segments of time.* Treat each segment as independent and worthwhile in itself. Once you've broken your work down into components, you can launch yourself into one thing, get it done, then go on to the next task. You give yourself a change of pace and a renewed sense of accomplishment.

Begin by analyzing your workload in a *positive* way. I emphasize positive because when most ambitious, hard-working people analyze what they do, the tendency is for them to throw up their hands in despair. This is a defeatist attitude and must be avoided. An example: For years I began each work day in a state of anxiety-neurosis and rage. The desk I had left behind the night before, neatly arranged with completed (or, alas, half-completed) work, was already a sea of messages and mail when I arrived in the morning. Telephones were ringing, and people were already lined up waiting to see me. I plunged in, but by eleven in the morning I was frazzled and overwrought, resentful that I had put in two hours of work without any visible accomplishment.

Then I decided that it was important to begin the day by accomplishing something, however trivial. I would spend the first hour of the morning answering mail. I would take no telephone calls, see nobody. I treated the mail as a separate, important but finite block of work. When I had read it, answered it, taken the necessary action where action was called for and gotten rid of it *all,* I had a cup of coffee, took a walk around the office to see what was happening, then went back to answer telephone calls on a priority basis. It was not very long before I began to look forward to my first hour—it gave me a sense of accomplishment and purpose. I could apply my energy to a limited task, instead of letting it dissipate early in the day by not being focused on anything.

The Self-reward System for Success

To develop energy, treat yourself as if you were a child! Reward yourself at every opportunity. If you smoke, don't light up a cigarette until you have finished what you set out to do, then leave your desk, sit down comfortably and *enjoy* your cigarette. If you like a cup of coffee and a Danish in the morning, make yourself answer your mail (or whatever else can be dealt with first thing), *then* drink your coffee. The secret is *conditioning*: By attacking small tasks with anticipation, zeal and concentration you are teaching yourself to develop and focus your energy potential. And if it takes a candy bar, or a cup of coffee, or a cigarette to do it, don't be ashamed. Not everyone is born with the ability to use his or her full energy capacity.

Controlled Laziness

Another way of developing an energy capacity is "controlled laziness." I am by nature lazy, and as a child wasted so much time that I was seldom prepared for examinations. Recognizing this as a liability (a discovery that is less common than it should be, since many people carry it through their lives), I put it to work for me. I would deliberately take on a major job and plunge into it so that I could get it out of the way and have nothing to do.

This sounds easy, but it's not. Most of us fail because we delay tackling the difficult jobs that would win recognition. We are held back by simple laziness, which produces a kind of permanent inertia if it's allowed to fester. It is almost hopeless to try to eliminate laziness from your personality if it's there. The trick is to use it, to transform a negative quality into a positive reinforcement.

Plan For Laziness

If you have a big report to write that will take four hours, tell yourself that when it's done, you can be lazy again, that the only thing that's *preventing* you from enjoying your laziness is the report. Then attack it as if it were the enemy, get it out of the way, and give yourself a spell of real, pleasurable *earned* laziness.

Don't be afraid of wasting time—simply make your-self do something *before* you sit down to waste time. By this method, even the laziest person can develop a measure of fiercely concentrated energy, if only for short bursts. Once you have developed a capacity for utilizing your full energy briefly, you can go on to use it for longer periods. The trick is to put yourself in touch with it in the first place. Once it's been tapped, once we know that we *can* turn ourselves on to work with energy, we soon discover that it is an inexhausti-ble resource.

Complete Every Action

One of the most common deterrents to developing energy is the failure to complete an action. Like elec-tricity, energy flows and must not be interrupted.

When you set out to do something, complete it.

If you don't think you can complete it, then don't even begin it. Energy thrives on achievement and de-clines as things drag on repetitiously. For this reason, it is sensible to begin your day with something that can be dealt with positively and brought to a conclu-sion. Pick a relatively simple problem from your list of things to do, and solve it. Then move on to a harder one, and gradually work your way up to the problems to which there are no easily identifiable solutions. You will now be attacking them from a position of strength, knowing that you have already achieved something in the day. If you start your morning indecisively, or with a failure, you are likely to continue the day on the same note, with a consequent ebb in energy.

The Energy Look

It is possible to simulate energy to a certain degree. These energy-developing habits may eventually help you become naturally energetic.

It is important, for example, to move decisively. Look as if you were on your way to do something, rather than moping along as if you had nothing to do. Most successful people walk at a fast, purposeful pace, even if they're only on the way to the bathroom or the water cooler. Posture is equally important. It's hard to seem energetic if you're slouched over, with your hands in your pockets and your stomach sticking out. Your entire body should convey energy. Stand erect, move briskly, hold your head up and pull your stomach in. You'll look alive and alert. Like it or not, we are usually judged on appearance, and if we appear

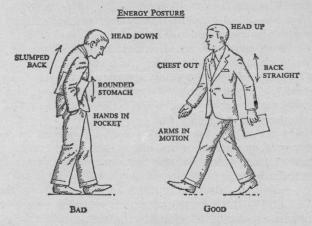

ENERGY POSTURE

HEAD DOWN   HEAD UP

SLUMPED BACK   CHEST OUT   BACK STRAIGHT

ROUNDED STOMACH

HANDS IN POCKET

ARMS IN MOTION

BAD   GOOD

listless, slow-moving and lethargic, all the hard work in the world will not convince people that we're worth promoting.

It is possible to convey energy even while standing still: simply square your shoulders—and keep your hands out of your pockets! One good way to do the latter is to make sure you're carrying something—a report, a file, a piece of paper—anything that expresses a purpose and keeps your hands (or at any rate one of them) in an active position.

Those who like gadgets may prefer to carry a portable dictating machine. This underlines the fact that you are always ready to dictate a quick thought or memo. A small electronic paging device (a "beeper") may be equally useful, since it implies that your importance is sufficient to justify instant communication. This beeper was greatly favored by White House aides in the Nixon era, since it provided visible (and sometimes audible) proof that somebody, maybe even the President of the United States, wanted to get in touch with them. John Erlichman has pointed out, however, that the ultimate status symbol in this particular area was the special device used by high officials of the CIA. Once, when he went to the theater and found himself sitting next to Richard Helms, then director of the CIA, Helms noticed the beeper in Ehrlichman's pocket and commented on it.

"That's very impressive, John," he said, "but noisy. We use a 'feeler' in the CIA." With that, he pulled out of his trouser pocket a small, rectangular device. When activated by an electronic signal from Langley, it silently scratched its owner's leg, indicating that an urgent message waited for him.

On the whole, the importance of all gadgets is determined by relative status, rather than by any rational need. Lately, it has become fashionable for executives to put computer consoles on their desks, the implication being that they understand how to use the office computer—which is seldom the case—and also that they have a vital need for instant information.

Pocket calculators, for some reason, do not perform the same function. They are too cheap and widely available. And who wants to show that he can't add or subtract without electronic help? On the whole, however, it is better to have something in your hand than to walk about empty-handed. In the absence of anything else, the newspaper will do, provided it is turned back to the business section.

The Language of Sitting

It's not only in walking that you can convey energy. It's just as important to know how to do so when you're sitting and at rest. Energetic people seldom slump. They transform sitting itself into an activity. They sit upright, conveying alertness and a sense of purpose.

As there is with every other body movement, there is a language to sitting.

The kind of huge executive chairs that are favored by Presidents of the United States seem to me to be a

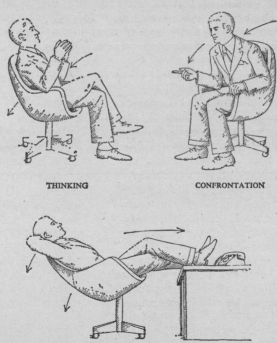

THINKING   CONFRONTATION

SELF-CONFIDENCE

mistake for the average person. Any chair so big that it towers above your head and holds you as if you were in King Kong's hand merely makes you look small and trapped. A chair should be of modest dimensions, with a low, comfortable back. You don't have to do business out of a seat that looks as if you are strapped into it for a moon launch. It should also be of some nice neutral color—*not* black, which makes most people look as if they were guests at their own funeral. And above all, it should be made of some material that doesn't make noises. Certain kinds of imitation leather have a tendency to squeak, and others stick to your body and whenever you change positions produce a sound that is embarrassingly similar to that of someone breaking wind. If you're going to use your chair for body language, you should also make sure of its limits; nothing looks sillier than being dumped on the floor by your own furniture.

Given the right kind of chair, and some control over it, you can swivel around suddenly to face somebody (confrontation), put your feet on your desk and tilt back (self-confidence and an "I don't care" attitude), lean forward suddenly and adopt the arms-on-the-desktop posture ("No more Mr. Nice Guy").

NO MORE "MR. NICE GUY"

THE <u>WRONG</u> CHAIR

THE <u>RIGHT</u> CHAIR

If you want to convey that you're relaxed and free, you can push the chair away from the desk altogether, and lean back in the classic American executive relaxation position, with the ankle of one leg resting on the opposite knee, one hand clasping the ankle.

CLASSIC "RELAXATION" POSITION

It is amazing how much movement people can put into the simple business of sitting, and how easy it is to project enormous energy and drive from your chair, instead of just sitting there like a bump on a log.

You should seem *dynamic,* as if your energy is only barely being held in check. The key is to convey restlessness rather than to fidget pointlessly. Finger tapping, head twitching and foot shaking are out— they merely indicate a lack of interest in the conversation or a bad case of nerves. An extreme example of this is to cradle two telephone handsets on your shoulders simultaneously, while writing a note to yourself and carrying on a conversation with a third party in your office. This requires a good deal of dexterity, but it can be mastered, and produces a powerful impression of zeal, drive and overwork.

Sleeping, an Energy Look!

Oddly enough, if you know the knack, even sleeping can be used to project energy. A good friend of mine occasionally takes a nap on his office couch in midafternoon. He does not sleep at his desk, as most people do after a heavy business lunch with too many martinis. Nor does he attempt to blunder through the afternoon heavy-tongued and glassy-eyed. He simply says that he's tired, has his calls held, and goes to sleep for half an hour. People conclude that his energy level has been depleted by hard work, since most of the time he gives a very dynamic impression indeed. Naturally, it is necessary to bounce back after a nap and show a virtuoso display of vitality in the remaining hours of the late afternoon. But this is no great trick in most offices, where the energy level of the executives declines rapidly after four o'clock. Even if you produce a brief closing rally of activity just before the bell, it will stand out by contrast with everybody else's languorous preparations for departure.

Energy Eating

One of the surest ways to deprive yourself of energy is to break up your day with an enormous meal. I am not suggesting that your way to success should be paved with crunchy Granola or organic nuts, but the traditional two martinis with a full luncheon is a mistake for most people. Successful people tend to eat sparingly during the day, not just to keep slim but to avoid that after-lunch slump that extends, in so many cases, to quitting time. Most restaurants have recognized this fact. If your business requires a lot of lunching out with clients, make sure you go to a restaurant where you can impress them without eating a four-course French meal.

In the East, restaurants like the Four Seasons and "21" in New York have taken to providing a light grill-room lunch for businessmen, which allows your guest to use one menu and you another. In the West, restaurants like the Polo Lounge of the Beverly Hills Hotel or the Brown Derby in Los Angeles specialize in superb salads, which serve much the same purpose. Wherever you live, it is usually possible to order a small grilled piece of fish or meat and a salad, and to have a glass of Perrier water with a slice of lime. (Club soda has less status but will do.) Do not be led into the common trap of feeling that you must eat as much as your guest (or worse yet, drink as much as your guest). Remember: he or she may be going home to relax after lunch, while you are going back to work.

If you eat in, it's worth trying to make that an enjoyable experience, instead of ordering a heavy sandwich at the last minute, and eating yourself into a comatose state on potato salad. Bring what you like to the office with you—some of the most successful people do—and eat a pleasant lunch at your desk. In the winter you can enjoy a Thermos full of good soup, in the summer some cold cuts and a little fresh fruit. The object is keep your energy level high, not to succumb to the midday collapse.

Early Birds

Some advantage can be gained by getting into the office early, though you have to be careful about this. If you get in so early that you have finished answering your mail and doing most of your morning paperwork before everyone else arrives, they are likely to find you sitting there reading the newspaper and drinking coffee at nine o'clock. One way around this is to leave memos on your colleagues' desks to greet them when *they* get in. These serve as visible proof that you have already been hard at work while they are still commuting, or even asleep.

This can be carried too far. I know one executive who got in to work at six o'clock in the morning. The president of the company was incredulous when he heard about this, and decided to verify it with his own eyes. He came in at seven and found his man hard at work. The next day he came in at six, to find his man hard at work.

By now the executive, who felt he was being watched for some mysterious disciplinary reason, decided that he had better get into the office before the president. He began arriving at five-thirty A.M., which forced the president to come in at five. News of this soon seeped through the office, and everyone began to come in early, unwilling to arrive later than the president. Unfortunately, the secretaries saw no reason to join in this madness, nor did the mailroom staff and the service departments. The executives were there bright and early, all right, but there was no mail, nor were there any telephone operators, filing clerks or accounting personnel. Sleepy, ill-tempered and grouchy, the executives put in two wasteful hours in the early morning, began real work at the same time, as usual, and were so tired by four o'clock that they went home early.

Productivity and morale dipped, and the executive vice-president was finally forced to announce that nobody was to enter the office before eight in the morning. My friend, a man who gets up at four and does his best work before nine, quit when this new regime was announced. He now works for another company, in which he has sensibly kept his early morning activity a secret. Just before nine, he puts on his coat, picks up his brief case, and goes down into the lobby of the building so that he can come back up again at the same time as his fellow executives. His prospects for promotion, he tells me, are very good.

In any case, it's worth noting that very successful people with a high energy level do tend to get an early start, though they may not get to the office early to prove it. A recent survey of executives earning more than $200,000 a year indicates that most of them are in the office by eight in the morning, but have been hard at work for hours before. Lew R. Wasserman, chairman of MCA, Inc., "sleeps on a couch next to his wife's bedroom in their Beverly Hills home so he won't disturb her when he rises at five A.M. to place calls to New York." [1]

He is not alone. André Meyer, of Lazard Frères & Co., gets up at the same hour to place calls to Europe. Charles B. Thornton, the president of Litton Industries, sometimes gets up at four, and the late Gustave B. Levy, of Goldman, Sachs & Co. usually rose at four-thirty to work through his brief case. Nor do these eminently successful men shave time off the tail end of the day. Most of them are in their offices until six or seven in the evening, and their dinner parties are indistinguishable from business. You can feign a high level of activity and energy output, but the real thing is as awe-inspiring as Niagara Falls.

Don't Fight Your Natural Habits—Use Them

It certainly helps to *look* energetic, but developing creative energy habits is a bit more difficult. A certain amount of common sense will help. Most people spend their days locked in mortal combat with their natural habits and behavior patterns. Nothing is more counterproductive. For example:

- If you don't like making cocktail dates, *don't*. Invite people up to your office instead. You can offer them a drink and have a cup of coffee yourself, and talk business more quietly than you could in a bar.
- If you're not a morning person and hate breakfast, don't ever be persuaded to attend a breakfast meeting. You will not be in top form for the meeting, and it may ruin the rest of your day.
- If you like to go to bed early and rise early, then imitate Lew Wasserman and go through your "homework" in the early morning, in bed if necessary, rather than forcing yourself to stay up late to do it.

Naturally, you will have to make compromises from time to time, but the important thing is to learn to respect your own needs and patterns and impose them on others whenever possible. The more energy you spend fighting against your inclinations, the less you will have to put to work for you.

Sylvia, an active lady executive of my acquaintance, has one of those jobs that require working late most evenings of the week. She goes home at four in the afternoon, takes an hour-long beauty sleep, bathes, changes and comes back to the office with renewed energy to work for two more hours. Several executives I know take one day off a week—usually Wednesday—to work at home. You may not be in a position or a business that allows this, but if you are, and if it works for you, do it. You can often increase your work output and your energy by breaking the week up into two separate sections (hence Wednesday is the logical day to take off), but you have to guard against using your "home" day for household chores or going to the movies. Properly planned, it can be the most productive day of the week.

Creative Routines

If you are somebody who thrives on routine, build one that you can live with and enjoy, and make sure it is varied enough to give you a frequent change of pace. I know one company president who works best on a tightly scheduled, preplanned day, with each meeting and appointment timed to the minute. Every evening, his secretary hands him a card with his next day's schedule neatly typed up. Each appointment is recorded—time, place, people, subject and the length of time the discussion should take.

Personally, I have long since discovered that I can't work to a fixed schedule. I need open-ended time, especially toward the close of the day when I'm trying to get all my telephone calls completed before people

leave their offices. I make it a rule not to meet people
for drinks or to have any fixed appointments between
four and six. Knowing that I have these two hours
ahead of me every afternoon reduces the tension of
my day considerably. What works for me may not
work for you. Everyone has his or her own work me-
tabolism. Discover what yours is, and learn to live
with it.

The Dangers of Boredom

Energetic people are rarely bored. Boredom saps
one's energy like nothing else in the world. If you feel
that you're falling into patterns of boredom that reduce your energy try the following (but don't simply
turn these things into a new routine!):

- Make a bet with yourself that you can get done
what you have to get done before the end of the day,
and reward yourself when you have.
- Vary the order in which you do things. Try putting your mail off to the end of the day, for example, or setting aside the last quarter of each hour
for answering telephone calls.
- Give yourself *one major goal* a day, and accomplish it, whatever else you have to drop.
- Make one day a week a "catch-up" day so that
you can afford to put a lot of small, irritating things
aside.
- Don't be ashamed to delegate. You are judged
on results, not the amount of trivia you can handle.
The more other people can do for you, the more
you can get done.

HOW TO SUCCEED FACE-TO-FACE

When we discussed the difference between lions and
foxes, we learned that foxes work behind the scenes,
whereas lions have the courage to fight things out face-

to-face. If you're going to be a success, you must learn to endure "eyeball" confrontations and come out the winner.

Most people are held back by an inability to deal with another person whose interests are opposed to theirs, which explains why the telephone is such a useful instrument. The fact remains that you can't expect to get ahead unless you can sit down with someone and fight for your point of view.

In a face-to-face confrontation, a certain amount of strategy is permissible.

• First Rule: Don't Sit Opposite Your "Opponent."

Try not to have confrontations while sitting behind your desk with the other party in front of the desk. You are all too likely to feel mentally trapped if you let yourself be physically trapped. By facing him or her directly, you produce a kind of duel mentality. The combative instinct is inevitably aroused, and this may lead to a sharper confrontation than you are able to deal with. If you think there's going to be trouble, get out from behind your desk and sit down beside him on the couch, if you have one. If you don't, ar-

HOW TO BREAK BAD NEWS

YOU   SUPPLIER OR CLIENT

METHOD A (IF YOU HAVE A COUCH)

METHOD B (IF YOU DON'T HAVE ONE)

range matters so that his chair is to one side of your desk, if possible so you're both facing in the same direction.

● SECOND RULE: MOVE FAST, STRIKE THE FIRST BLOW.

Make sure you have some way of terminating the conversation rather than letting it drag on into specifics. The moment the other party begins to produce copies of invoices, documents and contracts to justify his position, you have lost the essential momentum of the confrontation. In a case like this, the details can and should be left to some later meeting, or allowed to work their way down to the lawyers, where they will eventually serve as the basis for tedious and expensive litigation. The purpose of confrontation is not to go over details of the matter at hand and see who is right (or which side is least wrong, generally) but to establish a firm dominating position as the basis for further action.

Since it is equally important to get your opponent out of your office before the shock has worn off and he's started to argue his case, it helps to arrange beforehand to have somebody telephone you five to ten minutes after the confrontation has begun. You can then claim to have been called to a meeting and firmly but politely end the discussion and walk your visitor to the door—even to the elevators, if you think there's a chance he may turn around and come back as soon as he has regained his senses.

- THIRD RULE: IF YOU CAN, PICK THE TIME FOR ANY CONFRONTATION CAREFULLY.

If you have to fire somebody, do it just before lunch, making sure that both of you have lunch dates. That sets a time limit on the confrontation, and prevents an endless discussion about the unfairness and brutality of the decision.

- FOURTH RULE: THE "CHESHIRE CAT ROUTINE."

If somebody is coming into your office to see you on a matter which promises to be distasteful to you both, ask the receptionist to let your visitor in, then vanish. Go to the bathroom, borrow someone else's office to make a few telephone calls, or go downstairs to the bank. Don't overdo it. If you keep anyone waiting for more than five minutes he will be legitimately angry. What you're aiming for is to have the person standing in your office alone for a couple of minutes so that you can make your entry in a forceful, dynamic way. Unless the person is a very experienced gamesperson, he will be ill-at-ease when left alone in a stranger's office. Not knowing whether to sit down or stand up, he tends to feel like a trespasser. If you time it right, you may even be able to surprise the person standing fairly close to your desk, trying to read your mail while pretending not to. This puts him in a position of acute embarrassment when you suddenly rush through to door, holding a file in your hand, and sit down at your desk. You can easily increase this embarrassment by carefully putting the file on top of your mail, in a polite but regretful manner, as if you wanted to prevent a further display of curiosity.

Of course, if you're in the opposite position—the visitor's role, as it were—and this trick is played on you, sit down in a comfortable chair, take out the

newspaper and begin to do the crossword puzzle.
When the person who has kept you waiting comes in,
you can immediately gain the upper hand by asking
him for a ten-letter word meaning "lizard's relative."

- ### FIFTH RULE: AVOID THE OTHER PERSON'S EYES.

  It is worth remembering that trained soldiers and
policemen very often find it impossible to shoot an
armed attacker at close quarters, and not a few of
them die as a result of this perfectly natural human
hesitation. There is something about the sight of an
adversary at close range that saps one's determination
to attack. Policemen, for example, are taught never to
look an armed opponent in the eyes. It weakens his
resolve if he concentrates on the most expressive and
alive of human features. (For that matter, quite a few
hunters would be unable to shoot a deer if they had to
look into its eyes at close range.) What is more, combat experience has shown that looking straight into
the other person's eyes is very likely to frighten and
provoke him. Finally, the eyes are an unreliable in-
dicator of human intention. They may seem steady,
unblinking and trustworthy, but the hand may already
be reaching for a pistol. Trained combat shooters look
at their adversaries' hands, with particular attention to
the right hand. If the adversary already has a pistol in
his hand, they look at the knuckles.

  You, of course, are not in quite that position, but
the same advice holds true. Avoid the eyes, and place
yourself at such an angle that your own are hard to
see. The mouth is a good choice as a point of vision
for business confrontations. It is much easier to dislike someone's mouth than his eyes.

- ### SIXTH RULE: DON'T FALL INTO THE TRAP OF
  SAYING, "IT'S NOT MY DECISION BUT . . ."

  The last thing you want to provoke is a discussion
of whether or not you personally agree with a decision, or who in fact made it. If you have the responsibility of carrying out the confrontation, you must

always take the full responsibility for the decision, even if it isn't yours. The best way to increase your courage is to make *yourself* responsible.

One executive I know, whose specialty was conciliation, was put in charge of a department that had gone to pieces. It was necessary for him to fire a great many people, demote others, and confront a whole host of outside suppliers whose services were unsatisfactory. At first the task seemed impossible for a man who was at heart a gentle soul and a reasonable human being. But gradually he found that it was not so difficult, after all.

"I learned," he told me, "never to discuss things in detail and drag them out. And I also discovered that one's fears about confrontation are pointless. What can happen, after all? The people you have to fire aren't going to attack you physically, and some of them may even feel they deserve to be fired. The worst the outside suppliers can do is make threats and go to their lawyers, but everybody thinks twice about that, given what it costs, and if they do, it's no longer my business. Their lawyer sees our lawyer, and the whole thing is taken out of my hands. I used to think it required extraordinary courage to run things, but it doesn't. It's easy, so long as you don't let yourself be drawn into a clash of egos. The moment you let *macho* enter into it—and there are plenty of *macho* women, so I'm not being a male chauvinist—you're lost. You have to do it fast and directly, instead of trying to persuade the other guy that you're *right*. After all, right or wrong, he's *going,* if it's your responsibility to fire him."

Taking Over: How to Succeed Before Anyone Has Noticed It

The best way to succeed is to take on responsibility quietly. The determination to take on responsibility implies a certain humility at the beginning. You may have to take on unwelcome chores, sometimes even degrading ones. It doesn't matter. Seek for things that *you* can get done, even if it's only firing people nobody else wants to face. My old friend Marge is now a powerful and important publishing executive who has become famous for her ambitions and daring deals, and in fact triumphantly brought off the first seven-figure paperback sale in publishing history.

Marge, like so many women in publishing, began as a secretary, and a good one—the kind of secretary that men of a certain age refer to as "a treasure." She worked for the head of the foreign rights department, a middle-aged man with a passion for making lists and charts. Marge was indeed the "perfect secretary," meticulous, hard-working, efficient and eager to learn. She was also ambitious, which in those days, before the advent of Women's Liberation, seemed to most men an endearing eccentricity in a woman. As a rule, their attitude was that she would "grow out of it." After all, women got married, had children, and if they continued to work, "settled down" to become permanent fixtures as secretaries.

Marge did not seek out confrontations. She simply took on responsibility, indeed made a fetish of it. She did not ask for the "right" to make decisions, she simply said (again and again), "Tell me what you want done, and I'll take care of it." Was it a question of arranging to fly the president of the company to the Frankfurt Book Fair, making sure that his accommodations were suitably luxurious, and lining up enough prestigious foreign publishers and celebrities to wine and dine him? She would do it, and in the process, she learned about the book fair, made contact with people abroad and earned the gratitude of the president. Whenever there was a decision to be made, Marge cleared it with the people above her, but she never failed to make a recommendation. If it was followed, fine; if not, she did what she had been told to do, efficiently and loyally. Her opinion was on record.

She took on a wide variety of such tedious tasks as list-making, record-keeping and scheduling, made arrangements for conventions and meetings to which she was never invited. One day it became evident that she was more necessary to the corporation than the man she worked for. Wisely, she made no attempt to take his job. She simply asked for a job with more responsibility, and even made herself responsible for finding her boss a new secretary as efficient as herself.

Her new job gave her leverage between several different departments. By making herself into a kind of central clearing house for information, she made it impossible for anyone to function without coming to her. But at no point did she demand the right to make autonomous decisions. "People are always afraid to let you have the right to decide things, particularly if you're a woman," she said once. "But what's so important about making decisions in the first place? Take on more and more responsibility until they can't make decisions without consulting *you!*"

And indeed this soon happened. No decision could be made without involving Marge. She had proved that she was effectively able to handle any task, large or small, up to and including the negotiation of million-dollar deals. But she began by training herself in responsibility with just those small, tedious tasks that nobody else wants. And this is true for everyone—responsibility has to be sought not by trying to make decisions for other people, which always leads to trouble, but by assuming a great many tasks and then following through on them.

The Memo As a Secret Success Weapon

One way to increase your responsibilities is to intercept memos. For example, what would you do if you read the following memo?

To: Manufacturing Department
From: Robert Townsend [department head]
Date: January 1, 1978

Re: Imported books

It has been brought to my attention
that books printed for us by foreign
publishers and imported in finished
form do not always meet the specifications agreed upon in the contract,
and that in some cases the foreign
supplier has either substituted
cheaper materials or neglected to
follow our house style in laying out
the copyright page or the title page,
etc.

I expect everyone in this department
to pay particular attention to this
problem when dealing with foreign
suppliers. Double-check everything,
and when in doubt clear it with me.
    [signed] Robert Townsend

Copies to :
C. Northcote Parkinson [executive
vice-president]

Adam Smith   ⎫
Margaret Glinn   ⎪
Robert Metz   ⎪
Leonard Silk   ⎬ [production staff]
Morton Janklow   ⎪
Jay Watnick   ⎪
Murray Ramson   ⎭

Several things can be concluded from this memo.
The first is that a major crisis has erupted over a book
that has been delivered which didn't meet specifications, and that the executive vice-president has used

some strong language in private to express his displeasure with the head of the manufacturing department. Further proof of this is the presence of the executive vice-president's name at the head of the check list. The memo has in fact been written *for* him, as a sign that the problem is being faced. Another thing that emerges from the memo is that the sender hasn't any clear idea about how the problem can be solved. He is hoping that his staff will somehow pull together and save him. In fact, he is asking for their support. After all, if they took greater pains to check, double-check and check again, he wouldn't be in trouble in the first place.

Unfortunately, the memo—like most memos—merely alerts those who read it to the fact that there's a problem. It doesn't tell them it's *their* problem, or suggest they do anything about it. Everyone is simply invited to check his or her name off, and send the memo on to the next person, which is exactly what they will do.

Now, let us assume that you are one of the production staff, or even the secretary for one of them. What you do when you see a memo like this (and we all see dozens every week) is to intercept it. Instead of checking off your name, or your boss's, and sending it on its way to oblivion, take it to the department head and suggest that *you* take on responsibility for clearing all such matters. Develop a system, set up a central file, make sure that you are in control. And, of course, alert everyone else to your new status with a memo of your own.

To: Robert Townsend
From: Margaret Glinn
Date: January 15, 1978

Re: Imported books

Henceforth no authorization to print will be given to foreign printers until the specifications have been

checked against the original agreement, a copy of which I have on file.

This procedure is designed to prevent
errors and to ensure that in every
case the original specifications are
met.
   [signed] Margaret Glinn

Copies to:
C. Northcote Parkinson [executive
vice-president][Etc.]

A few creative memos like this, and your reputation for responsibility will be firmly established in the
mind of your equivalent of Mr. Parkinson. No matter
how unpromising the material may seem, read every
delivery of mail as if your life depended on it (which,
in a sense, it may). Study the memos everybody else
simply passes on or throws away, look for the areas in
which you can be useful and responsible, and exploit
them intelligently.

SELF-CONTROL

Almost every successful person, when questioned
about the definition of character, stresses "responsibility and integrity" (Paul A. Miller, president of the
Eaton Corporation), or "energy and integrity" (W.
Michael Blumenthal, former chairman of the Bendix
Corporation and now Secretary of the Treasury).[2] Integrity is, of course, very difficult to define. It may or
may not imply honesty, depending on the nature of
the corporation and the job. But probably the best definition is that someone can be counted on to behave
consistently and reliably, whatever the circumstances.
   Nobody is going to expect an executive of a major
chemical company to come out strongly against the
dangers of food additives, just as nobody expects oil

company executives to admit that their profits are very high, or labor leaders to admit they have ties to organized crime. On the other hand, everyone can be reasonably expected to maintain their cool. And that ability comes from the vital character ingredient called self-control.

More than lack of integrity, it is lack of self-control that leads people into situations where their feet slip out from under them. How many times have you said, "If only I could go back and undo what I've done!" The trick is always to ask yourself one simple question before doing anything: "What's the worst that can happen?" If the worst is unacceptable, don't do it.

The Watergate defendants were perfect examples of the failure in ambitious, intelligent and successful men to ask that one question of themselves and answer it honestly. They may have assumed, of course, that the worst that could happen would be that the burglary and the subsequent cover-up would fail. In such cases, the question can be made a little sharper and more personal, and thus more powerful as a character-building device, by simply adding two words: "What's the worst that can happen *to me?*" In the case of the Watergate defendants, most of whom were lawyers, the answer should have been fairly clear: exposure, prison and disbarment.

Let us imagine that you are negotiating a contract and suddenly realize the person you are negotiating with has completely misunderstood a key clause, in a way that is obviously to your advantage. Do you gain points with your side by keeping quiet about it so you can later show that you made a terrific deal? Or do you point out to him that he's agreeing to something he doesn't understand and probably won't be able to deliver on? You simply ask yourself the vital question, and the answer, in almost every case, will be that the potential for embarrassment and bad feeling that will result from taking an unfair advantage of the other negotiator is not worth whatever the temporary gain might be to you. Remember the old Wall Street saying:

"Bears make money, bulls make money, hogs never make money." This is true. The wise person knows better than to go too far.

Self-control Exercises

Excercising self-control is by no means easy, as any dieter knows, but it can be done. I have already recommended that you increase your capacity for work by developing a series of rewards for yourself. Self-control can be learned in much the same way. If you think you talk too much, and people have criticized you for interrupting them (a common example of failed self-control), concentrate on really listening to the other person, however boring this may seem to you. Then reward yourself with a break, a cigarette or a soda when you have managed to hear him out fully without interrupting. Learn to *use* your temptations, instead of resisting them.

One of the best ways of learning self-control is to talk to yourself. I know this is usually seen as the first sign of madness. But you don't have to do it in public. A team of researchers has in fact been looking into the idea and has been finding it a useful device for those who lack self-control and suffer from anxiety.[8]

It works. When faced with a difficult decision or a crisis, sit down and act it out in your mind, if necessary actually do so out loud. Force yourself to say what you think the person who is angry with you, or disappointed in you or simply opposed to you, would in fact say in a face-to-face meeting. Present your arguments and his counterarguments. Act out the discussion and imagine it actually happening. Let us say that you have been asked to explain to a difficult client that he's not going to get what he wanted. Imagine what he will say, raise all the points that you think he will raise, answer them, look for the weak points in your counterargument, anticipate the rising heat of the discussion, test how you're handling the situation. Concentrate on making this preenactment as realistic as possible. If the confrontation is to take place in your office, then act it out in your office. If not, try to give yourself a clear mental image of where it will take place. By acting things out in advance, we do more than simply rehearse a situation. We prepare ourselves for it, we reduce anxiety by eliminating to the greatest possible degree the element of surprise, and we increase our capacity for calm self-control. Having prepared ourselves, we are much more likely to behave with integrity and balance, since the temptation to propose or accept something rash and improper has effectively been screened out in advance.

Sifting

Concentrating on something that requires little or no concentration is a waste of time. More wasteful still is to try and mix routine work with work that requires concentration. The key to getting things done successfully is to *sift*. Whatever your job is, begin the day by sifting through the problems and projects ahead of you, separating them into categories. Separate what can be dealt with as routine from what requires concentration. Put the latter to one side and *forget about*

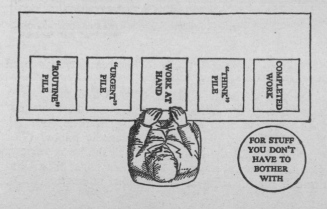

"ROUTINE" PILE   "URGENT" PILE   WORK AT HAND   "THINK" PILE   COMPLETED WORK

FOR STUFF YOU DON'T HAVE TO BOTHER WITH

it. This is not easy to do. The things you are putting to one side are likely to be more important, more interesting and more urgent than the things you're actually sitting down to do. There is a natural tendency to think about them. You have to avoid this. Tell yourself that out of sight is out of mind.

Learn Your Pattern of Concentrating

Now you have to discover your optimum pattern of concentration. Do you concentrate best in short spurts, or do you need a good long quiet period?

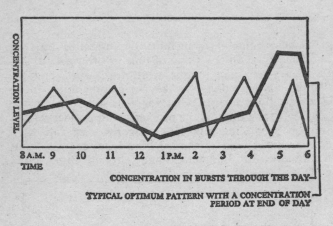

CONCENTRATION IN BURSTS THROUGH THE DAY

TYPICAL OPTIMUM PATTERN WITH A CONCENTRATION PERIOD AT END OF DAY

One way to gauge this is to observe how you read the newspaper in the morning:

Do you set aside a chunk of time and make your way through the newspaper in a methodical manner until you have read everything that interests you? Do you have a fixed pattern for reading the paper? (For example, I read the front page, then the book review, then the editorial page, then the city page, then skim through for anything else that looks interesting.) Or, are you one of those people who keeps the newspaper around all day long, and go back to it from time to time, saving up the crossword puzzle or the sports page to the last?

If you are the kind of person who has a fixed time and pattern for reading the newspaper, then you are probably someone who needs to set aside a regular scheduled period to deal with work that requires concentration. If you find it more enjoyable to read through the newspaper in bits and pieces throughout the day whenever there's a moment of leisure, then your pattern of concentration is better suited to short, intensive bursts. Another way of determining this is to analyze how you read a book. Do you wait until you have time to read it, then plow through it from page one to the end? Or do you leave the book around and come back to it whenever you have the time and are in the mood, without feeling that there's any pressure on you to finish it in one thrust?

If you feel that you need a specific block of time for concentration, hew one out of your day, however much this may inconvenience those around you. For most people, the early morning won't work. Your energy level may be high then, but unless you plan carefully to collect up work for the mornings, you are likely to find yourself awake, alert and intent, but with nothing to concentrate *on*. Most people find it best to put aside an hour at the end of the day, which also has the advantage of giving you some perspective on the day's events. For those who find it difficult to concentrate, there are other advantages to doing it late in the day. In the first place, you can goad yourself on by determining that you won't leave until you have dealt with your "think pile" effectively. This should spur you on (unless you have no desire to go home, in which case you'll need a different goad—a drink, a lover or just dinner). In the second place, it will be easier to set aside a fixed time for yourself, without worrying about interruptions.

Deadlines

The best way to concentrate is to give yourself a
time limit for each task. Most people concentrate best
with a deadline in front of them. Create deadlines,
even if they're artificial or self-imposed. You will work
more effectively if you allow yourself an hour, starting,
let us say, at five o'clock, deciding in advance that you
have to be out of the office and on your way to something at least mildly pleasurable by six. Open-ended
concentration may be all right for philosophers, but in
most of us it actually depletes our ability to reach any
useful conclusion. I have known several people who
were quite capable of sitting at their desks with their
eyes closed, in a posture of deep and intense thought.
When roused, they usually reply, "I'm not asleep, I'm
just concentrating." Heavy breathing, snoring and
snuffling are, however, seldom signs of real concentration. If you're tired—take a rest. But don't persuade
yourself that resting is concentration.

Think Piles

If you're in that lucky group of people who can
concentrate in short bursts, use this ability as a means
to break up the monotony of the day. When you have
the opportunity, pick up the first problem in your
"think pile," close the door and give yourself an uninterrupted fifteen minutes to solve it.

The Color Clock

Keep in mind that concentration is not meditation.
The aim of concentration is external not internal.
Good as meditation may be for you, it is to be guarded
against when you're trying to get something done. A
television producer I know recently bought one of

those mysterious-looking clocks on which the face changes colors in swirling patterns as the hands go around. This handsome and expensive toy nearly destroyed his career. Every time he sat down to think about something, his eyes moved toward the face of the clock, and in his own words, he soon found himself beginning "to float away in space and time."

This is a pleasant but unproductive feeling, and he began to realize that he was spending more hours looking at his clock than working. Being no fool, he put it back in its original box, had his secretary rewrap it, and gave it to his greatest rival at the network. "You never can tell," he said. "Jerry's an asshole, but once he starts getting hooked on that clock, even he may have a spiritual experience. I would guess it's got to cut down on his productivity by at least fifty percent. God knows, it cut mine down to nothing."

Day By Day

Half the reason people find it difficult to concentrate is that they regard each day as the extension of the preceding one. What doesn't get done today can be put off until tomorrow or finished "within the week." Successful people plan their lives for successful *days*. They know what they want to accomplish on a given day, and they set out to do it. This urgency to accomplish things leads naturally to an intensified power of concentration. Learn to think of the day as a vital unit of time, independent from the day before and the day after. Judge your performance by what you have done *today*, not what you did yesterday or what you plan to do tomorrow.

The Tools

Do not make the elementary mistake of concentrating in a vacuum. You need before you all the informa-

tion you can get, and above all you need a pencil,
paper and a dictating machine or tape recorder. A
surprising number of people ignore this simple rule,
and consequently can never remember a solution even
when they produce one. Just as all meetings fail without a formal agenda and somebody present to take
note of the decisions made, all attempts to concentrate
fail unless they result in a direct action.

The "Three-pass" Effect

Once you have the work you want to concentrate on
laid out before you, you have to perform a trick of will.
Eliminate everything else from your mind—*everything*.
Give yourself to the project at hand one hundred percent. Now you use what I call the "three-pass" effect:

- First, read whatever is in front of you quickly,
to familiarize yourself with the broad outlines.
- Next, read it very slowly. Underline the important points, facts and figures.
- Finally, put your mind to work on the specific
problem, and write it down on a separate blank
piece of paper *in one sentence*.

If you use a piece of paper with anything else
written on it, your mind is likely to be drawn to other
things. If you can't reduce the whole thing to one sentence, go back and repeat the procedure until you can.
This may take a couple of seconds, or it may take an
hour. It doesn't matter. Do it.

When you have reduced everything to a sentence
(it may be a question or a statement), think about the
possible resolutions. List them. Ask yourself if your
severest critic, past or present, would make the same
list. Imagine what kind of solution the president of
your company might suggest, or what Henry Kissinger
would do. Would they approach the whole thing differently? Put yourself in their minds. Consider every

alternative. When you have, apply the rule of "What's the worst that can happen?" to each of them. Then examine what the best that can happen would be. Pick the solution in which the maximum benefit coincides with the minimum "worst that can happen." In most cases it will be the right one.

Having solved one problem, accelerate and move on to the next. You will find that concentration, like energy, increases as you use it, and that you will pick up a rhythm of concentration that will carry you through even the most intimidating pile of work. Don't give yourself a pause. What you're aiming for is a kind of blissful state in which your whole being wants to get everything done. Truly successful people have this feeling. The sight of a vast pile of work excites them; they have an almost physical need to plunge in and get it all done. Above all, they know how sweet life is when it *is* done. These are the people who know how to savor their leisure time.

REALISM, FANTASY AND SUCCESS

To be a success you must be realistic and see the world as it is. In the sixteenth-century, Machiavelli, the Florentine philosopher of power, wrote:

> . . . This is to be asserted in general of men, that they are ungrateful, fickle, false, cowardly, covetous, and as long as you succeed they are yours entirely; they will offer you their blood, property, life and children when the need is far distant; but when it approaches they turn against you . . . and men have less scruple in offending one who is beloved than one who is feared, for love is preserved by the link of obligation which, owing to the baseness of men, is broken at every opportunity for their advantage; but fear preserves you by the dread of punishment which never fails.[4]

Your M-level

The Machiavellian succeeds because he is cool and detached with other people, *not* because he is devious, corrupt or treacherous, as most people wrongly assume. He effectively manipulates people and situations because he does not let his personal emotions color his decisions. He is therefore able to see things realistically in terms of the situation at hand. A high level of Machiavellian behavior is a necessary ingredient for success. We can call this component the M-level.

There is some evidence that we are born with a high or low M-level, or at any rate that it appears very early in childhood. In a study by Richard Christie and Florence Geis,[5] children were asked to eat a peculiarly nasty-tasting cracker and then told they would get a nickle for every cracker they could persuade another child to eat. The children with high-M scores in other tests (in other words, those who were manipulative mini-Machiavellians) invariably talked the low-Ms into eating a great many crackers. Those who have old-fashioned ideas about women will be discomforted by the fact that there were "no sex differences in scores or persuasive ability," though the rest of us will not be astonished.

Society tends to judge the Machiavellian rather harshly. Even the authors of the study—whose own test involved feeding small children inedible crackers, surely a disagreeable piece of manipulation in itself—comment rather severely in conclusion that "the High Machiavellian is an effective manipulator *not* because he reads the other person and takes advantage of his weakness, but because his insensitivity to the other person permits him to bull his way through in pursuit of coolly rational goals." [6]

The element of disapproval here seems inappropriate. It is an advantage in life to assume that a degree of competition, antagonism and opposed interests exists between ourselves and others. The insurance salesman wants to sell you more insurance than you want to buy, your employer wants you to produce more and hopes to avoid giving you a raise, your painter hopes to get away with one coat instead of two, your best friend will push you overboard, if only for the pleasure of rescuing you. Recognizing that life is like this is the first step to success.

Successful people generally have very low expectations of others. It is not so much that they manipulate people as that they never underrate other people's innate ability to make trouble, and allow for this factor in all their plans. A skeptical view of human nature sooner or later pays dividends.

A Lesson in M-thinking

Harold Behlert is the president of a thriving courier and messenger service that began ten years ago with Harold and his motorcycle, and is now a world-wide operation on its way to acquiring its own freight airplanes. But during the time he was expanding his business rapidly, things began to go wrong for him. "I couldn't see *why*," he told me. "I'm a meticulous planner. I had this whole thing worked out from the very beginning. I saw exactly where we could fit in, and how we could make a profit, and I had everything carefully scheduled. When I said we'd pick up something at ten, I meant ten, and when I said it would be on the eleven o'clock plane to Chicago, that's what would happen. The whole point of my business was that I could guarantee that.

"But as we got bigger, it just wasn't happening. Our pickups were late, we were missing flights. We even began losing stuff. At first I got paranoid. I thought the employees were out to destroy me. And that was a very heavy feeling, because most of my people were friends, in those days, guys I felt I could really trust. I kept asking myself, 'Why do they hate me?'

"Then I began to follow them around, checking to see if they were on schedule, and I suddenly realized that *they simply weren't me!* Because I knew them, I expected everyone to take the same kind of care that I did. But it wasn't their business, it was *mine.* There was no way they were going to hustle and perform the way I did, and they were going to make mistakes because they couldn't be as careful as I was. So I built supervision into my operation, and motivation, just like everyone else, but the main thing I built in was a calculated factor for error and delay. I simply *assumed* a certain amount of delay and error, and allowed for it in scheduling pickups and delivery. You might say I lowered my expectations, and that would be true. But it works, and I've discovered that it's what every business has always done. If you want to succeed, never take it for granted that people will do what they've been told, or even what's sensible and good for them." This is M-thinking of a very high degree.

Using M-thinking for Your Promotion

If you want a promotion, you have to be able to analyze your situation with total objectivity and dispassion—in other words, from a high-M position. What are your chances realistically? How strong is the competition? What would *you* do if you were in the position of replacing the existing department head? Would *you* be your own first selection? If not, why not? Concentrate on your defects, list them, analyze them, see if they can be modified or turned into advantages.

Study your position with realism. People waste an enormous amount of energy trying to get jobs and promotions for which they have long since been disqualified. If you want to be a department head, and you think you are qualified, then set out to discover whether this is the opinion of your superiors. The best way is to ask, frankly and simply. Take your superior aside and explain to him that you think you might be right for the job and *why* you think so. If you're smart, you will also dwell on the merits of other people, while tactfully and gracefully indicating that your own are slightly more impressive.

Be positive about yourself but *never run down anybody else!* High-M people are subtle, whenever possible, and know better than to criticize. Look for everybody's good points, analyze them in detail, and let it be understood that your own are obvious. Do not say, "Harry is a drunk, he couldn't stay sober long enough to do the job." Say, "Harry would be terrific for the job, first-rate, but of course there's always the question of whether he could do it as well as he's capable of, because of his problem . . ."

Learn from Past M-failures

The quickest way to develop a good sense of realism is to study your own past experiences. We are always told that it is a mistake to look back, or to dwell on the past. But in fact, successful people are usually those who have learned from their mistakes. It's not that they don't make mistakes like the rest of us. They do. But they make fewer mistakes, and they try not to repeat the same ones. Success is a matter of averages, not absolutes.

When something goes wrong, face up to the consequences, do what you can to put things right, then go away someplace quiet and think about how it happened. While you're doing this, keep an open and alert mind to the possibility that you may not have made a mistake at all. Once you call something a mistake, it becomes one. Be patient. Wait until the final assessment has been made. Many a career has been destroyed by giving in to defeat too soon.

I well recall the case of Charles H. Ware, a friend of mine who spent a good deal of his company's money investigating the possibility of going into the frozen-food business. This may not seem an unusual idea, except for the fact that Ware himself was a book publisher. He had published an extremely successful book of fast, cheap recipes for "instant" versions of great gourmet dishes (Ten-Minute Boeuf Bourguignon was one of them), using ingredients that almost anybody would have in the kitchen. The authors were so impressed by the popularity of their cookbook that they decided to go into the frozen-food business, using the book's title as a brand name.

Charles was fascinated by the idea. Like most book people, he nurtured a secret desire to break out into the bigger world of technology and modern marketing. And he saw no reason why the book salesmen should not have a freezer chest in their car trunks. After all, if a man has to drive to Nashville and visit a dozen bookstores, why couldn't he visit a dozen groceries at the same time, leave off samples, and come back the next time for orders?

Forming a partnership with his authors, Charles soon found himself in the food business. In the meantime, a variety of chefs were creating and testing frozen gourmet meals. Someone even began videotaping famous chefs preparing instant gourmet dinners in their own kitchens. These might later serve as commercials for the product.

Despite all this, the scheme was doomed to failure. The book salesmen refused to go near supermarkets and groceries, the freezer chests leaked and ran down the car batteries, and almost everyone who could be persuaded to try one of the meals expressed a strong preference for canned spaghetti or starvation. Charles' ambitious pilot project was a failure, and he was the first to know it. Manfully, he went back to his management and told them so. They believed him; after all, he had conceived the idea, and therefore should know. Taking him at his word, they exercised their option to get out of the deal, wrote off the expenses and waited for a convenient moment to fire Charles, which soon arrived.

In the meantime, a clever entrepreneur studied the project. While concluding that the frozen meals were a piece of craziness, he nevertheless realized that the "commercials" of famous chefs preparing instant gourmet meals were a potentially valuable commodity. He bought up the package, had the video tapes converted into cassettes and into a television show, and made a fortune. Unlike Charles (and his management) he studied the failure, and quickly discovered that while Charles was an amateur at food processing, he was a professional at communications. The tapes were worth more than the food. As it turned out, one of the by-products of the original idea was far more valuable than the idea itself.

Another case of failure being turned into success involves a Hollywood producer who went off to Africa a few years ago to make an elaborate and costly movie. The story was absurd, the script was unfixable and the actors and working conditions were impossible. It was obvious that the project was a failure, but not before the director and the two assistant directors had shot thousands of feet of background footage, at enormous expense. The producer canceled the movie, flew home and sat down to study the failure from every angle, if only because the psychic scars of the experience were so painful that he could do nothing else.

After a few days, it dawned on him that he had an asset. The footage of animals, jungles, deserts and natives was superb, and he proceeded to sell it off as background material to other producers. Since then, almost every movie with an African setting has contained hundreds of feet of film salvaged from his spectacular "failure." It had been, in his own words, "the most successful investment of a lifetime—gold from a bomb!"

Remember: *never walk away from failure*. On the contrary, study it carefully—and imaginatively—for its hidden assets.

The Fantasy Factor

This kind of realism should be balanced with a sense of fantasy. Successful people are able to entertain fantasies, then carry them out into reality. If your own private world of daydreams and fantasies is a barren world, then your activities and your approach to life are likely to be equally barren.

Fantasies, of course, are an essential element of human life. As one psychologist points out, people who have underdeveloped fantasy lives "become easily bored . . . [and] are also less relaxed and independent than highly imaginative people." [7]

Fantasy supplies a deep need, which, if it is ignored, makes other demands. A recent study of overweight male college students indicates that the grossly overweight "experience significantly less visual imagery in their fantasies." In every case these students needed to shut their eyes in order to summon up a day dream, whereas the thin students not only had a rich fantasy life but could fantasize perfectly well with their eyes open, while carrying on a conversation. An inability to fantasize may lead to "delinquency, violence, overeating, and the use of dangerous drugs." It may also lead to failure. [8]

Many successful people acknowledge that they daydream frequently, and that these daydreams inspire them toward a given goal. Allow yourself time for daydreaming, cultivate your daydreams, *enjoy* them. Above all, make them creative by linking them to your goal:

- *Imagine* what you'll do with the money you get from a raise.
- *Imagine* what your new office will be like when you've been promoted.
- *Imagine* how you'll live when you've made your first million.

We would go to bed with hardly anyone if we weren't spurred on by our sexual fantasies. And the people we *do* go to bed with tend to satisfy our sexual needs in direct proportion to the extent with which they coincide with our fantasies. Much the same is true of work. We work best, and most productively, when we are putting our fantasies into practice. Let yourself go, free your imagination, indulge your fantasies.

Set aside a moment of the day and dream—constructive, creative dreaming. There's nothing wrong with fantasizing about money, or going on a shopping spree, or fame or what it will be like when you've made it. The more you can dream, the more you can do.

MEMORY

Most successful people either have good memories or have invented a system to act as a substitute. If you want to succeed, you cannot afford to forget things, and furthermore you have to be able to remind other people of what they have forgotten. The art of management is partly that of creative, supportive nagging. Let's face it: successful people are generally "noodges," to use the expressive Yiddish word.

The "Tickler System"

Reiner Haynes, the highly successful president of a growing manufacturing firm, uses what he calls his "tickler system" (he's not into Yiddish words) to ensure that his executives don't forget anything. Every order or suggestion or inquiry he makes is written down, then typed up as a brief memorandum. The memo is dated, and a copy is sent out to concerned. When and if it is answere on some definite action) the

Otherwise, the original is placed in the weekly or monthly "tickle" file, and a copy automatically goes out to the person concerned and to Haynes at regular intervals until action is taken.

This works fine as a management device, but Haynes, who can hardly remember his own birthday, uses the same system to "tickle" his own memory. "It's because I have a bad memory," he says, "that I instituted the system. I had to be constantly reminded of things, so I set up the system to help me. Afterward, it was natural to extend it to other people."

Looking at the "tickle" memos on Haynes' own desk one day, I noticed that one of them bore the surprising message "Your dog's name is Brutus." This was sent out to him on a weekly basis, presumably so that he would know what to say to the dog when he got home.

Bananas in Your Easy Chair

Well, at least one can always say "Hello, doggie," if necessary. But people's names pose more of a problem. Those who are conscious of some deficiency in this respect sometimes go to memory courses and attempt to get by with a variety of mnemonic devices. The latter are cumbersome in the extreme. A recent article on memory by a Stanford psychologist suggests that a person with a poor memory might, for example, be able to remember the colors of the spectrum by coining a name in which the colors appear in the proper order by their first letter—i.e., "The ordering of the colors of the spectrum is suggested by the name ROY G. BIV for red, orange, yellow, etc." This is all very well, but how is one to remember Roy G. Biv?

The same psychologist also recommends visualizing the things you want to remember by "vivid interaction between the item and the things at a given location." [9] Positing a man with a shopping list to remember, he ~ ~n to suggest what sounds like a rather terrifying

Freudian fantasy as a mnemonic device: "Suppose a dagger-like loaf of bread piercing the refrigerator door, then large bunches of bananas piled up in your easy chair, and in the fireplace a large pack of cigarettes with several of them sticking out of the pack and smoking . . . Try to visualize a clear mental picture of the object 'doing something interesting' at the location where it is placed. Later, in the grocery store, you can recall your shopping list by an imaginary walk through your house, pausing to 'look at' what you've placed earlier at the standard locations in your route."

Well, maybe. I don't see this system working for me, or for most people, and it misses a salient point: it is a waste of memory ability to remember what you could just as easily write down. Better to make a list than to waste time visualizing a giant bunch of bananas in your easy chair.

Names present a more serious problem, since it is socially unacceptable to forget them. Here too, mnemonic devices abound, and are mostly useless. Some people may be helped by the suggestion that they remember "Mr. Carpenter" by visualizing him hammering "that long spiked nose of his into the wall." But apart from the unconscious sexual symbolism of this image, it would seem to me just as hard to remember the image as to remember the name. And this kind of memory device can be dangerous. A friend of mine, who was unable to remember anyone's name, took a course to learn how to use just such devices. Meeting a rather important executive whose name was Arliss, he noted that the man was both broad in the beam and sycophantic to his superiors. Proudly, he invented a sure-fire mnemonic device, just as he had been instructed. When he next saw him he warmly greeted the man by saying, "I'm delighted to see you again, Mr. Ass-kiss!"

A White House visitor to David Rockefeller's offices reported with astonishment that Mr. Rockefeller had two giant circular name files. The first contained 5,000 names, and the second, a more intimate address list, contained over a thousand. Each card not only bore the name, the nickname, the address and telephone number, but also the last occasion on which Mr. Rockefeller had seen or spoken to that person and what they discussed. "Just out of curiosity," my acquaintance told me, "I asked them to pull Nikita Khrushchev's card, and I discovered that David Rockefeller had talked to him far more times than the President of the United States had!"

The Key to Memory: Caring

All efforts to remember names—or anything else—depend on a simple fact: *we can nearly always remember what we care about.*

People do not as a rule forget a date which they have been looking forward to, or the name of someone they love, or the departure time of the plane that will take them on a long-anticipated vacation trip. They forget dates they don't want to keep, the names of people that bore them, and the departure times of airplanes that will take them somewhere they don't want to go.

The trick to remembering things is to care about them. If successful people have phenomenal memories (and most of them do), it's because they are totally wrapped up in what they're doing. It's no problem for them to remember facts, figures and names that are related to their prime interests. A man who can remember every figure from last year's corporate report and forget the name of his dog is more interested in his business than in the dog.

It's not memory that is at fault most of the time, but motivation. There are very few ways—if any—in which you can "improve" your memory. Memory is not like body building. Except for the occasional psychopath, most people have about the same memory capacity. The memory cells are there for most of us, unless they've been damaged by a stroke. We simply aren't sufficiently motivated to use them.

What's worse, we use them badly, by committing to memory a multitude of things we don't need to know. One public relations man I know boasted to me that he could remember every telephone number he needed in the ordinary course of his day; he never had to look them up. This was, in fact, true, but it did not prevent his forgetting where we were supposed to have an important luncheon meeting the next day, causing us both to be late, with embarrassing consequences. It is clearly not essential to remember telephone numbers when you can just as easily look them up, or even phone the operator.

The first task is to have an order of priorities:

(1) Things you must remember: mostly the names of people and certain key things, either information or obligations.

(2) Things it is useful to remember—provided you're not already overloading the circuits with (1).

(3) Things you hardly ever need to remember and could just as easily write down or forget.

Your Own Amazing Memory

Bear in mind that a considerable part of your mnemonic capacity is involuntary. Most people automatically remember their own address and telephone number, their spouse's and children's names, the bus routes they normally take, the way to the shopping center, favorite recipes, songs, poems or card games and a million and one other things that have floated into the system and implanted themselves there without any effort on their part.

Even people who claim to have poor memories in fact "remember" millions of things, without which they couldn't function at all. If you're convinced that your memory is poor, sit down and begin to list the things

you *do* remember, and you will soon realize that your
memory is just as powerful and retentive as anyone
else's, but not focused at all on any given area.

Making Lists

Begin to retrain yourself by eliminating what you
don't need. A good address book will do wonders.
Remember the adage of computer programmers: "Garbage in, garbage out." If you fill your memory with
useless garbage, it will produce useless garbage. Don't
depend on memory for dates and appointments. Become a list maker. Most successful people are, to put
it mildly, compulsive about written lists, and for good
reason.

If you are going into a meeting about a merger, you
want to be able to remember everything you need to
know to defend your position and understand what's
being discussed. Your ability to remember the essential information may be the key to success. Learn to
prepare yourself—the most successful people are invariably the best "prepped." But once the need for the
information is over, forget it. Give yourself a breather
and clear out your mind.

At the beginning of each day take at least five minutes to think about the demands the day is likely to
make on you, and prepare yourself for memory activity
in these areas. Whatever you can write down, write
down.

S-M-I-T-H!

When it comes to names, take an active interest in
the person who is being introduced to you, and write
down his or her name as soon as you conveniently and
tactfully can. Also write down the place where you met
and what his or her affiliation, business or profession is.
You are much more likely to remember a man's name

if you can recall that he's an architect and that you met him in the bar of the Madison Hotel in Washington, D. C., than by playing with elaborate memory devices that ask you to think of him hammering his nose into the wall like a spike.

Do not concentrate on first names. This is a certain way to confusion and embarrassment, since it makes it almost impossible to follow up on an introduction. You cannot telephone someone interesting you met if you can only remember her as Janice, and you cannot, as a rule, introduce her to anyone else either. It is best to think of the two names as a unit, but in a pinch it is more useful to remember last names.

When in doubt, try the letters of the alphabet until a likely one comes to mind, then try various sound combinations until you feel you're on the right track. This is usually sufficient to jog the memory into action. If it's not, don't apologize. Just say, "By the way, I've been wondering how you *spell* your name." If it's Smith, you will certainly seem like a fool (except in England, where some of the more pretentious Smiths are Smythes). But in most cases people will readily oblige, assuming that you're intending to send them a letter, or write the name down in your address book. In any event, a great many of them will be suffering the same agony of indecision, since they will be unable to remember *your* name. If you sense that this is the case, swiftly seize the high ground by saying, firmly and loudly, "My name is Michael Korda!" (if it is) and they will then be obliged to reintroduce themselves.

SUCCESS THROUGH COMMUNICATION

Dr. Herbert H. Clark, a psychologist from Johns Hopkins University, recently made the somewhat startling discovery that it takes the average person about 48 percent longer to understand a sentence using a negative than it does to understand a positive, or affirmative, sentence.[10] This is scientific confirmation of something that every successful person knows: *the secret of good communication is positive affirmation.* It is not what you won't or can't do that interests people, but what you will or can.

If you have ever left a meeting with the feeling that you failed to get your point across, or made no impact, if you think other people have a wrong impression of the kind of person you really are, if you know exactly what you want to say but it comes out in a way that doesn't satisfy you and leaves others uninterested—you have a communications problem. If you want to be a success, you're going to have to overcome it. Nor is this impossibly difficult.

Winston Churchill was born with a cleft palate. In his youth he stammered, stuttered and was taken for an idiot, even by his own family. He painfully set out to correct his defect, and went on to become perhaps the greatest orator (perhaps the last orator) of the twentieth century. King George VI was not only born with a speech defect but was also incurably shy as a young man, and stammered so badly that it was painful to wait for him to finish a sentence. When his elder brother, King Edward VIII, abdicated, George VI forced himself to make speeches. By the end of his reign he was an accomplished speaker.

Body Signals

In meetings, where the ability to communicate is of paramount importance and is the standard by which one is judged, many people find that they simply cannot get a clear shot to say what they want to say. Just as they start to talk, someone else begins talking. Or at the exact instant when they are about to make their point, someone interrupts and moves the discussion to some other topic. They wait for the right moment to make their move, then realize that it's too late.

There are various ways to set the stage for yourself. Elderly men, for example, are prone to throat-clearing as a preliminary to speech. It is a warning device, indicating that silence is requested, and most people understand the signal perfectly well. Many people rely on facial cues, but these are often ignored, and can easily be misinterpreted. Winking, grimacing, and sticking your tongue out may well attract attention, but not necessarily the kind of attention you want. The face is simply too small an object to dominate most groups, and its range of expression is ambiguous and subtle. It is better to use your whole body as a cue. Consider these simple yet effective body signals:

HOW TO SIT AT A MEETING

BODY SIGNALS INTENTION TO SPEAK

BODY MOVES BRISKLY AND DECISIVELY FORWARD, ARMS AND HANDS SUPPORT WEIGHT, AS IF YOU WERE ABOUT TO RISE TO YOUR FEET

• Instead of sitting at a table with your elbows on it and your head down, sit well back away from it, perhaps even lean back in a relaxed, but alert, posture if the chair allows you to do so. Then when you want to speak, sit up straight, move forward with your whole body and put your hands down on the table with a positive motion. This is a recognizable and effective way of signaling your intention to talk.

THRUST GLASSES
←— FORWARD

GLASSES USED AS A CUE

• If you wear glasses, it may help to take them off and hold them in front of you, in the direction of the most important person at the meeting. This is a widely understood signal.
• Chain smokers can sometimes make an elaborate display of putting out a cigarette prior to speaking. Pipe smokers can knock their ashes out into an ashtray, creating a noise which is bound to attract attention.
• If you don't smoke and don't wear glasses, my suggestion would be to buy a pair of glasses and have clear lenses put into them. They make an ideal instrument for signaling your intention to speak, and you can always attract attention by putting them on or taking them off in order to read something.
• Half-moon reading spectacles have the additional advantage of making it possible for you to glare over the top of them at people who interrupt you. But not everyone can get away with this. Unless you are capable of making a very severe face, forget it.
• Auditory signals are sometimes effective—throat

clearing, blowing your nose or cracking your knuckles.

• Many men run their hands through their hair and down the back of their neck preparatory to speaking, a gesture that gives the impression of concentration.

• Women with long hair can ostentatiously push it back, exposing their full face and their ears as a sign that they want attention.

• Women with short hair can remove their earrings, a signal that they mean to get down to real business.

• Those who wear a ring can remove it and place it on the table in front of them. Women who wear several rings can reduce a meeting to complete silence by taking them off one by one.

The following suggestions are for men only (see Chapter 5):

• At any meeting in which "serious" business is being discussed, it may be useful to write notes in pen on a yellow legal pad while other people are speaking. Do this as ostentatiously as possible, with a great many thick black underlinings, which will not only attract attention to you and show you're taking the meeting seriously, but will also make everyone else nervous. Then when you're ready to speak, put the cap back on your pen with as loud a click as you can achieve, and raise it like a pointer. This seldom fails to ensure an instant silence. On the whole, a bright metal pen is best. Most of the Parker fountain pens make a very satisfactory clicking noise when you put the cap back on them. A ball-point pen that can be sharply clicked will serve the same purpose for very much less money, though it has rather less class.

• Jingling the change in your pocket, or your keys, may work if nothing else is available.

The main thing is to get people's attention and give them a solid, comprehensible clue that you have something to say and intend to speak.

Bridging

Now that you have won yourself a clear shot, how do you begin? A suggestion: it helps to link what you are going to say to the last thing that was said. An abrupt beginning sometimes confuses your listeners, and also suggests that you haven't been listening to what everyone else was saying, but have merely been waiting for an opportunity to speak out. Begin, in effect, by repeating what the person just before you said, summarize the discussion as it stands before your intervention, then go on to relate your arguments to what has gone before. In other words, create a "bridge" between the last speaker and yourself. An example of such a "bridge" might be this:

(1) *Bridge:* "I think what Lynn just said—that we have to increase export sales—is perfectly true."
(2) *Summary:* "Up to now we've been discussing what markets to go into, and I think we've reached a consensus to take the rifle approach instead of the shotgun approach, which makes sense."
(3) *Your own message:* "Now, from my department's point of view, I think there are several things we could do immediately to get things under way . . ."

This is invariably the correct way to introduce yourself into a discussion, as opposed to waiting for a pause in the conversation and shouting, "Hey, I've got an idea!" Once you have begun, go slowly. Use your pen, glasses or cigarette to hold the attention of the others, especially when you're pausing for dramatic effect. This signal cue serves as an indication that you haven't finished speaking, and helps prevent interruption.

How to Structure Your Points

While you're actually talking, don't look at one person all the time. Switch your attention around to different people. When your remarks make it possible to refer to someone else by name, do so ("I think what I'm about to say will be of special interest to Ed . . ."), looking as relaxed and pleasant as you can. Unless you are the chairman of the board, do not try to be funny, and never try to be funny at anybody's expense even if you *are* the chairman of the board. Your aim is to hold people's attention, and draw them into agreeing with you.

If you have trouble making your thoughts clear, you should concentrate on reducing everything to very short sentences, broken by as many significant dramatic pauses as you can manage. This, by the way, is Henry Kissinger's approach to public speaking, and while it does not qualify him to stand among the great orators of all time, it never fails to hold the audience's attention and get his points across. Avoid complex sentences, and break everything down into numbers—you may even want to use your fingers—i.e.:

"They wanted a ten-year deal (*pause*).

We were against this for the following reasons (*pause*):

One . . . [*pause; statement*]

Two . . . [*pause; statement*]

Three . . . [*pause; statement*]

Instead we counteroffered a five-year deal (*pause*).

What are the advantages of this (*pause and signal cue*)?

One . . . [*pause; statement*]

Two . . . [*pause; statement*]

Three . . . [*pause; statement*]

"I think they are now willing to accept this (*pause*), and I think at this point we should go ahead (*pause and signal cue*).

"It's a good deal for us, as I believe I've demon-strated, and as I think some of you, like Ed, have already said, and (*pause*) I wouldn't look this par-ticular gift horse (*chuckle at cliché*) in the mouth (*pause and signal cue*)."

It is often effective to emphasize the numbers by using your fingers. (Do not break down whatever you have to say into more than five sections, or you'll over-whelm your listeners and get into some curious finger displays.) For instance:

"Number one (*pause*): How much will it cost us?

"Number two (*pause*): Should we use our existing personnel and facilities or build up a new department?

"Number three (*pause*): I've been observing what other companies have been doing, and I think we can learn from them."

Note in the above example that it is very useful to ask a question, then answer it yourself. The more questions you raise and answer, the fewer questions other people will ask, since after a while they will as-sume you have already asked and answered the important ones.

The Positive Approach

Always try to put things affirmatively—avoid nega-tives. Thus, instead of saying, "If we don't get the sales department to explore new domestic areas first, we'll never be ready for exporting," say, "*First,* let's explore new domestic sales areas, then we'll have a solid base to go after export sales."

Whenever possible, refer to other people present by name, and give them credit for what they've said, even when you disagree, as in: "I think Lynn put the need to increase export sales very well, BUT (*pause*) I think we have to examine the effect this is going to have on our (*pause; with emphasis*) *domestic* sales first."

Negative statements not only interrupt the flow of your remarks, they antagonize and depress your listeners. Remember: nobody is interested in what you *can't* do, *don't* know or *won't* agree to. Emphasize the positive, and let the negative points make themselves known unobtrusively, if at all.

Winding Up Strategies

When you have made your points, do not just stop and fall silent or allow your remarks to trail off. If people are to remember what you have said, you must anchor it in their minds. You must also ensure that what you have said becomes the theme of the following discussion. At long meetings, it may be useful to wait until just before the coffee break or the lunch break to make your remarks. You can then suggest breaking after you've finished speaking, which will effectively prevent any immediate opposing remarks, and leave whatever you have said on people's minds for the next hour or so. If you cannot do this, it is always possible to look around the room and say, "I'd be very grateful if anybody would like to comment on this, or ask any questions." This establishes your control over the meeting, and will usually moderate what might otherwise be fiercely expressed opposition to what you have said. Nobody likes to take up this kind of invitation, since it implies accepting a challenge on someone else's terms. Truly skilled success players will, of course, have arranged in advance for a friend to ask the right kind of question. This is the fox's approach to winding up a presentation. A more lionlike approach is to watch out for someone who doesn't seem to be listening, and put a question directly to him, e.g., "What do *you* think, Ed?" when it's almost certain that Ed has been daydreaming for the last half-hour. This will not only embarrass Ed but will also prompt him to agree with you hastily, rather than to risk making himself look foolish by arguing against something he hasn't even heard.

Clichés

When you get to the end of what you're saying, quickly summarize your argument, putting it into a solid, clear and memorable sentence. Don't be afraid of clichés. On the contrary; they help to anchor what you've said in people's minds precisely because they are familiar. If you think that going into export sales too fast is a mistake, in the example above, say, "I think going after exports while we've still got domestic sales problems is putting the cart before the horse." Your thought attached to a familiar cliché is instantly understood and certain to be remembered. It is a simple and reliable formula:

THOUGHT + APPROPRIATE CLICHÉ = INSTANT COMMUNICATION

When it comes to clichés, use down-to-earth ones. Avoid literary allusions. Don't be afraid to say things like:

"The ball is in our court."

"Fifty percent of something is better than a hundred percent of nothing."

"It's the last mile that counts."

"You can't make bricks without straw."

"The name of the game is profit."

I heard all of the above used by the president of a major manufacturing company within the space of a few minutes, and most effectively. Each one followed a precise summary of his point of view, and served to pin down in his listeners' minds exactly what he meant.

"I have no problem with that"

In a one-to-one conversation, you can apply most of these same strategies with very good effect. Sit as close as you can to the other person and keep your voice reasonably low. Don't mumble, of course, or whisper, but remember that nobody likes to be shouted at. The lower your voice is, the harder the other person will have to work to hear and pay attention to what you're saying.

Here, it is permissible, and even a good idea, to interrupt from time to time, particularly if the other person is talkative. You can do this with extreme politeness, simply by indicating your agreement with what he's saying. However, you must be very careful to signal when you no longer agree. It is vital not to let anyone go away under the impression that you have accepted his point of view if that is not the case.

This frequently happens to poor communicators. They are reluctant to talk, and therefore listen silently to things they have no intention of accepting, thinking they can make this clear later on with a letter or at the conclusion of the conversation. But this leads them into positions where they appear to be either stupid or treacherous.

Communicate your opinion continuously, whether you do it verbally or nonverbally. That way the other person knows where he stands. If nothing else, nod your head when you're affirming agreement, and shake it very slightly when you don't agree. Frown when you're doubtful. Be careful about mixing signals. A frown usually signifies that you don't agree with something the other person has said, but a frown combined with an up-and-down motion of the head means "It's a serious matter but I'm on your side." Keep your hands still when the other person is talking. It's all right to use them for emphasis when you're talking, but they merely distract the other person when he has the floor. It's useful to make an occasional comment, if only because it reminds the other person that the conversation is taking place between two equals.

My friend Morton L. Janklow, a distinguished New York attorney, has a superb desk-side manner, and uses a phrase of which I've become very fond. When you say something he doesn't find objectionable, he will comment, "I have no problem with that." This is encouraging and indicates both that he is listening and that the point you have made is one that can be negotiated. Note that his phrase very carefully stops short of complete agreement. The implication is merely that some common ground can be found in this area at some later date.

When you say something that he does *not* agree with, Morty takes off his glasses and says, "Let's leave that one until later." He does not say, "You're wrong!" or "Not on your life!" or "You must be out of your mind!" Instead, he very politely puts you on notice that on this particular point he is not in agreement, and reserves the right to come back to it in detail later on.

This is a helpful rule of communication. Get the things that you're agreed on out of the way first, then go on to the ones that are going to cause trouble. Don't go through a long list of points, agreeing to some but fighting out the others on the spot in the order in which they occur. When there is disagreement, make a note of it, indicate that you'll come back to it later on, and go on to dispose of the points on which there *is* agreement. You will find that the residue of things on which you haven't reached agreement is easier to deal with once you've gone over the affirmative points of agreement, and that a great deal of them will be found to be trivial after they've been isolated in a separate category.

How to Succeed with an Audience

When it comes to public speaking, most people find a quality of panic is introduced into the problem of successful communication. Nobody wants to "dry up," or lose the audience's attention, or make a fool of himself or herself, and the fear of doing so is perfectly rational. Just in case you feel you're special, a recent study indicates that 40 percent of American college students suffer from shyness as a social disease, all indications being that the proportion is not very different among adults.[11]*

Try to bear in mind that successful people are rarely shy, and that your own success is the best proof that you have nothing to be shy about. The mere fact that you are being asked to speak in public is a sign of success, and you must begin with the assumption that your audience really wants to hear what you have to say. You are doing *them* a favor by speaking to them. If you start to feel that they are doing you a favor by listening to you, you're lost.

Here too, aim for the numbered, factual and well-timed speech, if necessary a little on the dull side, but solid and informative. If you find it a help to write everything down and read it, do so, but keep the sentences short, look up at every possible opportunity, and use your right hand for emphasis, pointing the finger toward the audience to make an affirmative point, and showing the palm of your hand, opened flat, to indicate a negative point. If you have to read a speech, make sure the sentences are short, and never allow yourself to drone on with your eyes on the piece of paper in front of you. If you feel like making an extemporaneous remark, do so, but keep your finger on your place so you can find it again. As you develop the courage to break away from your set speech, you'll

* Oddly enough, the incidence of shyness among Jewish students is considerably lower—about 24 percent.

soon find that you only need an outline of what you want to say, and quite soon that you can speak without notes at all. The main thing is to regard the audience as your friend. Don't stare at one person. Select different people, look at them, project your whole personality toward them. Don't let your body get tense and immobile. Move about a little, turn toward one side of the room, then the other, and when you get applause, *stop,* back away from the podium a bit, smile, then take a sip of water and continue. Don't just plough right on, as so many speakers do, which is at once rigid and silly, since nobody will be able to hear what you're saying. Ask how long your speech is supposed to be, and cut that time in half. The shorter you can make it, without giving offense, the better off you are.

Be sure *never* to ask if there are any questions unless you have arranged beforehand for someone to ask you one. Nothing is more embarrassing than a speech that tapers off into a question-and-answer period that produces total silence. When all else fails, remember: You can't go far wrong as a rule if you end by thanking everybody for inviting you to speak and saying something nice about them, their company, their city or their dinner.

Finally, avoid grand oratorial gestures. They can lead to embarrassment. When CBS was presenting its fall season to the advertisers and the media, in the days when they took over "21" for the event, it fell to a man more noted for behind-the-scenes ability than for public charisma to make a speech to the guests, most of whom had been knocking back the free drinks at the bar for some time.

As he wound up his remarks about the wonders of the season's product, he paused for effect and pointed to the giant CBS logo above the podium. "THE C STANDS FOR CLASS," he told them in ringing tones.

A voice came up from the audience: "Tell us what the BS stands for!"

Communicating Under Severe Pressure

Unusual conditions make communication tougher. Television is a prime example of a stressful public-speaking situation. Even senior executives break down when called upon to appear on TV, in part because they're not used to defending themselves and tend to regard any form of challenge as overt hostility. The J. Walter Thompson Company has actually set up a telecommunications development course to teach businessmen to communicate effectively on television—particularly how to "cope with aggressive interviewers and defuse potentially damaging questions."

The methods used seem harsh, but no more so than the reality of being cross-examined on such questions as price fixing and oil prices. An observer described the training system used:

> As the pretest phase begins, a producer shakes your hand and disappears. A floor director who has little sympathy for your plight sits you down in a chair under lights that are three times hotter than normal. He slaps some make-up on your face and asks you to lean to the left and speak loudly because the sound is better that way. Also you're told it helps if you don't cross your legs (because that messes up the picture) and if you try to look at the camera the floor director is pointing to. In that condition— nervous, sweaty, unaware of what's coming and unprepared for what does, uncomfortably leaning to the left with both feet on the floor, talking louder than you usually do and spinning your chair in circles to find the correct camera—you make your debut . . .[12]

This rather Draconian approach to public speaking (which costs $1,200 per person for two and a half days) is probably well worth the money, and not just because you may have to appear on television some day. It is vital to learn how to communicate *despite opposition*. At meetings with your subordinates, when things are more or less under your control, try to encourage lively debate and opposition, not only because it's productive, but because it's a good way of learning how to think fast.

When in doubt, *shut up*. Many people who think they have trouble communicating are simply suffering from an inability to remain silent. Out of nervousness, they speak badly and hastily and without conveying anything of substance. Beware of this tendency. It is better to be quiet and attentive than to make a fool of yourself. Unless you're sure you're on solid ground, bite your tongue. Anyway, the less often you speak, the more important it will seem when you do.

- Above all, you have to be confident of your own value: If you're making a speech, remind yourself that you are doing the audience a favor—*they* have come to listen to *you*.
- If you're at a meeting, remind yourself that what you have to impart in the way of information and commentary is important to the success of the group.
- In a one-to-one conversation, remind yourself that the other person wouldn't be there unless he or she wanted something from you.

A great deal of nonsense is spread about "charisma" and who has or hasn't got it. But in most cases charismatic people have simply mastered the trick of using their body, their voice, their face and their hands to convey a message. The message is simple: "Pay attention to me!" You don't have to be Robert Redford or Jane Fonda to do this. Indeed, some very ugly people are astoundingly successful in this respect.

I know one powerful international business executive who is fat, bald and somewhat popeyed, and who can nevertheless dominate a meeting or conversation without any trouble. When he is listening, he leans far forward, his face rapt with interest, one hand cupped

PERFECT LISTENING POSTURE

pleasant expression

hand cupped to ear

body leans forward
to indicate submissive
attention to the speaker

legs comfortably crossed,
to indicate you are happy
and content to let the other
person talk, *not* tensed up and
waiting to interrupt or reply

hand relaxed
and loose

to his ear, hanging on your every word. This is very
flattering and tends to ensure that you will pay equal
attention to him when he speaks. When he is talking,
he sits up straight, his chest and whole body conveying
a manly self-confidence and an upright regard for
truth. His eyes are steady (none of that shifty, side-to-
side glancing that inspires mistrust), he keeps his
hands quiet and flat on his knees (unless he wants to

PERFECT SPEAKING POSTURE

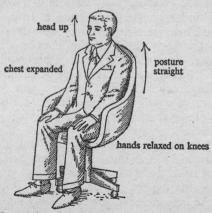

head up

chest expanded

posture
straight

hands relaxed on knees

feet solidly planted on floor

make a point, in which case he uses his index finger forcefully but without actually pointing it at you), and he keeps both feet firmly planted on the ground (which gives him an impression of solidity, as if his feet were saying "Here's a man you can believe"). Above all, *he pays attention.*

Good communicators know how to be good listeners. Learn how to respond to the other person as if you were his audience—watching Johnny Carson or Merv Griffin listen to their guests is a good way to learn. Learn to react appreciatively, without interrupting the flow of the other person's narrative. Smile, nod, use your hands to express disagreement or approval silently, use your body to indicate extreme attention (by leaning sharply forward) or doubt (by leaning back and away from the speaker). You needn't look like someone with St. Vitus' Dance, but *never* look like a wooden Indian, or you'll find that when it's *your* turn to speak, people will treat you like one.

THE SUCCESS GAME

Children are curious. They naturally explore everything, and find excitement everywhere. In the process, they learn. Then we send them off to school. It is at this point that many children stop learning, or must be made to learn by a series of rewards and punishments; for learning has ceased to be "play" and has become "work." For many of them, this work/play opposition will continue to condition their attitudes for the rest of their lives. It is almost impossible for such people to be successful.

The key to success is to feel that your "work" is "play." You are not doing it "to earn a living," or to fill up your time, or because your society, your family or your parents expect you to. You are doing it because it's the best game in town, the only one at which you can get paid for doing what's fun.

Educators have long since realized that one of the great dangers is rewarding children for something they like doing anyway. The reward (even if it's only praise) immediately turns what was enjoyable into drudgery. Adults have the same problem. When we are paid to do something, it seems to us natural to regard it as "work," and therefore drudgery. It is vital not to be caught in this trap. You expect to be paid for what you do—that's natural and healthy—but you aren't doing it for the money. Like a small child, you have to treat what you do as a game, one that involves play, curiosity, learning and experimentation.

The fact that the game is played in real life and for real stakes does not prevent its being a game. *Your chances of success are directly proportional to the degree of pleasure you derive from what you do.* If you are in a job you hate, face the fact squarely and get out. You may earn a good living, you may have a safe career, but you will never be a success. Find out what you enjoy doing, and your chances of succeeding will be dramatically better.

We play the game every day, sometimes without even recognizing that we're doing it. We compete with other people, or other teams, or other companies, not only because it is essential to business survival, but because we frankly enjoy competition. It's fun to be in the game, and it's even more fun to win.

Even making money is fun. One highly successful man put this very well when he told me, "I never thought of getting rich as a reason for working. I don't mean that I didn't want to be rich. Everyone does, but it wasn't my primary motivation. I had a lot of fun. I took over a small bankrupt company, I made it profitable, and I built up a team of good people while I was doing it, and we had fun. I used to say, 'Let's go beat the socks off the other guys in this business,' and damn it, we *did!* We were giant-killers. We went after companies ten times our size and beat them in the marketplace, and when we began to buy up other businesses and get into real growth, that was fun too.

I was learning, doing new things, finding that I could do all sorts of things I'd never thought I was capable of.

"I have it all now. There's a corporate jet and a corporate helicopter, I have an estate out in Bedford Hills, and it's terrific. We have our own building here in New York, with a private dining room and a French chef and an English butler. People say, 'Well, he works hard all the time. He's a millionaire, but he doesn't have enough time to enjoy it!'

"Bullshit! I enjoy my work, I still have time for living, for seeing my children, for vacations. I do a lot of work at home, sure, but believe me, I'd rather do it sitting by my own pool on two hundred acres of my own land, with a limousine to take me into town the next morning, than do the same amount of work for $20,000 a year. I don't work harder than people who aren't successful. But I enjoy it a lot more, and I do it in more pleasant surroundings, and I get more out of it. It's like winning all the marbles when you're a kid. It's not the marbles that count, it's the fun of winning them."

One of the many things that made the Kennedys so much more interesting as campaigners than Richard Nixon was the simple fact that they obviously enjoyed campaigning. Mr. Nixon, by contrast, gave the distinct impression that political campaigning was a painful duty. A "happy warrior" (to borrow the phrase that was always applied to Governor Alfred E. Smith) is always more interesting—and more likely to win—than a miserable self-pitying one. Like a campaigner who thrives on the "game" of politics, you will be a winner if you learn to love whatever game you're in.

The Positive Complaint

Successful people are, by and large, very seldom complainers. Your object is to project yourself as a person with a goal and a destiny. It is perfectly O.K.

to call attention to your difficulties, but in the corporate world it is very important to know *how* to do this. Always take a positive attitude. If you have a difficult task, make sure that your superiors know how difficult it is when you begin, and after you've succeeded remind them of how difficult it was, but never in the form of a complaint.

A good example of this would be the following memo to the president of a company:

> I am delighted to have been assigned the task of finding a new distributor for our products in Canada. I concur that this is a necessary step, though there will doubtless be a great many difficulties in finding just the right organization and negotiating a new agreement.
>
> Having studied the situation, I see the major problems as being: [list them in order of difficulty].
>
> I propose to begin in the following manner [describe].
>
> I am excited and pleased at being given this challenge, and well aware of just how much is at stake.

A memo like this, when written early on in any business situation, has many advantages. First of all, it lays a foundation for your success at the task, by pointing out that the job is not going to be an easy one. It also establishes that you are aware of your responsibility, and because you have listed the problems and the way you intend to face them, you cannot be accused later on of keeping your superiors in ignorance. They knew what you intended to do, and if they had doubts, they should have voiced them. Their silence is the equivalent of approval. In the event that you fail, which alas is always possible, you have

at least gone on record about the difficulties beforehand, so you have something to fall back on. This will
save you from the embarrassment of having to make
excuses in the future. You have already listed the excuses.

Finally, when and if you do succeed, you can now
send out a new memo—

> Despite the many difficulties, which
> I outlined in an earlier memo
> (attached), I am happy to report that
> we have now found the right dis-
> tributor for our products in Canada,
> and that an agreement has been suc-
> cessfully negotiated, subject to your
> final approval.
> There were many problems in the
> course of this search, and I think it
> would be useful to list them, since
> they may be instructive in similar
> situations in the future [list them].
> Nevertheless, we achieved our goal,
> and I think the experience alone was
> well worth the effort involved,
> though I am of course happy that we
> have established a firm basis, at
> last, for good service and real profit
> in this area. I look forward to re-
> porting on this to you in person
> whenever you have time . . .

This is what I call a "success memo," designed to
establish firmly that you did a good job. Note the use
of the word "experience" in the last paragraph, which
very subtly implies you've grown in the process, and
are ready for something bigger, but is also quite humble in tone. Note the suggestion that you'd like to report to the president *in person*. Each time you succeed
at something, you must use it as a wedge to increase

your personal contacts with the top people in your management. Note that in the first paragraph the words "your final approval," which strike a properly submissive note, make it clear that you are not trying to co-opt the final decision, or tread on your superior's toes.

Learning to put your problems to work for you is a vital part of the success game. Everybody loves a winner, it's true, but not many people are interested in someone who wins without any difficulty or opposition. In order to make your successes work for you, you first have to establish that the opposition is tough and the difficulties challenging. Nobody would go to a prize fight if the champion announced, "My challenger is a complete weakling and any ten-year-old child in reasonable health could KO him in the first round." On the other hand, you'd be reluctant to bet money on a boxer who announced, "My opponent is so good and so strong that I'm completely outclassed and expect to be beaten to a pulp in the first round, unless I'm lucky and get KO'd." You have to strike a happy medium in estimating difficulties, and make them part of the game, the enjoyable challenge against which you act.

The Risk Factor

You can't play games without taking risks. Most people find risk alarming—even terrifying. But successful people take risks. And those who are really successful are the ones who enjoy it, which makes winning the game easier.

A psychiatrist has recently described risking in terms of driving.[13] It is useful to see risks, he asserts, as the act of passing another car on the highway. When you do this you are confronted by a limited number of very urgent risk choices:

(1) You see an oncoming vehicle and fall back

into your original position—if you can. If you can't, you are dead.

(2) You see an oncoming vehicle and accelerate to pass before you collide. If you can, fine, you have passed safely; if you can't, you are dead.

(3) You see no oncoming vehicle, pass easily and speed on your way.

(4) You pull out, see an oncoming vehicle, and freeze in terror, neither accelerating nor dropping back to your original position. In this case you are definitely dead.

This metaphor may not necessarily work for you, but it is worth studying. If risks make you nervous, you'll have to train yourself until you are comfortable with them. The best way is to analyze very carefully what the risks *really* are.

Before taking a major risk, ask whether it is absolutely necessary to do so. Very often we take risks out of egotism (the desire to do something autonomously, without asking for advice or permission) or simple laziness (the impatient desire to plunge ahead before learning the full story or doing the necessary homework). When we eliminate these two factors, the number of risks we are actually obliged to take will be very much reduced.

Still, there will always be risks we can't avoid. In these cases, it is useful to spread the risk around as much as possible. Ask everybody for their advice, discuss the problem with your superiors and subordinates, lay out the possible consequences openly. When you have involved enough people, the risk factor is diffused, and any bad results stemming from the risk can be shared rather than borne singly. You will have to take some risks by yourself, and it's important to do so, but most risks can be minimized by simply being frank about them in advance, instead of keeping them a secret.

Remember: *Success is a game like any other*. And a large part of the game is making people see you as a success. As one friend of mine put it, surveying the

New York skyline from the thirty-first floor of a sky-scraper, his polished loafers carelessly resting on the rosewood top of his custom-designed desk:

"Before I'd made it, people thought I was an insignificant person. I was too serious, too intent, a kind of gentile Sammy Glick. I worried too much, and I tried too hard, and people wrote me off as one of those tight-assed guys who'd never make it. Well, I played the game the right way, and I made it. I've got the big office, and the big car, and the two secretaries and all the money I'll ever need, and now everyone thinks I'm a terrific guy. I pay attention to detail, I motivate people toward success, I set high standards, I work hard and expect other people to do the same. I get interviewed by the business press, and people say, 'He sounds like a real manager, a take-charge guy.'

"But the funny thing is: I'm the same guy. I haven't changed. The characteristics that people thought were bad, or ridiculous or abrasive when I was starting out, they're all still a part of me. Except as a success, people see them differently. They see *me* differently. It's not just the $400 suit, but all the things I used to do that offended people, or made them laugh, now impress people. Success is a game. You play it with deadly seriousness at first—because you're young, you're starting out, you don't know any other way. But once you're on your way up, you have to stand away from it from time to time and see just how funny it is. You get relaxed about it when you do. It's like Zen tennis—the moment you stop trying, it all comes much easier. There's a moment when it becomes a pure game, and when you hit that moment— you've made it, and nothing can stop you!"

4

The Sweet Look of Success

"All symbols of success ultimately tend towards simplicity."
—David Chang

LOOK LIKE A WINNER!

It may be true that beauty is only skin deep, but the fact remains that the world judges you on your appearance a great deal of the time. It will hardly help your rise to success if you look like a loser. If you're going to be a winner, you may as well begin by *looking* like one.

Obviously, a great deal depends on the field in which you want to gain success. An ambitious rock-guitar player may feel called upon to achieve some kind of distinction by striving for extreme eccentricity of dress and appearance, while someone whose ambition is to rise within the ranks of IBM would be well advised to buy some white shirts and get a haircut. Only you can be sure of what standards are most likely to apply in your profession or job. In general,

152

you cannot go very far wrong by adopting those of the more senior and successful people in your own organization.

If You're Not Paul Newman, Then . . .

Your face, of course, is what people see most of the time. There isn't a great deal you can do about *that,* nor do I believe that most men are willing to use make-up or resort to plastic surgery to correct any defects in this area. On the other hand, you can make the best of what you've got, even if you're not Paul Newman. A surprising number of men, for example, shave badly. This is odd, but I suspect that it's natural. Nobody ever *teaches* us how to shave. A great many otherwise well-turned-out men begin the day with patches of stubble that they've missed in shaving, and end the day with a heavy growth of fresh beard. This is not the way successful people ought to look. Learn to shave yourself carefully and well, switch razors and shaving creams until you find a combination that works. If you have a heavy beard, keep an electric razor in your desk drawer and use it.

The healthy outdoors look, which is perhaps the greatest success symbol of all, does not necessarily have to be acquired on a forty-foot racing sloop in Hobe Sound. Pouches under your eyes, as well as bloodshot eyes, will respond quickly to fresh air, exercise and a reasonable reduction in the amount you smoke and drink. Your face should project energy, not fatigue and dissipation, and given the fact that most of us work indoors, it needs all the help it can get.

Try to look at your face as if it were that of a stranger—which should be easy in the early morning —and ask yourself if you've really done the best you can with it. Would you look better if your hair were slightly longer? Do you part your hair on the left side because your mother always parted it that way, or is it really the best choice for your face? If your ears stick out, would it help to let your hair grow fuller at the sides? It may be a good idea to spend some money on having your hair "styled." But remember that the aim is a simple, natural appearance. If you end up with a hair style that requires hot-air combing, spray and antihumidity cream, you will not only get bored with the process, but it will almost certainly look artificial.

Understandably, those whose problem is baldness may want to give some thought to wearing a wig. But a word of warning is in order here. Wigs are not only objects of mirth to a lot of people, but also represent a kind of dishonesty, since you are pretending to have more hair than is in fact the case. If there is the slightest chance that your wig will be noticed, or even suspected, don't do it. Once you have been caught out as a wig wearer, nobody is likely to trust you about anything else. It will be the only thing that most people will remember about you. My own personal opinion is that it is usually better to accept fate and go frankly bald into the world. After all, you have plenty of company.

Fate may not have handed you a perfect set of teeth, and you may not want to go to the expense and pain of having them capped, unless you're an actor. But there is no reason not to have them professionally cleaned as often as is necessary. If you're a heavy smoker, the more often they're "scaled" by your dentist, the better. Yellow teeth turn people off. As far as nails go, I do not think that most men want a professional manicure, and I am myself inclined to distrust men who fingernails are buffed and polished. But they should at least be short, trim and clean, and surprisingly often they're not.

Glasses

It is worthwhile paying some attention to the glasses you select, not only because they serve as a useful prop or cueing device (see Chapter 3), but because it's one of the few areas in which you can legitimately develop a personal style or trademark of your own. Get a pair that does something for your face. Simple gold frames are usually best. However, the latest status symbol is the large Ray-Ban® aviator goggles. Fashionable as these are, beware: if you have a small face, they tend to make you look like a chipmunk. Avoid colored plastic frames—after gold, real or imitation tortoise shell is next best. One exception: In the world of high-WASP academia, the proper frame is made of transparent flesh-colored plastic, with very small lenses and very narrow sidepieces. Glasses with metal decorations or decorative inserts are out. Do not go to purchase a pair of frames without first clipping a few photographs of people wearing the kind of glasses that you think would look good on you. Unless you know what you're looking for, you are likely to walk out of the shop in a daze. The variety of styles available now is bewildering.

Clothes

Most business people worry a lot about their clothing. And looking at the average business convention, one can easily see why—the number of men who genuinely manage to dress for success is very small. If you want to be successful, you can speed up the process by dressing the right way. And it needn't cost you a great deal of money. Remember: *how you wear your clothes is almost as important as what you wear.*

One of the peculiarities of people's attitudes toward clothing is that they start to dress for success when they become successful. This is a mistake. Dress for maximum success *now.* Your object is to set yourself apart from other people, in a quiet, dignified but unmistakable manner, and to show that you are a winner.

If you look at the senior members of your organization or profession, you will almost always find that they wear plain dark-blue or dark-gray suits, with or without a muted pattern or a stripe. It costs no more to buy a blue suit than one in brown or green or some nubbly tweed pattern that looks as if it had been designed as an upholstery fabric for a chain of cheap motels. There is no occasion during the business day (or evening) when a dark-blue or dark-gray suit is inappropriate. In anything else, you have at least a fifty percent chance of looking out of place.

At the upper level of success a certain status is attached to such tailors as Morty Sills, Dunhill's or Roland Meledandri, in New York, and Huntsman or Hawes and Curtis, Ltd., in London. It is possible to spend nearly $1,000 on a plain suit, and if you can afford to, why not? The pleasure of having it made, and the fact that you're wearing a visible status symbol may make it seem like a worthwhile investment. However, this kind of perfection is only recognizable to a small number of people (most of them attired at similar expense), and is beyond the reach of the average person. You can spend whatever you normally spend, but make sure it is simple, single-breasted and either dark-blue (the darker, the better) or dark-gray. The cloth should not have any fancy textured pattern. It is also important to avoid contrasting stitching or piping, pockets with buttons on them and lapels so wide that they come out to your shoulders. Look for the kind of suit you would expect a banker or a clergyman to wear.

When you have found it, be ruthless about alterations. It is not all that important how much the suit costs, *but it must fit*. Nothing makes a man look more like a failure than a poorly fitted suit. If you are thin, have the jacket waist taken in to produce a slightly flared look. If you are not thin, adopt the old-fashioned "Brooks Brothers," look, in which the sides of the jacket hang more or less straight down. Do not go in for exaggeratedly suppressed waists (the so-called "Continental Look") unless you want to be mistaken for a bookie or a gigolo.

The left lapel of your suit should have a buttonhole.

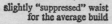

| slightly "suppressed" waist for the average build | "Brooks Brothers" type traditional look, suitable for a heavy figure | avoid at all costs |

It is correct, it is traditional and it belongs there. There should be at least three buttons on the sleeve cuffs of a suit, and if possible four. If the suit only has two, ask for a third one to be sewn on, or get it done yourself. Ideally, the sleeve buttons should be real—i.e., you should be able to button and unbutton them—but to get this small, correct touch, you have to go to a tailor.

Another thing to beware of in having a jacket altered is the collar at the neck. It is vital that the collar be raised high enough so that it's close to the back of the neck, rather than hanging away from it, as most do. This is the kind of thing you have to be firm about. Insist on putting down a partial payment on your suit, the balance to be paid when you are satisfied with the alterations, and make *sure* you're satisfied.

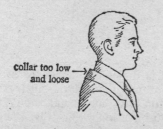 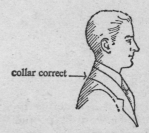

collar too low and loose

collar correct

Trousers are almost always worn too short. Nothing looks worse than a man whose ankles show when he's standing up. You must insist that the trousers be long enough to "break" gently over the shoes. Whether they have cuffs or not doesn't matter, though in fact cuffs make the trousers hang better by adding a bit of weight to the bottoms. If the trousers are cuffless, have them cut at an angle, as illustrated, so that they come down lower over the heels of your shoes than they do at front. Any alterations tailor can do this.

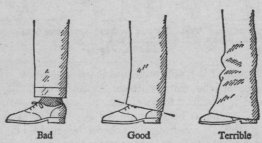

Bad   Good   Terrible

Beware of trousers that are too long or baggy at the bottoms, since this tends to give your legs a certain

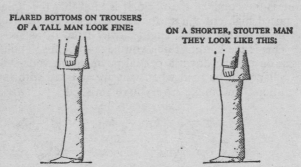

FLARED BOTTOMS ON TROUSERS OF A TALL MAN LOOK FINE:

ON A SHORTER, STOUTER MAN THEY LOOK LIKE THIS:

elephantine gracelessness. It is difficult to avoid trousers that have a mild "bell-bottom" these days, but try. It is not a flattering look for most men, and should only be worn by people who have long, thin legs. For short people, it is a disaster, since there is seldom enough length between the jacket bottom and the knees to give the long, sweeping flared look that seems so striking when the trousers are worn by a six-foot-tall model.

A carefully fitted suit is worth the time and trouble it takes, even if it means a certain amount of argument. "Off the rack" doesn't mean it has to fit like a sack.

A little bit of care goes a long way too. Successful people seldom appear rumpled and sweaty, and there's no reason why you should either. A sudden downpour can make your suit look like something an Arab camel driver wouldn't wear. It's useful to keep a freshly pressed suit in your office, ready for emergencies. In general, you should own enough suits so that you don't have to continue wearing them after the trouser crease has gone. If you suffer from dandruff, go see a dermatologist, but in the meantime, keep a clothes brush in your desk drawer and use it. Your object is to appear cool, unruffled and self-confident at all times. Dress as if you expected to be promoted to the board of directors at any minute, and perhaps you will be.

One way to appear cool is to avoid heavy fabrics. Most offices are overheated to begin with; don't compound the problem by wearing a "winter suit" that brings you out in a sweat. Buy the heaviest overcoat you can find, and wear the same lightweight suits year round. It's a good way to save money, and you'll increase your comfort at the same time.

Double-knit fabrics have the immense advantage of holding their shape, and are particularly good for travel. On the other hand, they never seem to look quite as crisp as ordinary fabrics, and most of them are manufactured in strange and unappealing colors. If you can find one in gray or dark-blue, add it to your wardrobe, and use it for traveling. If it comes with fancy buttons, as many seem to, have them removed and replaced with ordinary black ones.

Blazers should be dark-blue, single-breasted, with plain gold buttons. They should never, *never* have a badge on the right breast, and should always be worn with dark-gray trousers. If you're in the kind of business where you can get away with a sports jacket from time to time, pick a very lightweight tweed in a subdued and *small* check, and have the leather buttons replaced with plain bone ones. Personally, I think it's O.K. to have suede patches on the sleeves if you've owned the sports jacket for a decade or so and the sleeves are giving out. But it's ridiculous to buy a *new* sports jacket with suede patches on the elbows.

The Accouterments of Success

● SHIRTS

Despite much that is said to the contrary, a simple white shirt looks better than anything else when worn with a suit. If you can find plain white, 100 percent cotton shirts with button-down collars, you have it made. (The Orvis Company sells just such a shirt by mail, made of pure cotton with no artificial fibers.) There is a cult of fancy shirts, but my own experience is that men look best in plain ones, and that most successful people either wear white shirts or blue shirts, with an occasional very narrow, understated stripe in a muted color.

One basic rule: *Short sleeves are out.* A man who doesn't have a good inch of shirt cuff showing when he's wearing his suit jacket looks naked.

It is also a mistake to put anything in your shirt pocket (if there is one). Shirt pockets are purely decorative, and a row of ball-point pens and pencils clipped in one merely makes you look like a filing clerk.

Despite the contemporary passion for shirt collars that look like the wings of some giant bird, the successful look demands restraint and common sense in this area. The shirt collar should look natural and feel comfortable, and if it comes with little slots for plastic collar stays, use them, and keep a good supply. A crumpled shirt collar looks messy and unkempt.

I suspect that most men are happier with buttons

on their cuffs than with cuff links. But remember: *If you are going to wear cuff links, they should be as simple and inconspicuous as possible.* It doesn't matter how much they cost, they shouldn't draw attention to themselves. Plain gold ones are probably best, though these are usually worn by people who inherited them.

During the Nixon years, there was a great deal of status attached to the small, enameled cuff links bearing the seal of the President of the United States that Mr. Nixon gave away to White House visitors. These were kept in what John Ehrlichman referred to as "the Mickey Mouse" drawer of the President's desk, and can still be seen on the cuffs of Nixon loyalists. A number of organizations put out similar cuff links with small enameled devices on them. Any of these is likely to be more suitable than a pair of gold (or gold-plated) nuggets, a vast imitation gem or anything similarly clunky in appearance. You can even buy buttons made up as cuff links, in case you're sorry that you bought shirts with French cuffs in the first place.

- TIES

Restraint is equally important in ties. For those who have put on weight, a very wide tie has certain advantages. Noel Coward used to say that his ties got wider as he grew older, since they tended to conceal his stomach from view. In general, I would suggest not buying ties that are very thin or very wide. As to color and pattern, the less conspicuous and flashy, the better. Subdued stripes, checks, polka dots and paisley patterns are fine. But no tie should ever look as if you were wearing a neon sign on your chest. Color is O.K., but in moderation, and the design should be quiet—no sprawling geometric shapes, and no sunbursts.

I rather doubt that anybody really needs a tie clip, especially given the width of modern ties, but if you feel it necessary, it should be absolutely plain and inconspicuous, and worn well down on the tie, close to the belt, so that it doesn't show when your jacket is buttoned.

- ● HANDKERCHIEFS, ETC.

The pocket of your jacket should contain a handkerchief and nothing else. It should be plain white linen, or just possibly a muted silk paisley square, which should never match the tie. Very little of the handkerchief should be visible. It should be unfolded and slightly crushed, rather than arranged in neat little triangles or folded straight.

Under no circumstances carry pencils, pens or glasses in clip cases in your jacket pocket. As with a crammed shirt pocket, this is a very unsuccessful look. In general, it helps to cut down on the number and weight of things you carry, many of which can be put in a brief case anyway. Don't start off the day loading your pockets with a pen, a pencil, a thick wallet, keys, coins, a checkbook, cigarettes, a lighter and a pair of glasses. Eliminate anything you don't actually need, and whatever you must carry with you, put in your pants pockets, not your breast pocket.

- ● SUSPENDERS AND BELTS

Many successful people wear suspenders instead of a belt. This is an O.K. thing to do, but never wear suspenders *and* a belt, which is a sign of real anxiety. As for belts, the lighter and plainer they are, the better. Heavy tooled belts with fancy buckles are fine on cowboys, and look great with blue jeans, but serve no purpose when worn with a business suit—unless, of course, you're a Westerner, and combine them with cowboy boots and a Stetson hat.

- ● SHOES

Assuming you don't wear cowboy boots, take a good look at your shoes. Successful people are fussy about shoes, and you should be too. There's no point in dressing carefully if you wear heavy-soled shoes that make your feet look like King Kong's. One of the purposes of shoes is to indicate that the wearer doesn't need to plod through the muck and rain like ordinary people. This is an age-old function of shoes. The extreme form of cowboy boots, with their pointed toes and heels, was designed to make it evident that the wearer never had to walk, like a farmer or yokel, but went everywhere on horseback. Spanish grandees wore boots of such thin and supple leather that they were obliged to mount their horses directly from the marble steps of their houses, since they were unable to walk in the mud or dust. A simple rule about shoes: *The successful look is the absolute minimum of shoe.*

"SUCCESSFUL" HANDKERCHIEF IN POCKET

"UNSUCCESSFUL"

"UNSUCCESSFUL"

LOSER'S JACKET POCKET

On rainy, snowy days—until you become one of those very successful people we are trying to emulate who are driven in limousines and never get their feet wet—wear a good, stout pair of hiking boots to work, and keep your success shoes in the office. I have a pair of patent-leather Gucci loafers which seem to me ideal, since they never need polishing and always look elegant. But while Gucci has become a kind of success status symbol, any well-made, neat, light shoe is fine, so long as it's well-shined and not run down at the heels.

On the whole, I think black shoes are more useful for the success look than brown ones. You can wear black with gray and blue and almost anything else, which is not true of brown. And black is always correct, while brown is frowned upon by purists for evening wear. Avoid shoes with very pointed toes or heavy, square toes. They should look as much like your foot as possible, and should be free from welts, fancy stitching, patterns and ornamental straps. High heels are definitely out, and have no place in the success look. So are thick soles, "space shoes," "earth shoes," sandals and shoes made out of braided leather, like those of Mexican peasants.

● Socks

Apart from showing several inches of ankle by having your trousers hung at half mast, few things look worse than short socks, or socks that fall down in rolls around your ankles. Luckily, this is an area where the solution is simple and will free you from any further thought—buy black full-length socks. Black looks good everywhere and with everything, and takes at least one of the day's decisions off your mind. Stretch socks, particularly the ones made by Supp-hose®, never fall down.

● Hats, etc.

Personally, I am anti-hat. But I can see that in certain climates a hat makes sense. Very successful people don't need one—(they have limos)—and seldom wear one, but if you feel it's a necessity, don't get one with a very narrow brim, particularly if you have a full face. Avoid any hat that looks funny.

On some people, of course, *all* hats look funny. If you are in this category, buy a good umbrella, black with a plain handle. Remember that dressing for business success means looking your best even if it's five o'clock on a humid day, when everything has gone wrong, and you got caught in the rain on your way back from lunch. What you have to do is to project the appearance of someone who is never affected by the elements, and always manages to appear fresh, energetic and ready for anything. Most people work their way up to some kind of clothes sense by painful experience as they rise in the world. You don't have to. Stand in front of the mirror and take the first step today!

Dressing for Ms. Achievement

Women have far greater problems in deciding what to wear for success, if only because there are fewer guidelines and models for them to use. The women's clothing industry has not yet faced up to the fact that women need solid, reassuring and businesslike clothes as much as men do. However, women have one advantage over men in that men have no real idea of what a successful woman *should* wear, and are therefore in a poor position to criticize. Furthermore, their cultural background makes it difficult for them to express open criticism of any woman's clothes, though not of course impossible. In other words, if you're an ambitious woman in business and your immediate superiors are men, you can probably get away with a lot more than a man in your position could. That's not to say it's necessarily a good idea to take advantage of the fact, but it's worth remembering that a man who could quickly judge whether or not a male executive was appropriately dressed would find it hard to define just what *would* be appropriate for you.

So much of the clothing made for women is based on fantasy that it is hard to draw up any reliable set of guidelines. Most successful women, however, make a determined effort to find a simple style of dress that both suits them and seems appropriate to the business they're in and unlikely to arouse comment from men. Obviously, a lot depends on the business. An advertising agency or a magazine publisher would be very different from a bank or a government agency. But in general, successful women avoid extremes of dress.

Some years ago, my own bank abandoned its dress code and allowed its personnel to wear pretty much whatever they wanted to. Well, not exactly. In a burst of reverse sexism, they demanded that male personnel wear a suit and a tie, but allowed the women more or less total freedom. I notice that many of the women tellers wear skin-tight blue jeans, T-shirts and even halter tops, which is fine (I'm all for freedom). But the women who rise to become supervisors and vice presidents are those who wear a simple, rather formal dress or suit. And I think there is a lesson here: *By and large, women can wear what they want to, within obvious limits; but the women who get ahead take great care to dress unobtrusively and conservatively.*

Perhaps the best thing that has appeared for ambitious women is the simple shirtdress. It looks good on almost every figure and is acceptable under almost any social or business circumstance, assuming it is in a solid, businesslike color. It doesn't crease, it doesn't go out of style and it can be worn in any skirt length, from knee-covering conservative to mid-thigh shocking.

If I were a woman in business, I'd buy a dozen of them. I'd also think it worthwhile investing in a few classic, simple suits in dark colors, particularly grays and blues. The real classic seems to me the Chanel suit. But there are many imitations of it that will do just as well, and worn with a simple white blouse it not only looks good, but will seem perfectly appropriate at even the stuffiest business meeting.

Feminists may rebel at the suggestion, but I think a woman who wants to be a success could do a lot worse than to make a careful study of the women's fashion magazines, particularly *Vogue* and *Bazaar,* but also *Glamour* and *Mademoiselle* when they're doing a "working women" issue. You may pick up some ideas that will enable you to create your own "success look." You need all the help you can get, and it's a great advantage to see what other women are wearing in more or less comparable professions.

Avoid: very bright colors, "fussy" clothes, very tight pants suits, skirts so short they make you look like a high school cheerleader, plunging necklines and blue jeans.

Men naturally resent it when women take greater liberties in dress than men are allowed. They are also made uncomfortable in business situations by clothing that has an overtly sexual appeal. There may be occasions on which women can use an alluring outfit to their advantage, but generally speaking it's a *short-term gain* that will be paid for by a *long-term loss.* You will have problems enough in making your way to the top as a woman, without increasing them by the way you dress and present yourself.

For several thousand years, women have been dressed to answer the fantasy needs of men, and to prove that no woman could compete on physically equal terms. The vast dresses and wigs of the eighteenth century, the crinolines and bustles and hats of the nineteenth century, the eccentric "looks" of the great French couturiers in our own era, all made women into more or less decorative and static objects, in some cases hardly even capable of movement from point A to point B without the assistance of a man. There has been a natural and proper rebellion against this tradition and all that it implies in terms of constriction and role-playing.

Now, the main thing is for you to concentrate on putting men at their ease. You will rise faster this way. For this reason, the extremes of high-fashion make-up and hair styling are usually a mistake. It is important to make the best of yourself, but not to the extent of obscuring your natural identity and appearance. I can't help noticing, for example, that almost every successful woman I've met uses clear, natural nail polish, rather than the bright or dark colors. It makes sense. Many men feel threatened by the sight of long scarlet fingernails, even though this may be exciting to them as a sexual signal in other contexts. What is more, women with long, lacquered fingernails generally look as if they're incapable of performing any real work. Once again, they represent a male-imposed symbol of sexual possession—the proof that a woman is being kept and therefore doesn't *need* to work. It's a small point, but the kind of thing that gets noticed.

Women have one great advantage over men—their clothes are more comfortable. It is perfectly possible for a woman to wear a simple dress, minimal underwear and a pair of shoes that are hardly more than a strap with heels, and still look respectably dressed for a business meeting. These days, very few people will notice or care whether you wear pantyhose or not. Bare legs are not likely to cause a scandal, or even be noticed. When you consider that many men, in comparable circumstances, are wearing underwear, socks, a heavy pair of shoes, trousers, a shirt, a tie and a lined suit jacket, you will realize that not everything in life is in the man's favor.

Carrying Things

O.K.: A successful woman carries a handbag.
O.K.: A successful woman carries a brief case.
Not O.K.: A successful woman does not carry both.

Personally, I think a woman in business is better off with a good, solid brief case. It looks professional, and establishes her serious intent. Anything you would normally carry in a handbag can be carried just as easily in a brief case, and a good deal more besides.

I have the distinct impression that in a working situation men are made nervous by a woman's handbag when it is placed on their desk or in the immediate vicinity. Perhaps it's because the handbag is, in men's mind, a symbol of femininity, and contains God knows what intimate feminine possessions. In certain cases, a woman can use this to her advantage. If you have to negotiate a deal with a man, place your handbag on his desk as you sit down. It will almost certainly distract him and keep him off balance. On the other hand, if you're looking for promotion and success in the business world, never put a handbag on a man's desk or on a conference table. It strikes the wrong image, and will almost certainly be resented, even if unconsciously.

If you carry a brief case, pick one that's large and solid, as much like a man's as possible. It's effective to have your initials stamped on it. The sight of a woman with a Crouch & Fitzgerald attaché case strikes terror into the hearts of many older men, and this is something you can put to good use in negotiating.

SYMBOLS OF SUCCESS

The world is so full of success symbols that it is hard to know which ones, if any, are worth owning. It is possible to spend as much as $1,000 for a Vuitton attaché case. Hunting World in New York sells attaché cases in exotic leathers for prices that go as high as $5,000. Presumably there are people who buy them, or they wouldn't be made.

Status As a Private Joke

There are two different kinds of success symbols. The first consists of those things we want because they seem to symbolize or reward our success to ourselves. The second consists of the status objects that announce to other people that we have succeeded. A $5,000 attaché case is in the first category, since it hardly looks different from a $200 attaché case, and its value is known only to the person who is carrying it or the person who paid for it. The pleasure here is simply in *knowing* that your brief case is worth the price of a new car, even though it appears to any uninformed stranger like just another well-made piece of leather goods.

Certain success symbols have a built-in totemic factor. The Cartier "tank watch" for men may be bought at Cartier's for $750 plus ($350 for the hinged gold buckle on the leather strap). Exact copies of it, gold-plated and with presumably inferior mechanisms, may be purchased at any department store for $100 or less, and even bear the Cartier name. In this case, the pleasure lies in the owner's quiet satisfaction that only he knows whether he paid over $1,000 or less than a hundred, as well as the feeling that other people must surely realize that a successful man would never wear an imitation of the real thing. I once sat at a meeting and realized that every person present seemed to be wearing the identical "tank watch," including myself, but I would have been reluctant to ask which people were wearing the genuine article. Note: *the status of an object does not depend on the fact that it can't be copied*. Quite the contrary: Cartier sold more of their watches after the copies began to appear in the marketplace.

A great many people like to surround themselves with just this kind of status symbol. It is something in the nature of a private joke, like having your initials hand-embroidered on your undershorts. Even though the success symbols that most people covet are generally for attracting the attention of others rather than for some obscure private pleasure, sometimes the two can be combined. Ownership of a Rolls-Royce (the new Camargue version can be yours for about $90,-000) can obviously be a source of personal satisfaction *and* a public symbol.

Once you're a major success—that is to say, making more than $100,000 a year, and with every likelihood of continuing to do so in the future, you may feel inclined to gratify your individual taste and whim in choosing those symbols of success that please you the most. This is one of the major rewards of becoming a success in the first place. You always wanted a Porsche Targa 911E in dark-chocolate-colored lacquer, hand rubbed to a high gloss? Nothing prevents you from ordering one, once you have the $20,000. You want an office furnished with eighteenth-century English antiques, sporting prints and Bokhara carpets? As a success, this is your privilege. You aspire to own a triplex overlooking Central Park? Just the apartment you have in mind is available. Success frees you to make a reality of your fantasies. Some people can stand this, others can't—they find what was desirable as a fantasy becomes uninteresting when they can actually own it. On the whole, most people make the adjustment.

Over the years, it has always interested me to observe what happens to authors who make a huge movie or paperback sale, and find themselves suddenly rich. In each case, there is some fantasy object that they have always desired, and can now afford. The ones who go right out and buy it—whether it's a red Ferrari Dino, a pair of Tiffany Schlumberger cuff links, a pair of matched Purdy shotguns, a diamond ring from Harry Winston—survive and manage to handle their newfound wealth quite well. The ones who don't go out and make the vital, initial splurge frequently end up either losing all their money or going to pieces as a result.

Like these authors, you probably have a fantasy object, the one stupid, useless and totally desirable thing you have always wanted to buy and knew you never would. When you become a real success, you should be liberated to the point where you can bring yourself to purchase it. It's important to enjoy the pleasures that success affords you. If you don't, you're likely to find yourself halted in mid-career and unable to move further on.

Essential and Nonessential Status Symbols for Your Success Identity

On the way up, the problem is a little bit different. You cannot afford to indulge your fantasies. *Yet there are many symbols which can give you the aura of success in other people's eyes,* thus speeding up the process of establishing your success identity.

● CARS

In the old days, people worried a great deal about what kind of car they should own. A junior executive might drive a Chevrolet, for example, but would hesitate to buy an Oldsmobile or a Buick, on the grounds that his relative status within the corporate hierarchy would not entitle him to drive a car that was "out of his league." On the other hand, once he was promoted, he would feel obliged to "trade up" to a more expensive car. This kind of thing is much less true of American society than it used to be. The interest in ecology and the risk of a new energy crisis, combined with the popularity of foreign cars, have made the car *a very unreliable status object,* except at the highest level. Nowadays, a man may be making $75,000 a year and drive a VW Dasher. One of the most successful men I know drives to work on a Honda motorcycle, and Chester Davis, who used to be Howard Hughes' personal attorney, drives himself in a small foreign compact (though it has a phone with four lines and a hold button on the front seat). No, very few people are likely to care what you drive on the way up.

• BRIEF CASES

A good brief case is essential. Here is something that needn't cost a fortune, but definitely establishes your status in the business world. I have seen men come to work in the morning carrying A&P shopping bags or canvas barrack bags. This is a mistake. A good, solid brief case, either in black or brown leather, makes it clear that you are serious enough about your prospects to have invested $200 or so in one. My personal opinion is that a brief case that opens at the top, has accordion sides to allow for expansion, two solid handles and a brass lock is best at the under-$50,000-a-year level. Above that level, an attaché case is more appropriate, providing it's not too bulky. At the very top it is best to carry a slim leather portfolio or nothing.

Whatever you choose, this is not a place to skimp. Your brief case goes everywhere you do, and is a highly visible symbol of your status and success potential. Do *not* buy:

- Aluminum attaché cases with plastic handles (Halliburton Zero). However practical they seem, the effect is to make you look like a photographer carrying his equipment or a man on his way to the local pistol range.
- Fiberglass attaché cases.

If you can't afford leather, then vinyl will have to do. In fact, some of the vinyls don't look bad at all when they're new. Unlike leather, however, they do not improve with age, and become scuffed and faded, instead of settling down into a well-worn gloss. My advice, though, is that it's worth spending the money for a solid leather brief case right at the beginning. Well looked after, with a little saddle soap, it will help you

up every step of the ladder to success, until you reach
the final rungs when you can do without one altogether.

Never let your brief case be checked through as
baggage on an airflight. It will emerge tattered, shabby
and covered with stickers that are impossible to remove. Keep it with you, and even if you don't have
any important papers to put in it, you can at least
load it with all the things you would otherwise have
to carry in your pockets.

● LIGHTING A CIGARETTE

If you smoke, a cigarette lighter is a very useful
status symbol. Here again, you can spend several
thousand dollars for a Dupont, Cartier, or Dunhill
lighter, but this is hardly necessary. *The best status
symbol in the world is an elderly Zippo that looks and
works as if it's come through the wars.* If you have to
buy a new one, age it before using by scraping it back
and forth in gravel and sand, then banging it a bit
with a sharp rock.

The latest item in this area is a Braun electronic
gas lighter, which looks like a solid rectangle of black
steel. Everyone who owns one says that there are only
three people in the United States who have similar
lighters, a sure sign of a reliable, growing status object.

Many people carry prestige matchbooks in their
pockets for show. (It is always amusing to see their
expression when you make them tear off a match and
light it for your cigarette.) In Washington, the matchbooks that bear the legend "Air Force One" are a
very good status object. In New York, I once knew a
young man on Wall Street who went to the trouble
of having several hundred personalized matchbooks
made up on which he had elegantly imprinted the
name "David Rockefeller." He was always delighted
to give you a book of matches or light your cigarette
and attributes a great deal of his early success to the
aura his matchbooks gave him. Even today, he has a

reputation as a man with powerful friends. "It was," he said, "the best twenty dollars I ever spent."

On the whole, it's tacky to carry matches from "21," Lutèce, Scandia, Le Bistro or the Pump Room, if you haven't eaten there. The result is more likely to be a close auditing of your expense account than any immediate gain in status.

THE SUCCESSFUL OFFICE

As far as office furnishings are concerned, insist on simple, dark colors—blue for the carpeting, plain wood for the desk, dark leather or fabric for the chairs and sofa. Avoid vinyl, and anything fancy or overdecorated. The simpler your office looks, the more successful you will appear to be. By the way, if you're a messy worker, provide yourself with trays, boxes, drawers and cupboards so that you can sweep things out of sight. The more cluttered your office is, the more you give the impression of someone who has lost control of the work at hand and is drowning in a sea of paper.

Do not put your children's drawings on the wall if you can help it. But if you must, have them framed. Anything that goes on the wall should be framed, otherwise it gives the room a slumlike impression of impermanency, as if you didn't expect to remain in employment there for very long. Diplomas and certificates are O.K., provided they are not totally worthless. Beware of giving away too much information when you do this, however. One young man I know passed himself off as a Harvard graduate for some time (in a company where there were no other Harvard men to question him), then foolishly placed his degree on the wall in a neat frame—from which it was clear that he had, in fact, been graduated from Boston University. Your diplomas and degrees, if any, must correspond with your story, if not necessarily with the truth.

Gold pens and pencils are O.K. as success symbols, but it is essential that they look like gifts or presentations. It is absolutely out to buy your own, and if you do, you'd do well to have a suitable message engraved on the cap or barrel. The best kind are the Cross sets which are given away at special events. The executives of firms that become listed on the American Stock Exchange receive Cross pen and pencil sets with the Exchange's symbol in enamel on the clip. This kind of thing makes a nice success symbol even if you have to steal it off someone else's desk.

If you have one of those desktop pen sets, it must be a presentation set. If you feel you can't live without one, and haven't yet been presented with it, buy one and have it engraved with your name, a date and some imaginary occasion. Also make sure it works. Anyone who spends a good deal of time in other people's offices—as I do—knows that approximately 99 percent of the pen and pencil sets in the world don't work, either from neglect or because the pens have never been refilled. Usually all you get is a lot of caked ink on your fingers and trousers, and the apologetic offer of a felt-tip pen from your host's desk drawer. This is poor success planning. If you're going to have something in sight, it must work. This holds true of desk clocks, lighters and calendars as well. Nothing creates a poorer impression than something which is supposed to function and doesn't. If something on your desk doesn't function, it reflects on *you*.

Desk blotters, letter openers and correspondence folders are all objects that can enhance your status. None is genuinely necessary, but if you're going to have them, they should be simple, elegant and handsome, and always at least one cut above your actual status.

If you're an aspiring executive, keep your paper clips, stapler and Scotch tape dispenser out of sight. They are utilitarian objects, but you don't want to be thought of as someone who has to do these menial tasks for yourself.

In certain companies there is a major status distinction between those who have plain, printed business cards and those who have raised, engraved ones. If you're not entitled to the high status of raised engraving, go out and have your own made up. They look better, feel better and make an altogether more successful impression. Use them as much as possible. *The more business cards you hand out, the more people are likely to remember who you are.*

● FOOD AND DRINKS

If you can persuade your secretary to serve you coffee in a china cup and saucer instead of a mug or a Styrofoam carton, this is a nice touch of class, and makes an excellent impression. In David Mahoney's office, coffee is served on a silver tray, with cups, saucers, silverware and a small jug for cream. This may be too much for you (or your secretary), but it's a standard to which you can aspire. In all these matters, a little elegance is well worth the effort.

If you are having lunch at your desk with someone, keep a couple of plates to put the sandwiches on, and buy a couple of real linen napkins, rather than unwrapping them straight from the bag they've been delivered in, so your guest gets egg salad over his trousers, and has to make do with the one damp, flimsy paper napkin that most takeout delicatessens provide. It is also courteous to remove all the papers from your desk so that your guest doesn't have to place his sandwich on top of a freshly typed memo or the proofs of the corporate report.

All too often, "lunching in" is an exercise in slobbery. But it doesn't have to be. Even if you're not in a position to have a waiter serve a full meal from a trolley sent in by a nearby restaurant, as Lincoln Schuster, the cofounder of Simon and Schuster, used to do, it's easy enough to buy and keep a couple of plates, some knives and forks, linen napkins and salt and pepper shakers. If you have people in for a drink at the close of the day, then it obviously pays to have an ice bucket, real (as opposed to plastic) glasses, and a reasonable selection of liquors and mixes. Although it is often more conducive to business to have a drink in the office than to go out to a bar, nobody is really pleased to be presented with a plastic picnic glass full of Scotch, without ice or soda, when what they wanted was a well-iced bourbon on the rocks.

Many senior executives invest in a small refrigerator, a very nice touch, though it pays to have a lock put on it. If your office has a coffee maker, a supply of cups and a refrigerator, you can be sure it will become the watering hole for everyone on your floor. One successful executive I know gets in early every morning and turns on the coffee-maker, which he has prepared the night before. Almost all his senior colleagues stop by his office on their way and "borrow" a cup, as a result of which he knows them far better than he would ordinarily have the right to do, and hears most things of importance long before anyone else.

A woman executive in the same corporation brews a pot of tea every afternoon at four, and opens up a box of imported English biscuits. This is partly for her own enjoyment—she likes a good cup of tea in the afternoon—but also because she has discovered that a great many of the corporate officers "accidentally" walk by her office at four o'clock and sit down for a cup of tea. There are four executives of status equal to hers in the same "row," but she was promoted first, and continues to rise faster than the others. She is simply better known, and remembered in a pleasurable context.

Naturally, these things can be carried too far. It is a mistake to keep liquor in your office and throw a kind of office "open house" for departing commuters every afternoon at five, which I have seen happen. This merely gets you a bad reputation. But a certain amount of elegant intramural hospitality, if carried out in the right way, can be a small but significant step on the road to success.

● ODDS AND ENDS

Desk calendars can be used to good effect, if you
know how. Avoid the small ones that present a new
page for every day of the week. Go to the trouble of
buying a large one that presents the whole week on
two facing pages. Fill the pages up, then leave it conspicuously open, and consult it ostentatiously whenever anyone suggests a meeting of any kind.

Telephone logs are equally useful. Keep a list of all
the people you have to call, however insignificant they
are, and however unlikely it is that you intend to return their calls. This list should be left on your desk
where it can be seen—indeed, where it cannot be
missed—by anyone who comes into your office. It
pays dividends to use a special form, with space for
the time of the call. This gives a great impression of
efficiency with very little effort on your part.

Dictating machines can also be used as a sign of
success. Never mind that you don't dictate, and that
your secretary doesn't know how to transcribe. The
machine itself establishes your executive status. Certain machines, like the IBM portable dictator or the
small Norelco pocket tape recorder, imply superior
status. Packing a machine with you when you leave
the office shows a seriousness of purpose which is very
valuable, particularly if you are on your way to the
movies or taking a two-day fishing trip on the sly. Here
too, there's no point in saving money on a success
symbol. Invest in the best machine you can find, particularly if you never intend to use it in the first place.

I know one businessman who became so addicted to
the small pocket dictating machine he had bought (on
company money, of course) that he took to dictating
personal thoughts into it. He finally began taking it
to bed with him so that every night he could say,
"This is Bob Phillips, signing off for the night." Needless to say, his wife soon moved to a separate bed-
room. At one point in the gradual dissolution of their
marriage she began to steal the machine during the
night to dictate hostile messages to her husband on it.

The joke was on her. The machine was for show, not for any practical use, and neither her husband nor his secretary ever heard her comments on him and their marriage.

● THE TELEPHONE AS A SUCCESS SYMBOL

Status can often be measured by the number and type of the telephone instruments you use. A telephone without multiple lines is worthless as a success symbol, and one with buttons is slightly better than the kind that has an old-fashioned dial. There should be a separate telephone by your sofa (if you have one) and if you can afford to have a bright red "Hot Line" telephone installed for emergency and personal calls, by all means do so. Speakerphones have become very status-y, and in many corporations are a recognizable sign of élite membership. True, your voice sounds as if it were being dredged up from 20,000 leagues beneath the sea, but that too is useful. When people ask, "Why does your voice sound so funny?" you can reply, "I'm sorry, I'm on my speaker." Making conference calls by Speakerphone is one of the ego-satisfactions of success. You can sit in your office and talk to five or six people gathered around one telephone to listen to you at the other end, perhaps 3,000 miles away. If, as it has been wisely said, the true measure of success is the number of people you can inconvenience, the Speakerphone is one of the best ways of demonstrating success.

Both Presidents John F. Kennedy and Lyndon B. Johnson favored the kind of large "Call Director" phones that have several dozen lines, each with its own button. This enables you to rate your success by the number of people you can put on hold. Once a dozen or two people have been put on hold, you can move back and forth between them, ignore them altogether, or cut them off if they seem likely to be boring. In the hands of a successful telephoner, the instrument can be played with the virtuosity of an organ master.

You must beware of the fact that people don't *like*

to be put on hold. The late Jacqueline Susann once stormed into my office in a fit of rage. Pointing one heavily jeweled finger at me, she shouted, "I want the name of the girl that put me on hold! I want her OUT of here!" Her fury was real and represents a common reaction. Still, once a person has placed a call and gotten through to you, he or she will be reluctant to give up and start again, particularly if you're the kind of successful person who is always making calls, so nobody can ever reach you. It may take days to re-establish contact. People do not like to waste their dime, and will hang on long after it becomes apparent that you are never likely to get back to them, and that it's only a matter of time before the line goes dead. Personally, when someone tells me they're putting me on hold, I say "Thank you," then hang up. There's no greater waste of time than sitting at your desk with a silent telephone held to your ear, while the party at the other end takes his own sweet time getting back to you, and continues taking calls until they're stacked like airplanes at JFK airport on a rainy Friday night. Still, there is no doubt that *the more people you yourself can put and keep on hold, the more successful you will seem.* You can't have too many buttons.

I have seen telephones in cars, on yachts, in bathrooms, and in small compartments carved into the trees on a country estate. I have even seen one rather neatly installed on a motorcycle by a financier who likes dangerous sports, but doesn't want to be "out of touch." The classic example of this has always been people who get themselves paged at the pool of the Beverly Hills Hotel. If you can have your name called out frequently enough, as the legend goes ("Mr. Zanuck for Mr. Korda, New York for Mr. Korda, Dino de Laurentiis for Mr. Korda, etc."), sooner or later somebody really *will* call you, if only from the next cabaña. However, this can backfire. Mike Frankovitch, the producer, was once slumbering poolside when he heard the operator say on the loudspeaker, "Mr. Frankovitch phoning from New York for Miss Jane

Hampton." "I saw this girl get up from her mat," he later told me, "fix the top of her bikini and go off to the nearest phone to take the call. When she came back, I went over and said to her, 'Next time, play it a little more cute, Miss Hampton. Read *Variety* first, and pick somebody who's out of town. If you're not smart enough to do that, you're not smart enough to make it.' "

If you want to make an impression on someone, you can have yourself paged at a variety of places which may never have occurred to you. Airports are happy to page anyone, and so are many restaurants. One Hollywood producer I know was paged by his studio while he was sailing his yacht in the middle of a race off Santa Barbara. A fast speedboat came weaving through the sailboats, while a young man stood in the bow with an electric bull horn, shouting at him to get to the nearest telephone so Harry Cohn, the head of Columbia Pictures, could talk to him. Torn between the desire to finish the race and make a straight run for the harbor to take Cohn's call, the producer decided to finish the race. Needless to add, he never worked for Columbia again.

Cohn himself, like most people in the movie business, was a phone freak, constantly in communication with unwilling listeners at all hours of the day and night. Every success seeker could do well to imitate Cohn in this way; for one of the best ways to make a mediocre idea seem important is to give it urgency. Ideas which, if contained in a letter, would end in the wastepaper basket, are read with attention when they arrive in the form of a cable or telegram. Information which would seem dull and pointless at three in the afternoon can be made to seem dramatic and important if received in the form of an unexpected late-night telephone call.

For a long time office telephones, like the Ford Model-T, came in any color you wanted, so long as it was black. Garson Kanin, in commenting on the fact that Harry Cohn always had a telephone at hand, even at a dinner party, was awestruck to see that Cohn had a special *white* telephone to put on the table for very formal dinners—a touch of class that would be impressive even today. The first nonblack office telephone I ever saw in New York was specially ordered for Phyllis S. Levy, when she worked at Simon and Schuster. She insisted on a beige telephone and eventually got it, thus clearly establishing her special success status all over the other editorial assistants.

Since then, color has become a distinct mark of status in working telephones. As I have mentioned, a red telephone looks very impressive, but it must be a second phone, suggesting that you have a special number for emergencies (nobody unimportant has emergencies). Most men feel uncomfortable with white telephones, though for women executives they seem to add a special touch of class. One sees very few blue telephones; at present the "in" color among achievers seems to be a dark, rich chocolate brown, with dark-gray a close second. These days secretaries often get colored phones to match that of their boss, rather like livery for servants in feudal days.

Privacy—the Key to the Success Office

Of course, the ultimate in prestige is probably to have no telephone at all. When Charles de Gaulle was President of France, he refused to have a telephone in his office. The only telephone at Colombey-les-deux-Églises, his country house, was in the gate lodge, rather than in the house itself. Any emergency involving the French Republic would reach the President through this one ancient instrument, and an aide-de-camp would have to carry the message in person to De Gaulle, wait for an audience, then come back to the gate lodge to transmit the President's reply or comment, if any. Very few events short of World War Three seemed important enough to report, and De

Gaulle's ministers trembled in fear at the very thought of telephoning him.

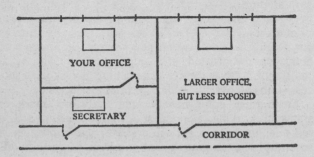

For less exalted people, this kind of splendid isolation is difficult to achieve. Perhaps the only businessman who attained the ultimate status of inaccessibility was the late Howard Hughes, who made a fetish of it, partly out of fear of germs, partly because he rightly felt that you couldn't be sued for anything you hadn't said or put on paper. One of his closest associates, a man who virtually managed Hughes' business affairs for over a decade, reported that while "he had known Howard Hughes closer and better than anyone," he had in fact never actually *seen* him. He had talked to him only once, and this was late at night in a motel room, where Hughes sat in the bathroom with the light off and the door ajar, talking to him through a two-inch crack. Nothing about Hughes is surprising. One friend of mine was invited to have tea with Jean Peters, and apparently surprised Hughes in the middle of an unexpected visit to Miss Peters. Hughes never showed himself, but during the hour my friend was there, a figure was painfully visible, standing motionless behind the drapes, with two dirty sneakers protruding from beneath the hem.

At the headquarters of one giant conglomerate, it is necessary to go through a security check in the lobby before ascending to the president's floor in a special, nonstop elevator, with built-in television security cameras. An armed guard in a neat red blazer greets you on the 57th floor, and you are then conducted to a large reception area, where a final check is made to ensure that you really *do* have an appointment and aren't an imposter. From there, you are taken to one of a number of small, comfortable sitting rooms, where you sit alone. This is very clever. It means that you never see who else is waiting, and therefore don't know who may have business here besides yourself. There you sit, until a secretary comes to guide you through a maze of corridors, up a flight of stairs, in and out of what seems to be a series of closets, and finally into the enormous office of the president. This kind of privacy does not come cheap, but it serves its purpose, which is to draw a demarcation line between ordinary people and those who are successful.

The more you can do this, even if it is on a more modest scale, the more successful you are likely to seem. If you have a choice of offices, take one that's a little out of the way. If possible, pick one which has a separate room for your secretary so that a visitor has to pass through that office to get into yours. Even if such an office is inconvenient in other respects, even if it has one small window overlooking a brick wall, it is still the one to choose.

If you don't have this kind of option available to you, a very good tactic is to *keep your door closed*. There is, after all, no reason why the door of your office *should* be open. It's merely one of those social conventions of American business life. Half the time it exposes the fact that you are doodling or daydreaming to everyone who walks past, the other half of the time it simply serves as an invitation to time-wasters and people looking for an audience to hear out their particular grievance or monomania.

If you simply close your door, you can work in peace if you're doing something, whereas if you're not doing anything it won't be noticed and held against you. Anybody who wants to see you will have to knock on the door, thus putting you in the position of

being able to control access to your person. It will soon
be taken for granted that your job is difficult, that you
work hard at it, and that your time is valuable to you
and to others. What is more, you will have created
some small but significant air of mystery about yourself, which is always valuable—the sense that you have
something held in reserve, that you're destined for
higher, better things.

When someone visits your office, it is always flattering to get up and close the door after he or she is
seated. It implies, first of all, that you are prepared to
cut yourself off to hear the other person out, and also
suggests that what they—and you—have to say is con-
fidential, important and worth dealing with in quiet
privacy. This is seldom the case, but people understandably like to feel that it is. It is the kind of small
touch that separates the potential success from the
potential loser. If your office has one of those semi-
opaque glass doors, get it changed. You need a good
solid door, preferably wooden. If this is impossible,
have the inside of the door painted.

Personal Touches

If you are going to have your name on your door,
do it properly. In many offices, the doors are fitted
with metal plates, into which a plastic nameplate can
be inserted—and from which it can, of course, be instantly removed. This is bad from your point of view,
since it creates the impression that you may be
removed, along with your nameplate, at any moment.
Unscrew the fixture and have your nameplate screwed
into the door. Most of the nameplates that go into
these fixtures are small and come with an initial and
your last name, i.e., "J. Silberman." This will not do.
Your name plate must bear your full name ("James
H. Silberman") *and* your title, if you have one. If you
don't have one, add a line that describes your function
or your department.

By contrast, a nameplate on your desk is something to be *avoided* at all costs. The implication is that someone entering your office may not know who you are, a possibility that reduces you to total insignificance

The personal items that people put in their offices often reveal a good deal about them—more, in fact, than many of them would want to reveal. It is perfectly O.K. to have photographs of your family. In fact, it's such a common practice that it is probably wrong *not* to have them on display. They represent visible evidence that you are a person of substance, with mouths to feed, and therefore reliable and trustworthy. As one executive told me, "I wouldn't trust a guy who didn't have a photograph of his wife and kids somewhere in his office. It shows he's got a reason to work hard and toe the line." (Interestingly enough, women executives, though they usually have photographs of their children on display, seldom if ever show a photograph of their husband, presumably because they don't have to provide for him. We generally show those people we have to support, as if they served as proof that we need our jobs.)

So strong is this tradition that many unmarried people put up photographs of other people's families, just so as not to be different. Dogs and cats will not serve the purpose, and vacation pictures are definitely a mistake, since they suggest you dream of sunny beaches and palm trees rather than the welfare and support of your nearest and dearest. If you own a house, by all means have a photograph of it on display. Everyone trusts a person with a mortgage, and a house is the ultimate hostage to fortune.

Be wary of photographs that are overglamorous. I once knew a young executive who attracted considerable ill will from his superiors by displaying photographs of his wife, a beautiful fashion model, in a bikini and in various evening gowns. They were jealous of him for having a professional beauty as a wife, and paid very little attention to his requests for a raise. It was widely assumed that she must be making a fortune. It took him a long time to fathom this hostility toward him, but when he did, he sensibly moved to another company and put up an unflattering Polaroid snapshot of his wife, and a picture of someone else's baby, since he didn't have a child. He has since been promoted at regular intervals, and encounters no problems in getting the appropriate raises.

How to Create a WASP Office

High-WASP status usually involves ship models, photographs of one's family on horseback and antique *bric-a-brac*—a ship's clock, scrimshaw, 18th-century desk implements, sporting prints and ancestral portraits of a more or less genuine character. John F. Kennedy's personal decorations in the Oval Office of the White House perfectly exemplified his vision of this style, as do those of a great many senior partners in old-line WASP law firms and brokerage houses.

The style is easy enough to achieve. If you don't own the basic elements, you can always find them in antique shops that specialize in supplying status climbers with a high-WASP background. But it must be appropriate to your job and your surroundings. A high-WASP background may look fine for an investment banker, but will certainly seem out of place in the office of an ambitious motion-picture executive.

Any suspicion that you have faked it will merely make you seem ludicrous to colleagues and visitors. So if you are going to opt for it, start early, at the very beginning of your career, perhaps with an inkwell in the shape of a horse's hoof, a whaling print and a photograph of a child on a pony. You can work up from there to full WASP status: photographs of your wife fox-hunting in Middleburg, Va., pictures of yachts, pewter tankards, needlework pillows on the sofa, a few leatherbound books, a couple of mounted heads of game trophies, and a wing chair or two. The important thing is to be *consistent,* right from the beginning, instead of blossoming out in full high-WASP style late in life, as so many people mistakenly do.

A "Jock" Office

Jock status is valuable in almost every profession, and transcends race, creed, color or national origin. Sporting trophies are excellent success symbols, and the more, the better. If you haven't won them, go out to the nearest pawn shop and buy them. Since golf and tennis are the most widely played sports among American achievers, it is sensible to mark your status in these areas. By all means display as many golf tournament trophies as you can, and if you have any tangible evidence of your superior ability as a tennis player, put it up where it can be seen.

It can do you no harm to keep a putter in your office, together with one of those little devices by means of which you can practice putting on your office carpet. An interest in golf is perhaps the most reliable way to establish contact with people, and is still likely to win you more friends than anything else. Bear in mind that it is by no means necessary to *play* golf. It is only necessary to show that you *care* about golf. If you are invited to play, you can always find a hundred reasons why you can't, but you should never let it be thought that you aren't a passionate devotee of the sport.

High jock status is usually achieved by careful reference to past triumphs in the sporting world. Football photographs are very useful for this, as are hockey posters, and a collection of sports trophies. Any major successes you may have achieved in the past in sports can be put to good use in gaining success in the larger world. After all, David Mahoney, the president of Norton Simon, Inc., first stepped out onto the fast track as a basketball player in high school. His later athletic triumphs brought him to the attention of the various power brokers who afterward sponsored his corporate career. Nothing is more universally respected than sports achievement, which is assumed to indicate strength of character and the will to win.

If you can lay claim to any achievements of this kind, display them with confidence. If you can't, pick a sport that nobody knows anything about and claim some achievement at that. Fencing is a relatively safe bet—a pair of crossed foils and a few silver cups will establish, in a modest way, your claim to sports status. Your chances of meeting a fellow fencer are comparatively slender.

The Jewish Success Office

Just as WASPs establish status by means of antiques and family memorabilia, Jewish success status in office furnishing is usually achieved by means of photographs, plaques and framed letters. I have been in offices where the walls are a solid mass of framed photographs and plaques. The photographs are usually of the achiever himself, shown in varying degrees of informality with an endless succession of celebrities and political figures. It is imperative that the photographs be signed, but this is not by any means hard to arrange. At one time almost everyone who counted for anything in New York had a photograph of himself or herself with Lyndon Johnson, and doubtless the signed photographs commemorating visits to Richard Nixon will make their way back onto people's walls very soon—after all, a President is a President, even if he did resign . . .

Plaques given out by organizations for fund raising or any other honorable service are extremely useful. A good start to this kind of success display can usually be made early on with little effort. This works exceedingly well in some companies, where proof of active interests in the outside world is taken as a visible indication of solid responsibility. More than one firm has placed its trust, and sometimes its future, in the hands of a man whose walls seemed to guarantee that he was a solid, responsible citizen and a pillar of his community. This trust is sometimes well placed, and often not, but it can work for you. Display your civic virtues, and if you have none, go out and get some plaques made for yourself, which will serve just as well.

Framed letters from political figures are very often used as a success display. This can be rather dangerous, unless you're absolutely sure of your management's political opinions. Presidents of the United States are always O.K. since the Presidency has an absolute status unrelated to the individual President. But senators, governors and congressmen are tricky, and their photographs may do you more harm than good. Those who pursue this kind of display are usually wise enough to cover all the bases. They will arrange to have themselves photographed with Mrs. Golda Meir *and* Cardinal Cooke, or with Senator James Buckley *and* Senator Hubert Humphrey. A framed letter from Lyndon Johnson will be placed next to a framed Christmas card from Dwight D. Eisenhower. They are careful to display status without committing themselves to an opinion. This is realistic. Status transcends party and religion. The object is to show yourself in the company of people who are more important than you are, and more important than the people you work for.

The important thing is to establish your method of success display early on in your career and build on it. Start small—one or two photographs, and perhaps a couple of plaques from some local community effort—and keep hanging. The walls of your office are waiting to be filled, and can earn you a good return on your effort if you go about filling them the right way.

Women and Success

The dominance of man over woman deprived him of the highest sexual pleasures, and must in a more highly developed civilization lead women to rebellion against their feminine role.

—Alfred Adler

THE SUCCESSFUL WOMAN

Difficult as it is for *anyone* to succeed, women carry the additional burden of a cultural and social tradition in which they were not supposed to compete against men, let alone win. An increasing number of women today are motivated to succeed, and more and more of them are in fact succeeding. Yet the pattern of success for women remains spotty, despite a few highly publicized cases. For example:

• There are no women chief executives among the nation's top five hundred business corporations.
• There is not at present a woman in the United States Senate nor on the U. S. Supreme Court.
• Very few women have reached the higher levels of American corporate life, particularly in the in-

dustrial and manufacturing area, where the big
money really is.

To be sure, there are a lot more women working,
and they are doing a far greater variety of jobs than
they used to. But the upper reaches of success are still
masculine.

In 1940, 4 percent of the executives of the United
States were women. This figure rose to 5 percent in
1950 and remained there in 1960. By 1971, despite
the effect of the women's liberation movement and the
fact that the total number of women in the workforce
had almost tripled since 1940, the figure had still not
exceeded 6 percent.[1] As one business weekly bluntly
puts it, "Companies shy away from giving women top
jobs because they fear the effect this will have on other
employees—particularly men."[2]

Progress, Yes, but What Sort?

From the way men talk about the progress women
have made, and from the triumphant tone of many
feminist publications, you would think that women
were neck and neck with men in the success stakes.
But as the figures show, nothing could be further from
the truth. All the claims and counterclaims about the
change in women's status must be viewed within the
context of a somewhat harsh reality:

• Women still make less money than men.
• Women still have a harder time getting interesting "career" jobs.
• Women have yet to make a significant dent in
the vast industrial-manufacturing-financial area that
is the very heart of America, and the source of
most men's success.

When men discuss the changing role of women, they
are usually talking about a woman doing a job that

was formerly thought of as a man's. There was a great
deal of publicity attached to the hiring of the first
woman pilot on a scheduled airline, but very little
when it later transpired that she had been fired in the
aviation industry's slump. Several women have been
awarded their general's stars, but the Joint Chiefs of
Staff, like most of the institutionalized apparata of
success, remain predominantly masculine. Nor is the
revolution near at hand, as so many men seem to fear.
The fact that West Point and the other service acade-
mies have begun to accept women students is not likely
to make any significant change in the make-up of the
armed forces for several generations, any more than
the hiring of women telephone installers and "lines-
people" is likely to affect the upper management level
of AT&T within our lifetimes.

Book Publishing

Admittedly a rather special and minor industry,
book publishing nonetheless provides some interesting
insights into the dynamics of female success. Originally, publishing was a male-dominated business.
Rather old-fashioned and paternalistic, it consisted
mostly of small privately owned family companies
competing against each other in a very limited and
"gentlemanly" way. The executives, owners, managers
and editors were nearly always men, while the secretaries were invariably women. Very often the
daughters of men in the upper ranks of publishing,
these women had college degrees and "good" family
backgrounds. The book business hit the technological
revolution very late, with the result that firms merged,
families sold out to entrepreneurs, and these in turn
later sold out to conglomerates. What had been a
small cottage industry became a large and very profitable business.

At the same time, the publishing industry continued
to pay low salaries and neglected to develop any ra-

tional way of training young people, or even recruiting them. The young men who might have gone from Harvard to the book business in their fathers' footsteps found they could make more money, lead a more actively committed life and rise faster by going to law school, or by going into industry, television or the news magazines. The Vietnam war, by encouraging young men to stay on at the university and go through graduate school, in effect overqualified many of them for book publishing. Because of all this, it became necessary to promote from within. Publishers did not set out to promote women as a deliberate policy; they simply had no choice.

Although there had always been women in publishing, those who were famous were mostly the wives of publishers, like the late Blanche Knopf, or women who held jobs that were regarded as "appropriate" for women—mystery editors, children's book editors, crafts and cookbook editors. Now women emerged as executives, as the heads of service departments and as star editors, and even took over whole areas of the industry, like the sale of book club and paperback rights, in which they proved to be far more innovative and aggressive than men had ever been. Within a decade, the most powerful people in the industry were predominantly women, for the women who succeeded in the first wave, by rising from secretary to executive, tended to hire and promote women, thus institutionalizing their success.

And yet, by and large, women in publishing still *do* earn less than men in comparable jobs. And with perhaps one or two exceptions, they are still very underrepresented at the highest levels of management. Even in an industry which has found itself unable to recruit men in any significant numbers, women have generally found there is a ceiling to their success. It is easy for them to get to the $25,000 mark, possible for them to get to the $50,000 mark, and extremely difficult to rise above that. Doubtless this will change, but it is likely to be a long and slow process.

One woman I know, a powerful and successful/editor, has worked her way up from secretary to editor-in-chief of a medium-sized, but growing, publishing house. Its growth is largely credited to her energy, knowledge and aggressiveness. She began as the owner's secretary, and is now his highest paid and most valuable executive, virtually running the company for him, while he cultivates his garden and travels around the world in pursuit of ever more challenging golf courses. She has been offered prestigious jobs at far higher pay. But she stays where she has always worked, believing that when he retires, she will become the president, or that if he decides to sell out she will get a block of stock and a high-level position in the purchaser's executive hierarchy. On both these points he has given her full, if rather ambiguous, assurance.

Any keen student of the relationship between the sexes at work would hardly be surprised to learn that his personal view of the situation is somewhat different. His opinion of his trusted and valued employee is colored by the instinctive male fear of successful women. One night at the Players Club in New York, I overheard him explaining his plans for the future to a fellow book publisher. "Jesus," he said, "I can't get on without her, and I don't know anybody who could replace her. I mean, she's a tiger, and she really knows how to run the whole thing. But there's no way I'm going to put a woman in the driver's seat when I go. My wife wouldn't let me anyway, and the companies I've talked to about buying me out, they're even more adamant. They want to keep her there, it makes sense in profit terms, but they all want to be damned sure one of their men gets in on top of her to control things. One of them said to me, 'If she were a man, given what we know about the business, we'd give her carte blanche to run the thing, and maybe make her a director of the parent corporation. But no way we're going to do that for a woman.' You have to face facts: the stockholders don't like women in high-level positions—they just don't trust a woman with their money.

"So there it is. I string her along, and I rely on her, but when I finally make my move, she's going to find out that in that league, being a woman is striking out. I mean, she should *know*. When we had merger talks with a big conglomerate, their president came around to visit our offices, and when he saw her in the hall, he stopped and asked. "And who do *you* work for, little lady?' He couldn't believe there was this woman running our company, basically, and when he found out, he didn't like it one bit. In fact, I think that's what soured the deal—especially when she replied, 'I don't work for *anybody*. I work for me!' He laughed, all right, but it wasn't the kind of laugh that makes you laugh back. No, I'm afraid when it's big money, men just don't trust women."

Another woman, one of the "hottest" and most successful editors in the business, left her job, because, as she put it, "I don't have any say in things no matter how much money I make for them, or how much they pay me." In her new job, she was offered complete autonomy. She could hire, fire, buy and control everything that had to do with books. "But," she reports, "when it comes to the long-term management of the company, the curtain comes down. As long as I can make money for them, I'm their darling girl. But what they do with the money, the real business of running a business, that's still being done over a drink at the golf course or in the steam room. I can spend a million dollars to buy a property, but when it comes to things that involve real corporate matters, I'm frozen out. A woman is still 'talent.' Nobody wants to believe she has a real head for business."

The Exceptions

In a recent survey, *Business Week* was able to come up with a list of the hundred most successful corporate women in the country, spread across such diverse industries as banking, broadcasting, cosmetics, fashion, electronics, financial services, food, manufacturing, petroleum, public relations, advertising, publishing, retailing, services and utilities. With a tact rare among magazines, *Business Week* did not note whether or not the women were married and had children, and also did not comment on their appearance, as most of the media, including the *New York Times*, still feel obliged to do. "It makes me sick," said one woman banker, "that whenever I get mentioned in the press it's always as 'the attractive, blond mother-of-two.' I notice that when David Rockefeller makes a speech, he isn't described as 'the handsome, balding father of six.' It's as if nobody can overlook a woman's domestic persona. If we ever get a woman President of the United States, they'll still be writing, 'Dressed in a charcoal Mollie Parnis suit, the attractive and vivacious President, mother of two, today pressed the button that set off World War Three.' "

Start with a Law Degree

This is the best way to the top for women in business, according to *Business Week*, which describes the degree as "the principal tool in their rise."

Banking and financial services would also seem to offer excellent opportunities for women, accounting for 23 percent of the women on the list. Madeleine Mc-Whinney, the president of First Women's Bank, in New York, got a great deal of publicity when she opened the first bank to serve women predominantly, giving women the possibility of backing feminism with every check they write. But her bank's assets ($8 million) are far eclipsed by the $20.8 million of deposits controlled by Catherine Cleary, president and chief executive officer of First Wisconsin Trust Co. of Milwaukee, the only woman in the United States to head a major bank she did not inherit. Juliette M. Moran, executive vice-president for communications services at GAF, is one of the highest-paid woman executives who have "made it through the ranks" to success. Her salary and bonus of $120,000 a year is an impressive figure, but it does not compare with the salaries of the highest-paid male executives, which, as we have seen, go up to nearly a million dollars a year.

Still, the presence of these women effectively proves that there is no limit to the financial and business responsibilities a woman can handle. If Ms. Cleary can handle $20.8 million of banking assets, or Camron Cooper (of Atlantic Richfield) can manage an investment portfolio of $700 million, there is little reason to suppose that women are lacking in any of the abilities that make for business success.

KATHARINE GRAHAM

If there were any doubt about this, it would surely be answered by the career of Katharine Graham. The publisher of the Washington *Post,* Graham is also the owner of a large corporation that not only controls one of the country's major newspapers, but *Newsweek* as well.

It's a pity in some ways that Katharine Graham was born rich. Otherwise, as probably the most powerful and successful woman in America today, she would present a stronger argument for the equality of the sexes than she appears to. At an early age, her mother told her, "You can't just sit around the house and be rich, you must do something." What she did, in fact, was to marry an ambitious man, whose death left her the owner of the Washington *Post* and its properties. She was the owner, but in her own words, she "had deferred to men for ages. They knew better." Even though she was in a unique position to exercise power over her husband's empire, there were legitimate doubts that she would choose to do so, or be able to.

But she set out to learn. Money may have been a help, but the world is full of rich people who own things and destroy them. And Palm Beach is full of absentee owners who are happy to let their salaried employees do the thinking and the work. Kay Graham studied the newspaper business and finances. When she wasn't satisfied, she fired people, much to the astonishment of her executives. She learned about Women's Liberation, which at first she didn't understand at all. (It is hard for someone who is rich and powerful to think of herself as part of an underprivileged group.) But when she understood what it was about, she made trouble and she made changes. When Gibson McCabe, *Newsweek*'s then-president, warned her against bringing women into meetings, she threw an ashtray at him. And she learned about politics when the *Post*'s discovery made her Enemy Number One of the Nixon administration.

Shy, doubtful of her own abilities, widowed unexpectedly, she transformed herself into a major success, toughening herself up enough so that she could keep right on talking to Lyndon B. Johnson while he undressed in front of her as he prepared for bed.

Katharine Graham is a lesson for men and women alike that being born wealthy is not enough: success is not handed to anyone on a silver platter. The special lesson that women can learn from her example is that even though they haven't been trained to or brought up to, women can play by the same rules as men—and win!

THE "MYTH" OF
SUCCESS AVOIDANCE

If it is true that society does little to encourage the success instinct in women, and on the whole rewards it less well than it rewards men, it is also true that women themselves are not always convinced that individual success is all that valuable a goal. There seems to be a factor that Matina Horner referred to as "the desire to achieve [being] often contaminated by what I call the motive to avoid success."[3] This is a logical result of the conditioning and education to which women are still being subjected at home and at school. Then, too, women have always been in a better position than men to understand the dark side of success. They know—if only through their mothers' experiences—what the penalties of success and failure are, from the domestic point of view.

Women are intimately familiar with what men are like to live with when their careers have failed. And some of them are also familiar with the penalties of a successful career: the late hours, the relentless drive, the growing ego, the nervous anxiety and the inability to share the pleasures of achievement. One only has to look at the wives of political successes to see what one person's ambition can do to another: Mrs. Pat Nixon allegedly threatening to divorce her husband if he ran for office again; Mrs. Betty Ford apparently visiting a psychiatrist because she spent long years alone bringing up her children while her congressman husband traveled through the country speaking to Republican fund-raising groups; Mrs. Jacqueline Kennedy, by all accounts, agreeing to maintain a marriage because she was a necessary ingredient of her husband's successful bid for the Presidency.

The wives of successful executives, writers, journalists or actors are not always better off. For years, Vivien Leigh was, publicly, the smiling, radiant, happy wife of Laurence Olivier. In private, though, she lived in a tormented hell, fearful that her identity was being submerged in Olivier's enormous and growing success.

An element of caution on the subject of success is not altogether a bad thing. It is never useless to examine the price of success. Still, that same element of doubt holds back many an ambitious woman at the very beginning of her career. This is compounded by the fact that a great many women begin their careers later than men do, having gone through the wife/ mother experience first. And even in mid-career, they often find that achievements count for less in a woman.

Part of the trouble is that women are commonly thought to have *lost* something in becoming successful, while men are almost universally assumed to gain in stature. Women generally *do* have to sacrifice something, whether it's a family, a marriage or simply a noncompetitive relationship with men. One very successful businesswoman, now in her mid-forties, complained that success had made her "a pariah" in the eyes of other people: "When I decided that I wanted to go into business and succeed," she told me, "my mother was worried that I wouldn't get married and have children. It was all right for my brother to go to medical school and become a success. We were all supposed to be proud of Bernie and pick up his socks off the floor every time he came home. But it wasn't all right for me. Every time he succeeded, there was family applause. My successes just made my family more angry with me. Well, I succeeded anyway, and I got married, and I had children.

"Until we had the children, my husband was all in favor of my career. And why not? I put him through law school, and paid the bills! Then, after the children, he thought I should stop and settle down to becoming 'a good mother.' Never mind that I paid for the sitters and the nurse, and made sure the kids were O.K. My career was suddenly all wrong. And the more successful I was, the more unhappy he was with me."

A recent psychological study showed that when

women were asked to explain the reasons for another woman's success, they tended to attribute it to "luck," whereas they mostly assumed that men had succeeded because they were "capable." [4] The women were also more prone to suffer guilt and self-recrimination after failure. By a curious reversal of thinking, the men in the survey attributed their own failures to "bad luck," while the women attributed *their* failures to their own inadequacies. Success-motivated men managed to retain their pride even after they had failed, while the women almost invariably were ashamed of failing.

There is, therefore, some evidence to support the thesis that women have a rather ambivalent attitude toward success. It is vital to overcome this. *You have as much right to succeed as anybody else, and probably just as good a chance . . .*

THE NEED FOR THE REWARDS OF SUCCESS

There is no doubt that women are, in general, somewhat more timid about pursuing the *rewards* of success than men, though there are signs that this is changing. As the president of one large corporation put it, "You used to be able to promote women without worrying too much about how much it was going to cost you, particularly since their base salaries were usually much lower than a man's. You could give them a big increase, percentage-wise, and you'd still be ahead of the game. But women are beginning to learn how to job hop, just like men, and they're also learning to find out just what the job is *worth,* in other words, how much we would pay a man for the same job. The days when you could figure a woman would cost you less are just about over."

Jane Doheny, a senior vice-president in the head office of a big conglomerate, is an example of a woman who fought for her rights. The fact that she is beautiful should not, of course, be mentioned, except that it makes her success all the more remarkable. Many men will accept the presence of a middle-aged lady of formidable appearance within the power center of a corporation, but find it difficult to cope with an attractive and well-dressed young woman in their midst.

"Everybody was very nice about my promotion," she said, "but there was a good deal of quiet embarrassment. At that level, you get a contract, which was no problem, and a car. The car was a problem. You get to pick what you want. So the vice president in charge of transportation suggested that I ask my husband what kind of car I should order. I thought that was pretty odd, when you consider that they were making me responsible for a huge financial operation.

"Then, there was the shoe-polish question. I hadn't realized it, but on the executive floor they have a man who comes around every morning and polishes the executives' shoes. I used to feel there was something humiliating about the whole performance. But then I noticed that the shoeshine man never came around to see *me*, once I was on the executive floor. I decided to ask why.

"Well, there was a lot of embarrassment about that. Everybody asked if I really *wanted* my shoes polished, and one of the executives said he didn't think women ever had their shoes polished—his feeling seemed to be that they bought these flimsy things and wore them until they were dirty, then threw them away. I said I had as much right to have mine polished as anybody else did. That was true enough, and nobody could argue against it, but the executive vice-president finally put the thing out front by saying, 'Look, Jane, it's a little tough on old George. I mean, you don't want him down on the floor looking up your skirts every morning, do you?'

"Frankly, I could care less. But I said I'd compromise. I'd leave my shoes at the door, and old George could take them away and polish them. And that's what I did. Now everybody is happy.

"But it's funny. When you get to the top, you realize how many of the things that successful men take for granted, women have never even thought of asking for. All these years they've been living better than we have, and all they ever told us about was how hard they worked—just like my father, who complained to my mother every day of his life. He never told us about the *compensations* of success. Now I've discovered that men really take care of themselves up there, and it's not so bad. And why shouldn't a woman want the same, whether it's a limo or having her shoes polished every day?"

The lesson to be learned from Jane Doheny's story: By demanding the same privileges and rewards as men, women will be taken more seriously in their careers.

BARBARA CAWLEY: THE NEW WOMAN

I recently sat next to the head of a successful television production company at a dinner party. Barbara Cawley, a woman in her late forties, now runs a business with over two hundred employees, and runs it with an iron hand. Having begun her career with a program aimed at women, Barbara was, in her own words, "a woman with a product aimed at woman, which is to say a nobody."

When her program developed into a whole series of services, and took on a more commercial aspect, she found herself obliged to reexamine her view of herself and her possibilities. "You have to understand," she said, "that we had a nice program, designed for nice women, and that I was 'a nice woman' myself. I was charming, enthusiastic, hard-working, and grateful for the fact that what I was doing seemed to be successful. I was treated like a good little girl, and I didn't know any better. Then one day I realized that I was a lot smarter than the men who were running things around me, and that I could put together something really unique and successful. I'd come a long way from being a housewife. I had a career, and I was making good money with an idea of my own. But I was still being humored.

"For me, the big moment was when I realized that it doesn't matter whether you're a woman or not. At a certain point you have to have the guts to say 'Fuck you, I'm doing it my way'—and I did. I got out of the network, took a small office, became my own person, raised money and went back with a series of packages which I knew I could sell. When I went in to see my former employer, I said to him, 'Forget the fact that I used to work here, forget the fact that I'm a woman, I've got something you need, and you're going to buy it!' And he did. It was such a joy to discover that I could take risks and be tough, that I could build something of my own and make it *work*. I'd always felt like a wallflower at the party in my business career. But suddenly I was out there on the floor, dancing with everyone else.

"I want it all—the Lear jets and the corporate headquarters with my own private elevator, and the limousine with two telephones. A lot of it may be silly and funny, but men have had it all these years, and now it's my turn to enjoy it. For years we were told that we wouldn't *like* it, that it was all more trouble than it was worth, that all the luxury and the comforts and the perks couldn't make up for the strain and the tension and the responsibilities. And you know something? It isn't true. It wasn't ever true. It's like being told that money can't buy you happiness. Of course it can't, but that's no reason to stay poor. Success can't make you happy either, but it's a lot of fun; it's exciting, and it makes you feel alive, active and terrific. I don't think you can have too much of it, and I'm looking forward to a lot more!"

The need for success is as strong in women as it is in men. Why wouldn't it be? The curious thing is that we ever supposed it to be otherwise. We have simply taken our view of society for psychological reality, and concluded that because in the past women were excluded from the success game they were permanently disqualified from playing it, or if really given a chance would play it less well than men. Even women's magazines approach the question of success as if there were some different set of standards for women.

A recent survey in *Glamour* concluded that successful women would describe themselves as "exhibitionistic, dominant . . . and with a low tendency to feel guilt," characteristics which most people would regard as having a certain negative quality, and commented that the successful woman "may have little insight into the type of threat she imposes on others" and "may place excessive demands on others." [5] It is doubtful that a poll of successful men would rate exhibitionism, inability to feel guilt or the making of excessive demands on others as the characteristics of success, or that successful men would feel they imposed a threat on other people. Even the women's media fall into the trap of suggesting that a woman can only succeed by adopting disagreeable character traits. Men, on the contrary, tend to feel that the prerequisites of success are intelligence, drive, energy and the ability to get along with others, i.e., charm.

For women who crave success, as for men, the desire to acquire fame, money and power, or some combination of the three, is the motivation, and the strategies used are not greatly different from those of their male colleagues—and rivals. The notion that "women [may] make poor leaders because their personalities do not allow them to be assertive" [6] is as false as the assumption that women are impossible to work for or with—in the words of the same study, that "women . . . are presumed to fit the mold of the dictatorial, bitchy boss." [7] One thing that Women's Liberation has produced is ample evidence that women can be just as assertive as men; increasingly, it is also giving a great many men the opportunity to learn that having a woman as a boss is not different from having a man in charge. As one psychologist says, "It's not the sex, it's the clout!" [8]

Success with a Vengeance

Perhaps as a reaction against their upbringing, there is today a generation of women whose ambition, drive and toughness far exceeds that of most men. Many successful men use their health as a weapon of defense; they are not embarrassed to plead a cold, the flu or a headache to postpone a discussion or a decision. Successful women, on the other hand, are never ill. They simply will not allow it to happen, and if it does, they refuse to show it. It is as if they were reacting against those generations of women who complained about cramps, dizzy spells, difficult pregnancies and nausea, and are determined to prove that a woman can be physically tougher than any man. One management expert points out that when men reach the corporate level where a free yearly physical examination is offered to them, they invariably take the half day off and go through the tests. And they are usually interested in the results. Women, on the contrary, often go to great lengths to avoid the examination, and show little or no interest in the results. They simply refuse to acknowledge the possibility of being ill.

What is more, successful women are invariably harder-driving than their male counterparts. "Maybe it's generations of repression, the need to be 'a good girl,' that does it," says a highly successful magazine editor, as we talk about success in her beautiful white-on-white apartment, filled with books, prints and two perfect Persian cats, themselves the epitome of successful felinehood. "When women set out to become a success, they do it with a vengeance, there's no holding them back. Men have a kind of serene confidence in the notion that the world owes them success, that it's their right. But women don't. Look at Julia Phillips, for example . . ."

Indeed, look at Julia Phillips, who while still in her twenties, collected her Academy Award for *The Sting* from Elizabeth Taylor, saying, "This is a great evening for a Jewish girl from the Bronx—getting an Oscar and meeting Elizabeth Taylor at the same time." One of the most successful producers in Hollywood, she received a check for $2,500,000 as part of her share in the profits of *The Sting* as if it were an everyday event.

She emerged from the copy-editing department of *McCall's,* a vast dim place where young women toil to correct the editors' grammar and punctuation, and got a job as an assistant in the editorial department of the *Ladies' Home Journal,* at $8,000 a year. Bright, sharp, pretty, trendy, she had, in one observer's words, "the look of success, a kind of steady, self-confident glitter to the eyes that tells you, 'This kid is going to make it.'"

By and large women stay longer in jobs than men. Not Julia Phillips. She was no sooner settled into her job at *LHJ* than she managed to get herself taken on as the East Coast reader for 20th Century-Fox, at $15,000 a year. Most story readers stick at the same job for decades, gradually building a reputation and securing so many "contacts" in the publishing world that they become indispensible. Julia acquired her contacts overnight, fixed them with the white-hot glare of her ambition, and within six months was in a new job, buying properties for Redford, Poitier—the great ones. She bought successfully, and she bought for herself as well.

When she produced her own movie, it failed. But before the failure had even been noticed, she was producing *The Sting.* "She never lets up and she never lets go," says a friend. "Her whole life is devoted to winning. Hollywood is a tough town for women, except as actress sex symbols. Julia set out to be a producer, which no woman had ever been, and made a fortune. Now that she's done that, she's naturally going to become a director, which she's never done, to prove that she can do that. And she'll probably succeed at that too, then move on to something else. It's the challenge of trying that excites her, not the money or the success itself. Just the other day she was having lunch with Joanne Woodward, who was begging her—*begging* her—for this part, and Julia cut her off by saying, 'No, but I could use you for the mother.'"

From the very beginning of her meteoric career, Julia Phillips has taken the world by the horns, motivated by a fearless and totally unquestioning desire to succeed. She has no doubts, a quality that is still rather rare in women, most of whom feel it necessary to keep their competitiveness concealed or held in check. Since men need not operate under such self-imposed restraints, women are frequently placed at a disadvantage by their own cultural conditioning—and when they throw it off, as many do in mid-career, it may be too late. Now, however, women are beginning to come out of the starting gate at the same pace as men. And their instinct for the jugular stroke is an indication of just how far they have come. "Women," as one male executive puts it, "are formidable infighters, far more stubborn and determined than most men, and far less likely to be bought off or deflected."

When a woman makes up her mind to succeed, her drive is likely to be far greater than most men's. Men take the success drive for granted; it's been their prerogative for generations. But for women it's a revolution.

"Women may still find it harder to get interested in success," says Linda Gray, a successful advertising executive, "but once they do, there's no stopping them. Look at me. I went to college because everybody did, in the days before women's colleges were co-ed or radical or anything. I was Daddy's little girl. My brother went off to Yale to get good grades and become a success, and God help the poor bastard if he hadn't. But all my family expected of me was that

I wouldn't get pregnant or fall in love with somebody unsuitable. When I graduated I didn't know *anything*. I was supposed to spend the summer in Europe, then get a 'nice' job in New York, and share an apartment with a couple of other 'nice' girls, and come home to play tennis in Bronxville on the weekends. And that's what I did. I became a secretary in an advertising agency which was full of 'nice' upper-middle-class girls putting in their time at a job and using their salaries to shop for clothes at Bloomies.

"Everybody had always asked my brother 'What do you want to be?' but nobody had even *suggested* the question to me. I went right through college thinking that I wanted to be beautiful. Well, I don't know how beautiful I was, but I was mostly *bored* as a secretary, and I began to look for things to do.

" 'Linda's projects,' everyone called them, and they were happy to have me pull together reports, make up charts, eliminate dead files—I mean, why not? I was this bundle of energy, consuming everything around me and waiting to be put to good use.

"Before long I realized that I was smart—something nobody had told me at home or in college, by the way—and I also realized that no matter how hard I worked, nobody was going to help me. At the back of my head, there was this notion that somebody would realize how good I was and give me a break. But twenty-two-year-old young women don't get breaks, or anyway I didn't. So one morning I nerved myself up, and I went into my supervisor's office all prepared to make this persuasive, *nice* pitch about wanting more responsibility and opportunity, and so on. When I got into his office, my courage failed. I was going to be charming and sincere and *winning*. But here I was in this office with a man old enough to be my father, and I knew I was brighter than he was, and harder working. I got angry, angry at him for being in a position of authority over me, angry at myself because I was suddenly afraid to explain that I didn't want to be a secretary any more and wanted a break. In fact, I was so angry at my own cowardice that when he asked me what I wanted, I blurted out 'I want your job!' I could have died, right there on the spot. I stood there in my fake Courrèges suit and my real Gucci shoes (one week's salary for status) and waited for God to strike me dead. But He didn't. Instead, after an embarrassing silence, this guy shook his head and said, 'That's the first sensible approach to getting promoted I've seen for a long time.'

"He asked me to sit down, and we talked about what I'd been doing, and what I'd learned, and what I *wanted* to do. He was really very nice, and when we were through, he turned to me and he said, 'Linda, I think you're going to go a long way, because you're smart and you're ambitious and you've got guts, and I'm going to make sure that you get promoted to a job where you can really put all that to work for you. The only thing is that it's going to be a job in somebody else's department, not mine. You're going to make somebody the best assistant he ever had, and he'll wake up one day to find he's been scalped. I know just the guy who's looking for someone like you, and I'll set it up right away.'

"And he did. He was right. I became an assistant to an account executive, and within a year I had his job, and now I'm way up at the top. I could go two ways—either for the presidency of this place, or out on my own. I think I'm going to go on my own, because it's more exciting, and when it works it's *yours*. But I learned a lesson about success when I lost control. If you're a woman, you can't charm them. You've got to hit them hard!" When Linda, aggressive tennis player as well as a formidable executive, met Dr. Renée Richards, the transsexual tennis star, she was astonished and displeased to hear Dr. Richards admit that her serve had weakened since her operation. In short, she now played "a woman's game."

"A woman's game!" Linda exclaimed. "What the hell is she talking about? Just because she's had an operation to become a woman doesn't mean that she shouldn't be able to hit as hard as she used to when she was Dr. Richard Raskind. Why should it? She should be hitting even *harder*, for God's sake, instead of falling into the same old trap about women not being able to hit hard. Somewhere at the back of her mind she's still a male chauvinist."

WINNING FOR WOMEN

Hitting hard is perhaps the first rule for success, as far as women are concerned. Ambitious women must learn that they can't win by charm, persuasion and tactful pressure.

Men can get away with it, and many do. They learn how to ingratiate themselves with their superiors, they take up golf and play it with the right people on the right courses, they re-create themselves in the image of what they're expected to be. For years men were sent to prep schools like St. Mark's, St. Paul's, Andover, Phillips Exeter, and to colleges like Yale, Harvard or Princeton, in order to acquire just those characteristics which would please their future bosses. Young men who graduated from huge Midwestern high schools in places like Lincoln, Nebraska (like TV personality Dick Cavett), reached for the coveted scholarships that would take them to the great Eastern colleges, where they would not only learn something, but transform themselves into the type of person who looks, in the phrase of senior executives, like "our kind of person."

This process always takes place without much discussion, since we give lip service to "equal opportunity" and don't like to admit that every stratum of American society has its own membership rites and standards. Fathers prepare their sons for membership in their own union local, not just by getting their sons a union card but also by showing them how they should act to be accepted by their peers in the union. It was not just that it was easier to get a job in the

Police Department if your father or your uncles were cops, but you were also prepared by family example for life as a cop. You "knew the ropes," you picked up by the imperceptible process of male example the tricks you needed "to get ahead." Young men going into the garment business learned "chutzpa" and hypertension, while men going into an old-line brokerage house learned to be cool and unruffled under pressure. It is apparent, then, that to a startling degree men succeed by observing how their elders succeeded, or by learning from their failures, which comes to the same thing.

The Winning Style

By comparison, there are few models for women. John and Robert Kennedy, for example, grew up in the world of Boston politics. From the very beginning they were surrounded by examples; they learned what you had to do or say to please the older men who could get you nominated. Bella Abzug, to take one of the few nationally prominent women in politics, had no such training, no comparable models on which to base herself as a politician. Even in matters of dress, a woman has to make decisions which a man is automatically spared. Most male politicians know enough to wear the kind of quiet, inconspicuous suits that attract no attention. But a woman always risks being overdressed or underdressed, or even a bit eccentric in her dress, like Ms. Abzug. What is not an issue for a man remains one for a woman.

Nor is it an inconsequential issue. At a recent meeting of the National Society of American Bankwomen, Marilyn Bender, an editor of the *New York Times* and a distinguished financial reporter, stated that one of the major obstacles to success was the problem of appropriate dress. Ms. Bender's feeling was that most women looked "sloppy," and that men resented their sloppiness, and reacted strongly against it. To a degree, this is undoubtedly true. Men have a clearly defined image of what neatness is for men, and an acute perception of just what a man's clothes and bearing have to say about him. With women they're at a loss. What is more, the clothes designed for women are deliberately frivolous, and a rousing cheer came up from the audience when Marilyn Bender criticized the fashion industry and fashion designers for this state of affairs.

Also present during the discussion was the Army's first woman general, Jeanne Holm. She pointed out that one of the reasons for *her* success was quite simply that women in the armed services wear uniforms, and that rank is all that matters. "If you're a colonel," she said, "people look at your shoulders and see the eagles, and that's it, whether you're a man or a woman." She noted that one of the advantages of an Army career is that status as an officer outweighs sexual distinctions. "Nobody ever asked *me* to go out and get coffee at a meeting," she remarked, "because I was an officer, and that's an enlisted person's job. Of course, now that I'm a general and have stars on my shoulders, men have finally stopped asking me whether I intend to make the Army a career!"

At the White House, the general soon found that clothes have become an important matter to her. After a lifetime of wearing a uniform, she was surprised to find that she occasionally gets mistaken for a secretary, or asked to perform menial chores—something which clearly astounds this dynamic woman who, until recently, enjoyed all the prerogatives of a general, including a chauffered car with general's stars on its flag, aides-de-camp, the use of military aircraft, a crisp salute from everyone below her rank, however old, combat-decorated and male chauvinistic they might be, and the general respect the Army and the public gives to senior military rank.

It is difficult to imagine the general being mistaken for a secretary. Her bearing, posture, commanding voice and piercing blue eyes would have seemed to me sufficiently intimidating to prevent anyone from making that assumption. But men tend to assume automatically that women are subordinates in most working situations. The general strongly believes in confronting this kind of thing head-on, and while she does not believe that attack is the best form of defense for women ("Always go around the enemy if you can, rather than attacking head on, but if you have to attack, fight and win") she clearly knows how to stand up for herself. Small as she is, Jeanne Holm is capable of a penetrating stare that would freeze any man in his tracks who asked *her* to get him a cup of coffee or type a letter. "If you want to succeed," she said, "you'd better look as if you mean business."

SUCCESS TECHNIQUES FOR THE AMBITIOUS WOMAN

● YOUR EYES

Develop a steely, uncompromising gaze. It helps to have large, expressive eyes, and the one area in which a little make-up can be used to good effect for success is right here. Men find it difficult to look a woman in the eye under the best of circumstances, and when it's a business situation, particularly a competitive one, it pays great dividends to simply outstare them. This should not be done in an obvious way, like children playing a staring game. But in any encounter or negotiation with a man, sit directly in front of him and look him in the eye, calmly, firmly and self-confidently. You have little to lose by challenging him, since in most cases your very presence as a competitor, supplicant or superior has already irritated him, even if it's only subconsciously. Nor does it hurt to be stubborn. Where a man might approach things from a tangent, and offer a persuasive compromise that will satisfy everybody, a woman does best by sticking to her guns and facing men down. You may also find that it helps not to wear glasses—nothing should detract from the eyes themselves.

● THE SECOND-STRIKE WEAPON

Tears are generally much underrated by feminists. This is a mistake. If there is one thing men fear more than anything else, it is tears. Oddly enough, it is possible to combine the suggestion of tears with absolute and uncompromising firmness. If you can learn to keep your eyes steadily on target and to let one or two teardrops appear at the corners of your eyes at the crucial moment in a negotiation, you have it made.

It is necessary, of course, not to *weep* or show any other sign of weakness. The mouth should be set, your gaze should not waver or falter, and your hands should not acknowledge the tears by trying to wipe them away. You have to be able to ignore them if they're going to be effective as a threat. What you are projecting, after all, is your determination to have your way, coupled with the promise of massive emotional retaliation if you don't.

Tears are essentially a second-strike weapon, but once the technique has been understood, they can be extremely useful in playing for success. Men find it difficult enough to deal with ambitious women, but the embarrassment of having reduced them to tears, and thus having undercut their image as equal competitors, is more than most men care to take upon themselves. You may find an occasional man who will resist, or simply ignore the whole thing, but very few. If the tears are subtly handled, most men will surrender quickly enough. Needless to say, this technique should not be attempted on another woman, where it would be useless and self-defeating. Remember: *there is no such thing as humiliation if you want to win.*

● Your Hands

Keep your hands still. In moments of stress, men have a way of placing their hands palm down on their thighs, with the thumbs sticking up toward the waist, as if they were bracing themselves. This is usually a sign that a man means serious business, just as the

appearance of his hands anywhere near his face indicates thought or hesitation.

Women should *avoid* all these hand signals, whenever possible. They should particularly avoid pointing their index finger at men. This is usually taken as a sign of overt aggression and is likely to produce hostile and violent retaliation. The best thing a woman can do with her hands is to keep them folded neatly in her lap. Leave the dramatic hand gestures and positions to men. A certain amount of immobility and restraint can work well for women.

- How to Sit

Avoid large, low chairs. They are difficult to get in
and out of gracefully, and if you're not careful they
tend to push your knees up in the air, exposing most
of your thigh. Make a beeline for the most upright,
simple chair you can find. Sit straight, with your knees
together and your feet firmly planted on the ground.
Remember: your aim is to present a model of determination. It is easier to argue from an upright position
than if you are slouched back on a low sofa, wondering what to do with your legs and constantly pulling
down on your skirt.

If you're in a position to choose what kind of desk
you have, insist on having one that is closed, rather
than an open table-desk. It will save you the trouble
of worrying about how you're sitting. Men have long
since discovered that with a closed desk the upper
half of their body can present a businesslike and respectable appearance, while below the waist level they
can stretch out their legs in a comfortable sprawl and
even take their shoes off.

● YOUR VOICE

Avoid any hint of prissy, nagging, schoolmarmish tone in your voice. For many men the voice of a woman is emotionally disturbing. They fear correction from women, and what might be a casual suggestion from another man will be taken as an unpleasant reproach when it comes from the opposite sex. The more you can develop a low, strong, firm voice, the better, since it is the relatively higher pitch of a woman's voice that triggers off this reaction in men. Voice control is important—never be shrill. However, many men will still resent your suggestions or criticism even if you sound like Tallulah Bankhead. The way around this is simple: be aggressive. Suggest radical innovations, talk tough, accuse other people of timidity and "good guy" behavior, learn to use phrases like "bottom line mentality," "profit motive" and "numbers realism." *Take the hard line on every occasion.* If a man suggests that the situation calls for a stiff letter, say, "Stiff letter, hell, let's sue." Go for the jugular, and at least you'll never be accused of feminine weakness. Your objective, after all, is not to be loved, but to succeed.

INDEX OF FORBIDDEN OBJECTS
● glasses dangling from your neck on a chain
● hats
● high boots in the office
● white gloves (they make you look like a temporary secretary from the 1940s)
● harlequin glasses
● sequins on anything
● blue jeans
● turbans
● T-shirts with comic or pornographic messages printed on them
● heavy dangling earrings

(Note: Never play with your hair or your earrings if you're negotiating a serious piece of business. It

gives the wrong impression, since men regard it as a
sign of sexual interest, rightly or wrongly.)

● YOUR BEST SECRETARY—A MALE
Hire a male secretary. He will increase your prestige
enormously. With the current rate of unemployment
what it is, there are plenty of well-qualified, college-
educated young men who are happy to work as secretaries. One of the great surprises is that they are just
as efficient, careful and subservient as any woman,
and if anything, rather less competitive. Executives
are discovering that men can type, take dictation,
make coffee and reserve a table for lunch for their
boss just as efficiently as a woman. They can even answer the telephone and open the mail.

There are few things that strike a more direct terror
into the hearts of male executives than the sound of a
masculine voice saying, "I'm sorry, but Mrs. Judson is
on the phone, may she call you back?" Each of them
sees himself in the subordinate role, as a kind of night-
mare vision of the future, taking dictation instead of
giving it. A woman's prestige is considerably magni-
fied by having a male secretary, and it costs no more.
Equal opportunity works both ways—many men are
now willing to work for the same wages as women.

The "Perfect Secretary" Myth

Women started out as secretaries for so long that
men have become inclined to see in every successful
woman a kind of supersecretary. They assume that
women are possibly efficient and organized, but basically unimaginative and inflexible. This is pure myth.
Very few jobs are as ego-destroying as that of secretary. The better you are at doing it, the more you have
to suppress your own opinions and your personality, so
the perfect secretary, whether male or female, is in
fact the person who is most able to see the world from
somebody's else's point of view. Every effort you can

make to dissociate yourself from this myth works to your advantage.

● Do Not Answer the Telephone Yourself.

If there's nobody there to answer it for you, let it ring.

Do not allow yourself to be put in a secretarial relationship. This is quite a common practice. A woman is promoted to an important job but still continues to perform functions for her male colleagues and superiors that no man in a comparable position would do. Men have been used to service from women, both at home and in their working lives.

● Do Not Become a "Go-for."

I remember attending a meeting at which a very successful young woman was presenting a complicated project to the head of a large company. In the middle of her presentation, he stopped and said, "Look, let's continue this over lunch. Why don't you order us something to eat? There were three male executives present, with lower salaries and positions than hers. But the instinct to associate food with women, and a woman's presence with service was simply too strong for him. And, unfortunately, for her. She wrote down what everyone wanted to eat, then went out to give the order to a secretary. She should not have done so. She could, after all, just as easily have called a secretary in, without being in the least impolite. It might even have been a perfect opportunity to *be* impolite. Men can afford to take a step backward. Women cannot.

● Avoid Note Taking at Meetings.

Taking notes of a meeting, or performing the subsequent chores, merely tends to reinforce the view of women as having subservient roles by nature. It is very common for women to be invited to meetings on an equal basis, then asked to "keep the record" or be assigned to the task of "following." In most cases, this merely means the drudgery of implementing whatever has been decided, without any of the glory. Any failure of action or implementation will naturally be your fault.

- REMOVE FROM YOUR DESK TOP SUCH MENIAL OBJECTS AS STAPLERS, SCOTCH TAPE DISPENSERS, PAPER CLIPS AND FILING CARDS.

If you have occasion to use any of these things, keep them in a drawer, and use them when nobody is looking. If your memory is fallible, invest in a small leather diary, with a gold pencil, and make notes in that. Never carry a steno pad (the ultimate symbol of servant status, since it implies the mindless recording of other people's ideas). If you sit down at a conference table and there is a yellow legal pad in front of each person, *get rid of yours*. If you don't, you will almost certainly be asked to "take a note," or "follow up" on something.

Nice Girls Finish Last ...

This is the most important thing to learn: *Nobody wants you to succeed except you*. The odds are stacked against you.

Learn to challenge. Start small. When someone makes a mistake, *point it out!* When you're not satisfied, *say so!* When you've got a point to make, *make it!* The world will not come to an end if you make a scene; the way up consists of a long series of challenges and confrontations. Nobody will stand up for you except yourself.

Start now! Begin your day by making a list of the things that annoy you, hold you back, seem to you patently unfair, and systematically train yourself to deal with them one by one. Never mind how trivial or unimportant they may be to *other* people. They are important to *you,* and the fact that they are not that important to others makes it all the more likely that you will get your way. When your "A-priority" conflicts with someone else's "A-priority," there is always a problem (as when you are after someone else's job), but when your "A-priority" is somebody else's "C-priority," or hasn't even occurred to him or her at all, you have a very good chance of winning. And winning is a habit. Once you begin, you will go on winning, and rise to larger and larger gains.

For example: in one office I know of, the women executives invariably were excluded from having office couches. Originally, this curious tradition derived from the belief that a couch in a woman's office was an open invitation to sex. But the prohibition remained long after it was obvious that the distinction was ridiculous and demeaning. When one woman executive set out to get a couch put in her office, it was felt to be a revolutionary move. But in fact, of course, her strong feelings on the subject were shared by very few of the senior male executives, to whom it seemed an irrelevant and comic demand. They fought it out of instinct for the preservation of male chauvinist traditions, but they hardly cared. When she won on this point, she established an equality with her colleagues and a reputation for toughness that gave her the base on which to build a successful career. Remember: *minor victories can lead to a major triumph.*

Courage

What men really don't expect from women is courage, which men have always assumed to be a masculine virtue. Given the general level of cowardice prevalent in business life, it is by no means difficult to acquire a reputation for boldness. One of the extraordinary things about human nature is that people will generally accept an order if it's expressed with self-confidence and authority. They may be resentful afterward, but by then it's too late. You have already established that you're in a position to give orders.

The reverse is also true. I recently met a woman who

had emerged from fourteen years of marriage and motherhood to work as an assistant producer on a West Coast television news program. Unfortunately, she was eager to please, rather than determined to be firm. On her first day, she found herself confronted with a busy camera crew at seven o'clock in the morning, and watching them struggle with the coffee machine, she volunteered to take on the task herself. This earned her the tolerant friendship of her crew, but totally undercut her authority. Gradually the coffee job became a part of her routine, reducing her to the servant level at which many men find it comfortable to "accept" a woman colleague, but effectively destroying any chance she may have had of making a real success of her job. After six months, she realized that nothing would help—the only solution was to get a job on another show, and start all over again.

"This time I learned my lesson," she told me. "I arrived on the set, made myself a cup of coffee, turned to the biggest guy on the crew and told him to move the number one camera closer in. It was fine where it was, and I could see he was thinking about it. I just looked at him straight in the eyes, not aggressively but firmly, and after a beat he shrugged and moved the camera. Since then, I've had no trouble. But my God, what it cost me to have that first encounter! I couldn't believe that I could tell a six-foot, forty-year-old father of two what to do, and make it stick, and I didn't have the slightest idea what I'd do if he'd said no or ignored me. But he *didn't!* And I've discovered that most people don't. If you give orders, people presume you have the right to, and more important, they assume you know what you're doing. It's all a question of style and courage, and fourteen years in the kitchen and the home aren't the best place to learn those things. But I'm learning fast, and these days people are bringing *me* my morning coffee, as if it were the most natural thing in the world, and maybe it is, because I really think I'm on the way up at last . . ."

ON THE WAY UP . . .

If you are obliged to start as a secretary (as many women still are), don't feel that your position is hopeless. The world is full of women executives who began as secretaries and have come a very long way indeed. Just follow these six simple rules:

(1) *Horizontal movement can be as valuable as vertical movement.* If you begin as a secretary, it's difficult to get into the promotion pattern, since the only real promotion possible for a secretary is to stop being one and become somebody who needs one. You can, however, give the impression of upward mobility by switching jobs within the company or the department. In the first place, you learn more this way. But more important, you can make each move *look* like a promotion by treating it in a positive manner. *Don't* get yourself assigned to one person and stick there until you become a permanent fixture in his or her life. Do as good a job as you can, but keep your eyes open for a secretarial job with someone else, and switch to it when you can.

(2) *Do not depend on your boss to help you upward.* The more perfect you are as a secretary, the less reason there is for promoting you. Once an executive has found a devoted, loyal, intelligent, competent person, who never forgets messages, types perfectly, runs errands, keeps a pot of coffee percolating and can balance a checkbook during the lunch hour, he or she is most unlikely to let go, even in the higher interests of the corporation or your career. It is important to do your job well, but not so well that it becomes unthinkable for those who depend on you to move you upward. So far as secretaries are concerned, this means brisk efficiency rather than mothering and errand-running. And that efficiency should be directed out-

ward as much as possible. You have to keep your own boss reasonably happy with your work, but if you want to get promoted, what you must do is get the attention of people higher up in the hierarchy. Here, one of the small factors that make a difference is to avoid the interoffice mail. When your boss has a memo or report to be sent to his immediate superior, hand carry it yourself. Do this at a moment when you can be reasonably sure of giving it directly to the senior executive it's addressed to. In doing so, be specific and informative. Don't just put it on his desk. Hand it to him and say, "This is the report you requested on regional marketing costs. It's broken down by region, but I've also indexed it in case that's more convenient. May I be of any help to you?" Contrive to make it clear that you *know* what the document is about and what it's for. This will contrast with the attitude of most of your rivals, who will generally be handling pieces of paper they have typed but not read.

It is not, of course, necessary to *understand* what a document means—very few people in business do—but it helps to know what it's supposed to be about. Reading the first and last paragraphs will usually give you as much information as you need. The main thing is to make contact with management people as soon and as often as possible.

(3) *Seize control of communications.* The more information you have at your disposal, the more people will have to come to you to find out something they need to know. Convince your immediate superior that he or she should have more time to get on with the business of solving problems and thinking up new solutions, and that you should take over the role of keeping lists, recording information, drawing up schedules, etc. Gradually, if you take over enough information, your immediate superior will be unable to go to meetings without you. You will be the only one able to answer practical questions like "When are the goods actually being delivered?" or "What date was the contract

signed?" When your boss begins to have to look at you for answers, you are halfway there.

(4) *Dress as if you were already an executive.* It costs a little more and takes some effort, but it is well worth the extra time and trouble. The important thing is to look as if you will fit in with those *above* you, not those at your level.

(5) *Stay a few minutes late.* It is better to leave at the same time as the executives than to arrive early, when the only person to notice your devotion will probably be the mailroom boy. Ideally, you should leave later than your immediate superior and time your departure to that of the senior executive whose attention you are trying to attract. If possible, make sure you are carrying a brief case, an appropriate industrial journal, and a bundle of envelopes, properly addressed and stamped. These can be kept in your desk drawer and used over again every night, as long as you are always careful never to actually mail it.

(6) *Eat in at your desk whenever possible during lunch.* This never fails to create a good impression. Having breakfast at your desk, though, always produces a strong impression of sloppiness, late rising and doing something private on company time. When you *do* eat lunch at your desk, don't spread out a newspaper or a magazine—that will only spoil the effect. Open up a file or a report. You have to give the impression that you are staying in to *work,* not simply because you can't be bothered to go down to the coffee shop and want to catch up on the day's news in peace.

(7) *Keep your personal life out of the office.* Never sew, knit or crochet at your desk, write greeting cards or attempt to balance your checkbook. These things strike the wrong note, as do photographs of dogs, cats

or small children. A neat wall chart of some kind, however meaningless, may pay dividends, and nobody is likely to inquire very closely what it's supposed to be in aid of.

At each stage of your journey to success, remember to look as if you know everything about your present job and are ready to move up to another. If you're stuck and can't think of anything else to do, move your furniture around in some new arrangement, or put up a new wall chart. Always give the impression of change and momentum.

SEX, MARRIAGE AND SUCCESS

It is one of the clichés of male chauvinist thinking that ambitious women are usually single, seldom happy and are driven to compensate for their sexual deprivation by aggressive careerism. Male executives will explain a single woman's success by saying, "What the hell do you expect, the job is her man, right?" Wrong. In the past, successful women were apt to be elderly and single, simply because few marriages were arranged to cope with two people's having successful careers, and because it took women many years of secretarial work to become noticed as executive talent, if indeed they were lucky enough. Men always looked elsewhere for a woman's success, and sexual repression was the reason most flattering to the male ego. It had the further advantage of turning successful women into freaks. Men got married, had children, and were, in effect, whole persons. Women who succeeded did so by giving up their status as human beings. This also served as a useful face-saving device for men when a woman was promoted over them. *She* was a driven neurotic, with no life or family or love to blunt her ambitions and take up her time, while *he* had to fit his career into the larger demands of children, wife and domestic life.

The Married Look

As a woman, you may actually find that a single-minded determination to succeed works against you, in terms of promotion, by arousing in men the fear that they are dealing with a woman who is wed to her job. Work as hard as you like, but be sure to let it be known that you have another life. Even in an age when half the marriages in the country end in divorce, corporations still have a touching faith in domesticity as a sign of steadiness and promotability, though they are rather more subtle in informing themselves about such things than they used to be.

Men do not, as a rule, trust bachelors after the age of thirty, on the assumption that any man who hasn't married by that time must either be dissolute or homosexual. (It's generally all right to live a bachelor life after being divorced.)* Still, a marriage, or marriages, and children are the living proof of responsibility and normality, and a male executive without them would do well to keep his bachelorhood quiet.

The situation is a little more ambiguous for women. Men tend to feel that a single woman is dangerous, either because she's frustrated or neurotic or likely to commit an unexpected folly like running off with some guy at a crucial moment in her career. At the same time, they tend to feel that successful, ambitious women who *are* married must in some way be ignoring their husbands or children, and possibly both. "How does your husband feel about your working late?" they are likely to ask.

I'm not suggesting that you ought to get married in

---

* This view was perfectly expressed in the British Army saying which ran: "Lieutenants *must not* marry, majors *may* marry, colonels *must* marry." A young executive, like a junior officer, may make his way single, but there's a point at which he is expected to pay his dues to his superiors' domesticity, and offer his own hostages to fortune in the shape of children and a mortgage.

order to succeed. But if you're not married, it is important to give the impression of having an active—but not *too* active—social life of your own. This will give you the reputation of being a "well-rounded" person, while at the same time protecting you from any number of sexual importunings and suggestions. It is not a bad idea to keep a man's picture on your desk, provided he looks suitable, solid and of the right age. One young woman I know, who lived alone and was tired of being treated as one of the dropouts of life by her male colleagues, bought an expensive leather frame for her desk and put a photograph of her sister's husband, a football player, in it. Both the questions and the aggravations ceased. Another, more daring young woman put the picture of the chairman of the board on her desk, in a silver frame. Since the company she worked for was one of those huge financial institutions with thousands of employees, none of her immediate colleagues or superiors felt in a position to ask whether or not she was in fact related to the chairman. Her opinions were listened to with cautious deference, and it did not take long for her to get promoted.

Even if you're not going anywhere for the weekend—especially in the summer or on holidays—take a suitcase to the office, if you're single. Once again, it gives the impression that you have a reliable, conventional life outside the office. If you can possibly avoid it, you don't want to be thought of as a swinging single, or as someone who lives in an apartment with three other "girls."

Of course, these minor protective subterfuges are unnecessary for many women, since they are married in the first place. For married women who want to succeed, the cardinal rule is to talk of your husband with the deepest respect and affection, whatever your real feelings are. Make sure your executives have the impression that your husband is pleased to have you working, that he's happy in his job himself and that he values your success. It may not be true (Alas, it so often isn't), but you have nothing to gain from letting this be known. Never complain about the difficulties of being married and holding down a job. Men believe that's exactly why women make poor executives, and will often cite the pull of home and marriage as a reason for promoting a man instead of a woman.

Of course, it is still difficult for men to accept success in a woman, and all the more so when it's their wife who is the success. There is a learning process that has to take place, and it's sometimes slow and painful—nor does every marriage survive it. It takes a great deal of preparation before a man is likely to take a woman's ambitions as seriously as his own, or to understand that it matters as much to her as it does to him.

"When I went out to get a job," says Barbara Weiss, a successful office designer who is married and has two children, "I made a deal with my husband. No whining. He's a lawyer and works like a dog. I've never objected to that. For years, he did what he wanted to do, and got a bonus of sympathy as well. That was fine when I wasn't working too. But now it doesn't work. We both had to face up to the fact that we liked working hard, long hours, that we needed the tension and the aggravations, and that we wouldn't whine or complain to each other about how hard we work. I understand him a lot better since I'm doing the same thing myself, and we've developed a mutual respect, which is a lot better than what we had before."

Ms. Weiss is not alone is discovering that success is a positive factor, and that the old myths about women and work are both erroneous and demeaning. Far from taking anything away, success *completes*. As more and more women enter the working world, they have the right—in fact, the obligation—to succeed on the same terms as everyone else. It isn't necessary to make a choice between marriage and ambition, or to stay single if you want to get ahead, and it isn't reasonable to accept second best. Society being what it is, it may still be necessary for women to approach success by different techniques, and it may be a harder struggle for them than it is for men of equal talent and drive. But the truth is that success knows no sexual distinctions.

Overcoming the Fear of Success

Patients with success phobia . . . may become very passive and submissive and avoid success, or may appear very assertive, but still inhibit the executive end of the aggressive or self-assertive act."
—Morton Friedman, M.D.[1]

"Failure too is a form of death . . ."
—Graham Greene
A Sort of Life

You Don't Have to Feel Guilty!

It may seem paradoxical to talk of the fear of success. But it is in fact an enormous obstacle, because success implies change, and change is frightening. People build comfortable, predictable lives around failure. They are reluctant to give up its assurance and familiarity, in much the same way as people with a physical complaint are often unwilling to have it cured. How many people do we know who use illness as a lever to get what they want? Pain and suffering, whether real or self-created, give them a reliable excuse for not doing the things they don't want to do. Asthma, impotence, ulcers, sciatic pains, a bad back, migraine headaches all may be used as powerful weapons to defend a way of life that is comfortable and secure. Family, colleagues and friends are forced to make concessions to the sufferer, out of pity, sympathy or the simple fear of provoking another attack. Pain can even be used by the neurotic to achieve success, miserable as this would seem to be as a technique.

Dr. George Engel, in a remarkable study of "Guilt, Pain and Success,"[2] describes a patient who suffered agonizing pains in the foot for years, and rose to great success as a business consultant, working himself to the point of exhaustion, and terrifying everyone around him. His very real suffering gave him "justification for his rudeness, aggressiveness, impatience and ruthlessness, while those who worked under or with him excused his objectionable behavior on the grounds [of his pain], for the dramatic character of the attacks and his exhibitionistic stoical suffering aroused admiration and tolerance."

This symbiotic relationship between the sufferer and his colleagues lasted for nearly twenty years, became in fact a life style in which the pain itself gradually became institutionalized as a productive and useful phenomenon, driving the patient on, and excusing in the eyes of his colleagues those character traits he was unwilling to give up and on which he thrived. Unfortunately, the pain was finally diagnosed as a glomus tumor under a toenail, and removed (it says little for modern medicine that it took twenty years to make the discovery), and the patient was instantly cured. Not only was he unable to sleep because of the absence of pain, but he returned to the office to find that his secretary had been transferred without his knowledge, since he was no longer regarded with fear and respect, now that he was cured. In Dr. Engel's words, "Others were less tolerant of him, since he was no longer seen as the unfortunate but admirable man suffering pain [and] neither the foot nor the ulcer were any longer publicly recognized sources of pain and distress." Shortly afterward, he took to drink, became confused and depressed, and given to rages and wife-beating.

Needless to say, he no longer has his job; he now runs a chicken farm. His pain had provided him with what Dr. Engel describes as "a built-in bank account, from which guilt could be atoned for and success paid for in advance," and without that pain the patient's carefully constructed world fell to pieces overnight.

It can be argued that it was not a very happy world to begin with, but that is not the point. Like so many people, Dr. Engel's patient had fashioned an atmosphere in which he was comfortable, using his own pain as the foundation. Granted that there is, in Freud's words, "a quota of suffering" that is necessary to maintain the balance of our lives—and is, in any case, unavoidable—but to build a life around suffering is a distortion of reality, and so it is to build a life around the security of failure.

The Will to Fail

Reik has described masochism in modern man as "victory through defeat." Life being what it is, we can assert ourselves in two ways. One is to succeed, to justify or even exceed other people's expectations of us. The other way to assert ourselves is to *fail*. By failing we demonstrate our own power, even at the cost of total self-defeat. In the words of one psychiatrist, "Many of the shortcomings and inadequacies we ordinarily attribute to someone's being 'shiftless' or 'lazy' are in reality expressions of a driving and urgent hunger for power . . . In doing 'nothing' [these people] were indeed doing a very important 'something,' and that was maintaining a sense of power by balking, by *not* doing what people expected them to do." [3] It is vitally important to realize that failure can be a mechanism, that it constitutes a productive and satisfying way of life for a large number of people, of whom you may be one.

Children are often impelled to show their power by proving that they can't or won't do something; infants, in fact, have no other way of asserting themselves. It is an easy habit to fall into, and the rewards can be substantial to the ego. You can punish your parents by not eating, by not succeeding at school, by not making the most of yourself. As an adult, you can punish your wife, your children and yourself by failing. Yes, *yourself!* For guilt too is part of the mechanism of failure, perhaps its strongest part. And guilt is an addictive drug as strong and as destructive as heroin, and far more widespread.

Freud commented that "people occasionally fall ill precisely because a deeply rooted and long-cherished wish has come to fulfillment," and concluded that "the forces of conscience which induce illness on attainment of success, as in other cases on a frustration, are closely connected with the Oedipus complex, the relation to father and mother, as perhaps, indeed, is all our sense of guilt in general." [4] Fenichel too noted that the fear of success was strong in some patients, in whom "a success may not only mean something that must bring immediate punishment but also something that stimulates ambition and thus mobilizes fears concerning future failure and future punishment." [5]

The Icarus Complex

Strong as the Oedipus complex may be, it is almost worth inventing an "Icarus complex," named after the unfortunate youth who fell to his death after flying too high and too close to the sun. And it is not insignificant that Icarus died not only because he had flown too high (i.e., overachieved) but also because he had disobeyed his father, and soared higher than his parent.

Many of us feel, profoundly and unconsciously, that "the higher you climb, the harder you fall," and solve the problem by not climbing at all. Dr. Daniel B. Schuster has commented on the common phenomenon among most people of "the inability to enjoy good fortune, even though passively acquired." [6] It is common enough to talk about "paying the price" for some piece of good fortune, or "paying one's dues," as if it were somehow necessary to suffer in a measurable quantity for every gain or achievement. We fear that other people will resent our success, that our every advancement will create hostility and envy, that our every step upward will provoke some form of punishment. In many people, success is a country full of ill-defined but potent dangers, and the closer they come to their goals, the greater their fears. Failure thus becomes a kind of security blanket, a warm, enveloping, familiar comfort that answers a deep, yearning need for punishment, and protects against the uncertain, but dreaded, consequences that success might entail. By failing, we satisfy the inner need for suffering and expiation, while at the same time avoiding the pain that other people might impose on us if we took the risk of offending them by succeeding.

Hubris, or pride, was the one sin the Greek gods never forgave and always punished, and half the Greek legends involve the elaborate and ruthless strategems by which the Olympians clipped mortals' wings and taught them the futility of human ambition and achievement—poor, blind Oedipus was punished as much for being a successful king as for inadvertently killing his father and marrying his mother. The fear that success will bring down on our heads the revenge of the gods, that by failing we are protecting ourselves against a dreadful Olympian vengeance, still holds us back, even in an age when material success is supposed to be the common denominator of human behavior.

The epic tragedy of the Kennedys was taken by many people as a moral lesson, and seen as a naturally fitting end to overwhelming ambition and success. Joseph Kennedy, according to popular legend, acquired great wealth with singular ruthlessness, and drove his sons hard to achieve greatness, which they did with equal ruthlessness. They were also handsome, popular, energetic, courageous and sexually successful to an extraordinary degree. Joseph Kennedy, Jr., was killed in the war; Robert and John Kennedy were assassinated; Edward Kennedy's political career was destroyed by the Chappaquiddick scandal, and his domestic happiness, such as it may have been, shattered by the problems of his wife and the illness of his son. When a great many people answered a national poll by arguing that the Kennedys "deserved what they got," they were not talking out of right-wing fanaticism as much as out of a basic, moral feeling that the consequences of success are always tragic. Hubris must be punished. Pride goeth before a fall. The price of ambition is death. These are popular fallacies.

Stop Punishing Yourself

Before you can be successful, you have to rid yourself of these fears, and learn to stop punishing yourself. The methods by which people assure their own failure are subtle, devious and complex, so much so that you may be unable to see just how you have done it. People consistently choose the wrong kind of job for themselves, submit themselves to masochistic relationships with employers who hate and use them, behave in ways which are guaranteed to ensure they will not get a raise or a promotion, ignore their strengths and follow their weaknesses. *The instinct toward self-defeat is strong and insidious.* Like all rationalizations it disguises itself as common sense most of the time. Except in rare individuals, the instinct to do nothing, to stay put, to accept the second-rate, is far stronger than the urge to succeed, and has been built into the personality so solidly and purposefully that it is in any case hard to overcome.

The fear of success is not necessarily fanciful or unrealistic. Success does imply risks—the risk of new responsibilities, the risk of living up to new and greater expectations, the risk of losing what one has in the pursuit of what one wants. It is, however, important to recognize these fears as realistic, and to confront them in a sensible and organized way:

- Ask yourself how much responsibility you are prepared to take.
- Don't set your expectations so high that you are bound to fail.
- Assess just how willing you are to lose what you have in order to rise up the next step.

What you must do is to separate the rational fears from the irrational and neurotic ones. It is sensible to wonder if your attempt to win a vice presidency may cost you your present job if you're unsuccessful in the promotion race. If the odds seem heavily weighted against you, wait for another try, or change jobs and try somewhere else. On the other hand, if you feel that you won't get the vice presidency because you have always been "unlucky," or if you feel, like so many people, that the promotion can only bring you trouble, grief and possible retaliation, then you're holding yourself back out of *unnecessary* guilt and fear.

One telling sign of this is the attempt to placate hostility in advance or to exorcise disaster before it has even happened. Do you preface a remark or an opinion by saying, for example, "I may be wrong about this, but . . .", or "You may disagree with me, but . . ." or any variation of these rather common disclaimers? This kind of self-minimalization can become an ingrained habit. If you do this in conversation, you are almost certainly doing it unconsciously on a larger scale.[7]

The first step to success is to accept the consequences of knowing that you're *right*, when that is the case. It is not so much a matter of being assertive, as of giving up the comfortable cocoon of apologies and guilt in which most of us have chosen to live.

Turning Failure into Success

The freedom to fail is vital if you're going to succeed. Most successful men fail time and time again, and it is a measure of their strength that failure merely propels them into some new attempt at success.

We all know the clichés: the branch that bends does not break, the building that sways in the wind does not collapse in the storm, the ship that creaks and moves in every timber withstands the heavy seas. Yet, obstinately, most of us are unable to apply these rules to our lives. We are determined to be inflexible, to maintain a straight course, to find some way to anchor ourselves in a secure system of beliefs. We are comfortable with the predictable and the familiar, and will go to incredible lengths to manufacture make-believe worlds in which we can pretend that everything is normal and under control. This is a dangerous illusion, and a deep-seated impediment to success.

Some of our best-known folk heroes have in fact been experts at failing big until, as it were, they fall downward to success, fame and a place in the grateful nation's memory.

Winston Churchill, for example, failed at school, very nearly failed at Sandhurst, where he was regarded as hardly bright enough to become a cavalry officer (bearing in mind that little more is demanded of a junior officer in the cavalry than that he be brighter than his horse) and failed to win promotion once he was commissioned. Fame came to him because he was inept enough to be captured by the Boers, and eventually made a historic escape. But being captured in the first place was a kind of failure, by military standards, and he can thus be said to have failed his way into the limelight.

Once there, Churchhill repeatedly failed. First, he failed to win elections. Then, as a Minister, he single-handedly forced the government to send a British Army to the Dardanelles, where the troops met with a military failure of colossal proportions. Far from its ending his public career, he was next allowed to fail as Chancellor of the Exchequer, from which post he managed to precipitate the world monetary crisis by returning England to the gold standard, despite the advice of older and wiser men.

This failure was so great that he became a widely respected public figure and was the natural choice to become Prime Minister in 1940 when it looked to most people as if the whole country was going to collapse. A lifetime of failure and public disasters brought him to "the top of the greasy pole," perhaps in part because it is easier to trust a man who has failed than one who has an unbroken string of successes.

General Ulysses S. Grant, though unkempt, drunken and a confirmed failure (he had failed in school, failed as a young officer, failed as clerk in a harness store and was in the process of failing in real estate when the Civil War rescued him), seemed far more trustworthy, both to the troops and President Lincoln, than other, more dazzling generals like Mead and McLennan. A country in the process of losing a war needs a man who isn't afraid of failure, and is in fact familiar with the process.

Even George Washington, the Father of our Country, was, in the words of Neil Hickey, an early practitioner of "upward failure." [8] So notorious was his reputation for losing battles ineptly that John Adams called him "an old muttonhead" and Thomas Jefferson commented, with great and polite understatement that Washington was "not a great tactician." As a young officer, he once constructed a fort at Great Meadows, Pennsylvania, on a swampy creek bottom, hemmed in on all three sides by wooded hills. This position for a fortress was so ludicrous that the French, in this case Washington's enemies, captured him immediately, and generously released him with the advice to take up some other line of work.

Giving up fortifications, Washington then used his failure to become the personal aide to Lt. General Edward Braddock, whom Washington persuaded to divide his forces at the seige of Fort Duquesne. The result? Braddock lost the battle, his army and his life.

Washington, whose advice had been so conspicuously wrong, went on to blunder in larger matters.

On the record of these alarming defeats, and also because he seemed so stupid as not to be ambitious, the Continental Congress, hoping that they had at least avoided the possibility of creating a military dictator like Caesar or Napoleon, gave the command of its army to General Washington, who proceeded through 1775 and 1776 to retreat from Long Island to Brooklyn Heights, from Brooklyn Heights to Kips Bay, from Kips Bay to Washington Heights, from Washington Heights to White Plains, and from there across the Hudson into New Jersey. As Hickey points out, it can truly be said that like the great General Kutuzov, whose strategy against Napoleon consisted of retreating, Washington beat the British by retreating faster than they could advance. Washington's record of failure was sufficient to carry him to the very top. He eventually accepted the Presidency and lived afterward in great comfort at the expense of the taxpayer.

Richard Nixon, to take a more recent example, failed as a civilian, failed as a high school football player, failed as a junior naval officer, failed when he applied to join the FBI, failed to win the presidential election in 1960 and later failed to win the gubernatorial election in California. Widely regarded as a loser —even a *bad* loser ("You won't have Richard Nixon to kick around any more")—he was elected to the Presidency and proceeded to mismanage things to the point of impeachment. He lives comfortably in San Clemente, while his associates serve jail sentences. His scale of failure was large enough to ensure his eventual success.

At a lower level, the same process can be observed. A perfect example of sustained success through failure is Robert McNamara, the "whiz kid" who took over the Ford Motor Company in its hour of need and helped to create the notorious Edsel. Years of market research, engineering and "creative thinking" led to the production of a car so unsalable as to become a national joke, even a kind of national legend. It is therefore not surprising that McNamara should have been chosen by President Kennedy to do for the Defense Department what he had done for Ford. There, through two Presidencies, McNamara presided over a series of ever more disastrous failures. In terms of procurement the Edsel was repeated on a gargantuan scale, billions of dollars flowing down the drain for such ill-fated projects as

- the TFX variable-geometry fighter, which not only failed to fly but almost brought down the governments of Great Britain and Australia, who had committed themselves to buy it;
- the B-71 bomber, famous for the fact that it crashed spectacularly in front of the national news media;
- the notorious Sheridan Main Battle Tank, which consumed billions of dollars over more than a decade until the Pentagon finally threw in the towel and adopted a German tank;
- the AR-15 rifle, so prone to jamming after the first few shots that American infantrymen in Vietnam took to carrying the AK-47 Kalashnikov rifles they captured from Viet Cong and North Vietnamese.

In terms of policy, McNamara failed on an even grander scale. He was among those involved in the Bay of Pigs invasion, a failure of sizable proportions. His experience in that disaster naturally persuaded the President to rely on his advice about Vietnam, where McNamara conceived the notion that the war could be won with no more than six divisions of American troops, i.e., about 250,000 men. When this proved not to be the case, McNamara became one of the fiercest of hawks, recommending not only increased American participation, but even suggesting the construction of an electronic barrier across the DMZ to halt infiltration. As the leading spokesman and salesman for the massive bombing of the North, he disregarded the record of the U.S. Air Force and its documented study of bombing in World War Two that made it perfectly clear that bombing the Germans had merely hardened their resolve. When American troop levels reached nearly 600,000 men, at which point it was also obvious that there was no "end to the tunnel," McNamara commissioned a study of the situation, a tactic common to all executives and public servants when things go badly, which is generally designed to show that the man who commissioned the study was not personally responsible for the failure. In this case the report, which later became famous as the Pentagon Papers, was written to prove that the D.O.D. had had little or nothing to do with the disaster at hand, while at the same time providing the Secretary of Defense with an opportunity to escape from the Johnson administration back into the liberal camp, leaving the President with the war McNamara had urged him to fight.

McNamara illustrates one of the most important abilities an "upward failure" must have—that of being able to move quickly off the situation that has failed. No sooner, after all, had McNamara given the Ford Motor Company the Edsel than he accepted the call to public service, leaving Ford to deal with its own problems. No sooner had his public service been crowned by multiple disaster on the largest possible scale than he heard the siren call of international duty and moved swiftly to accept the presidency of the World Bank, thus, as Hickey trenchantly points out, "sinking to the top."

To be a successful failure on this scale, one must master the art of escape. This requires a precise feel for the exact moment at which it is necessary to abandon the sinking ship and its crew to fate, and a ruthless lack of sentiment about getting off in time. They are not tempted to go down with it, or send the women and children first. They do not waste energy, emotion and time in attempting to justify their own role in a disaster. They get out as quickly as they can, and

move on to something else. The great failures know
how to look the other way at the right moment. They
do not become emotionally involved with those who
choose to stay on board. They know better than to
identify themselves with a losing cause: they may have
been the captain of the ship, but not its owner. As one
executive put it succinctly, "I'd rather run something
than own something, and if you want to stay on your
feet you'd better learn that you don't try and put out
a fire in the store unless you own it. If you run it, you
get outside and watch the damned thing burn."

Failing Upward

The ability to succeed even when things are going
badly is highly rewarded, and has shaped the careers
of many of the most successful corporate executives.
One of the most interesting examples is that of
Matthew J. Culligan, the adventurous and colorful
salesman turned business executive, who presided over
the last years of the Curtis Publishing Company and
its flagship publication, the *Saturday Evening Post*.
His career is worth examining in detail.

"A tiger of a salesman" was, in fact, the usual description of "Joe" Culligan, who like many men, pre-
ferred the more punchy and aggressive name he
adopted to his own. Culligan looked every inch a dynamic success, with his craggy, handsome face, his
trim physique and his brisk, self-confident manner. He
is a perfect example of how important it is to *look* as
if you know what you are doing. Culligan had the
right kind of ego for a supersalesman, and the right
kind of life style and energy. He boasted of being up
and at work every morning at five-thirty, and electrified the directors of Curtis, most of whom were
scarcely out of the horse-and-buggy age, by commuting to Philadelphia every morning from Rye, New
York, in a helicopter.

Joe Culligan was in every way "the paradigm of

the romantic, go-getting salesman." [9] He started his career as a pitchman at the New York World's Fair in 1939, and went on to take over NBC's radio network at just the time television was about to destroy radio. In 1957, he managed to convince a reporter that television had already peaked, was "a bit passé" and that radio was the natural medium for hard news and the scoop. He also predicted that what he called "the jukebox stations" would drown each other out, leaving room for "a few Tiffanys." [10] Culligan picked the right moment to walk away from NBC (and radio) and join the board of Interpublic, Inc., the parent company of the McCann-Erickson advertising agency. From this secure position, he won a considerable reputation as a man who knew Madison Avenue. He carefully honed his own legend, eating daily in the downstairs barroom of the "21" Club, and praising his own capacity for work in flamboyant terms: "One of the legendary things they say about me," he confided unblushingly to a reporter, "is this capacity for work I have . . . If I work 18 hours a day, the others will work 14! Flaming leadership, that's what's needed." [11]

By 1962, the Curtis Publishing Company, one of the oldest and most distinguished corporations in America, owning among other things the *Post, Ladies' Home Journal, Holiday, American Home* and *Jack and Jill,* was terminally ill. A company existing on magazines in the age of television, it was committed to a vast and cumbersome system under which Curtis owned everything it needed, from the presses to the very forests from which their paper came. In 1962, Curtis lost $4,727,000 in the first quarter, and even the *Post* was down 19 percent in advertising in one year, while the total ad revenue of Curtis' four major magazines had dropped by $9,200,000 in less than twelve months. The board of directors looked at the past and thought ahead to the future, and there seemed no reason to believe that the company would not simply bleed to death, left to itself. They virtually deposed Mary

Curtis Bok Zimbalist, eighty-five, the daughter of founder Cyrus H. K. Curtis, as well as her son, Cary Bok, and the president of Curtis, Robert E. MacNeal, who was vacationing in Europe when the ax fell.[12]

"Flaming leadership' was just what they were looking for, and Joe Culligan seemed to fill the bill. In the press the reaction was favorable, if only because Culligan was a picturesque personality. He immediately took off on a whirlwind "barnstorming tour" of the United States, to see the "heads of 75 companies, the top 30 ad agencies, bankers and security analysts," and talked expansively of adding to the Curtis list of magazines a competitor to *Time* and *Newsweek*, a teen-age magazine, and of eventually transforming Curtis into a "multi-billion-dollar worldwide communications network."

Culligan left behind him his "inside man," Clay Blair, formerly the *Post*'s managing editor and now promoted by Culligan to vice president. "It's a two-man job," Culligan said, announcing Blair's promotion, but he instantly added, "As long as it's clear who's running the show." [13] This seems an odd decision to have made: the *Post* was such a disaster that it threatened to bring the whole company down with it, and it was therefore somewhat daring to promote the man who had been running the *Post* to a position of greater responsibility in the parent company.

Having announced that "failure is unacceptable," Culligan went on to fire 1,000 of Curtis' 6,800 employees and predicted that the *Post*'s ad revenues would rise a startling 60 percent in the first half of 1963. Then he was quoted as saying, "I think that most of the attrition . . . has already taken place. *Collier's, American Magazine, Women's Home Companion* and *Coronet* have hit the dust, but remember the *Post, Life* and *Look* have survived television's growing years, and television is not going to get that much bigger so far as numbers are concerned. Also, TV is beginning to fragment . . . The next step in television is color. When it goes to color it will be even more expensive. That in turn will shake out advertisers, who will use magazines again. For certain types of advertising, like food, color television will never be precise enough. Therefore there will always be a large amount of advertising that needs magazines . . . Television has reached its peak." [14]

Having made this remarkable prediction, Culligan beat the woods for the advertisers while delegating much of the editorial decision-making to Blair. Blair, in what was perhaps an unfortunate decision, set out "to restore the crusading spirit, the sophisticated muckraking, the exposé in the mass magazines," and added that "we're going to provoke people, we'll make 'em mad." [15] Making people "mad" very soon produced what may have been the world's record libel judgment. Blair himself had even more swash-buckling attributes than Culligan. An ex-submariner, he was one of the world's most famous skindivers and was said to kill sharks "with pleasure" near the wrecks he worked. He once remarked that "treasure diving was like editing the *Post*—pursuing the truth amidst sharks." But this dramatic vision of an editor's position was not perhaps as striking as his later comment to a questioning colleague that "God wants me to save the *Saturday Evening Post*." [16]

By 1964, Culligan was traveling around the country selling the idea of a "new" *Post*, while his editor-in-chief pursued an editorial policy which seemed likely to offend the *Post*'s remaining readers. Though it might be thought that Culligan had some legitimate reason for complaining about the hostility of his subordinate and rival, it must be remembered that Culligan himself had hand-picked Blair to be his second-in-command, knowing full well that Blair was disappointed at not having been named president of Curtis himself. (It is an elementary rule of business and of life not to give power of any kind to people whose hostility is known to you. It's hard enough to deal with the people who *secretly* hate you and are after your job, without putting weapons in the hands of your known rivals.)

Curtis lost a staggering $7,624,000 in the first quarter of 1964, for a total loss of $13,974,000 for the entire year, and was forced to postpone interest payments on its $9,970,000 of outstanding debentures. At this point Culligan resigned, while continuing to draw his now $150,000-a-year salary "to work on special assignments, such as preparing a company history . . ." Though he professed to long for "obscurity," he remarked to one reporter, who asked whether he had a premonition of disaster, "Was the captain of the *Titanic* prepared for hitting the iceberg?" [17] The difference was that the captain of the *Titanic* literally went down with his ship, having failed to obey one of the basic rules of successful failure.

By 1966, Culligan turned up again in the public eye as a full-time consultant for the William J. Burns International Detective Agency, in order to study "the possible use of closed-circuit TV, microphones and other modern gadgets in advanced security systems." [18] At this time he was still drawing severance pay from Curtis, in addition to $24,000 annually for ten years. The ship had sunk, but the captain was not only in the lifeboat, but also very comfortably fixed for survival.

There are many things to be learned from a career like Culligan's, but the crucial one is never to lose self-confidence. No matter how bad the situation is, you can always announce plans for something new, something big, something even more ambitious than whatever it is that has just failed. The secret is to play for big stakes. Small gamblers find it hard to get credit, but big gamblers can always find someone to stake them.

The Perils of Optimism

Ebullient hope combined with bellicose enthusiasm will carry one far. No man ever tied together a more ambitious industrial empire with less stock control than Robert Ralph Young, the dynamic president of the New York Central, who was once described as "a pathological optimist." Optimism about railways is a form of madness that has been common to investors in every country over the past hundred fifty years. But Young was unique in persuading the public both that railways were viable in an age when it was already apparent that they were not, and that he could single-heartedly stem their decline. An aggressive, born fighter from the very beginning, Young failed at the University of Virginia and failed as a banker, even though his father owned the bank. He made a fortune by selling short in the stock market crash, thus making capital out of failure on a vast scale, and then went on to specialize in buying the assets of businesses that were failing. By 1937, so many of the businesses he had acquired were continuing to fail despite his ownership (or perhaps because of it) that he had a nervous breakdown.

He got back on top by gaining control of the huge Allegheny Corporation, and went on to fight a costly and highly publicized struggle to gain control of the New York Central, then in the process of coming to pieces completely as a carrier and a business. It was natural that a man who had made a fortune by acquiring failing companies should be obsessed by the possibility of controlling the largest failure of them all —Young pursued New York Central as Ahab hunted down Moby Dick, and with much the same result. It is worth noting that he bought his 120,000 shares of New York Central stock at $22 a share and that by his own proxy fight he drove the price up to $49.50 a share. He promised stockholders a new deal and a dividend of at least $8 a share. In fact, the highest dividend New York Central paid under Young's regime was $2 (in 1955), while its price per share tumbled from $49.50 to $13.50. By the end of his reign, Young himself had sold all but 1,200 shares of his stock—most of it, rather oddly, to his wife—and the railroad was on its way to a more or less complete disintegration and collapse.

Young lived well on the proceeds of failure and died (by his own hand, due to circumstances apparently unrelated to his business) in a magnificent twenty-five-room Palm Beach mansion. He left an estate valued at more than $6,000,000, in addition to such items as 225 acres of choice Newport property, which is not bad for a man who started work at General Motors in 1928 at $100 a week and had been zealously pursuing failure ever since.

Young's story teaches us that publicity and energy will very often substitute for any kind of real achievement. It is not so much a question of masking failure, which is what most of us do, as of exploiting it in a forceful and dynamic way. To do this, you have to realize, as Young did, that people are less interested in tangible results than in appearances, and that the appearance of action, when combined with optimism and promises, will effectively take the place of real success. Most horse racers would rather be on a long shot than a favorite, and the same is true in business.

Dealing with Your Own Failures

It is obviously more difficult to carry out this kind of success through failure in ordinary circumstances than when one is operating on the very highest financial levels. But it is by no means impossible for the ambitious upward-striver to apply many of these principles to a comparatively modest career. It is not enough just to fail—you have to fail in an interesting and ambitious way. No matter how small the job, no matter how relatively humble the circumstances, it is possible to turn your everyday failures into the equivalent of dazzling successes. There are several rules to follow:

1) *When in doubt, predict, announce and exagger-*

ate failure. It is the unexpected failure, which comes as a surprise to those above and around you, that does the most harm. If you have already predicted that something is going to fail, then on the whole you are at least likely to be given credit for some kind of intelligent realism and honesty.

2) *Apply the "Perils of Pauline" principle.* Account for failure in terms of a dramatic and lurid struggle, in which everything was done to stave off defeat. Always begin by explaining how hard you worked, how many hours you put in, and how badly you feel that they were wasted and it was all in vain. If it was a joint effort, emphasize how hard everybody worked, not just you. It is up to you to prove that you *tried,* and the sign of success is when your superior says, "Listen, you win some, you lose some. When you've done everything you can, you still can't win them all."

3) *Spread failure out.* Remember: "Success has a thousand fathers, but failure is an orphan." It is your task to reverse this truism. You must assume personal responsibility (i.e., guilt) *first,* if possible before all the facts are known, then gradually make the failure a team effort. There is a bad moment when you are stuck with the total responsibility for failure, but if you are at all adept, you can then move gradually to implicate everyone else in it, while retaining credit for your honest confession of guilt. The use of the pronoun "we" is a vital part of this technique.

The Infighter

Remember: *It is better to fail noisily than to succeed quietly.*

The case of James T. Aubrey is an excellent example of this. Aubrey, reputedly known to his foes— behind his back—as "the smiling cobra," set a high standard for what was generally held to be efficient ruthlessness while president of the CBS television network.

Cool, elegant, energetic, handsome and physically fit, Aubrey was a sophisticated Princeton graduate who set out to please the mass audience he once referred to as called "the soft underbelly of America." His reputation was such that people even assumed William Paley, the formidable founder of the company and chairman of the board, was frightened of Aubrey. Aubrey seemed to share this view, and once was said to have told a friend, "Paley can't ax me when I've made him $40 million—as long as I build up the stock and drive the ratings up, no one's going to give me a hard time." [19]

In 1963 Aubrey was paid $224,000, and produced $45 million of CBS Inc.'s $87 million of pre-tax profits. He was, in everyone's eyes, a winner, in fact, one associate remarked, "he doesn't want to win by a foot, but by a mile." [20] He was also described by one observer as "far more overbearing than a really successful man need be." [21]

He had, as Murray Kempton reported after his fall, a favorite story about himself as an absolute power:

"One Saturday in midterm, Aubrey invited CBS-TV's vice president in charge of programing to meet him in the office that morning. The vice president assumed that they were to discuss the program schedule and he began dutifully to recite the status and condition of each project. He had gone on for 40 minutes when Aubrey said softly, 'You're through, Hub.'

"The vice president answered that he was indeed almost through with his presentation but had a few things to add.

"'No, Hub,' Aubrey said, 'I mean *you're* through. I called you in today so you can get your things out of your desk and won't have to do it Monday in front of all the secretaries.' " [22]

This kind of thing may be satisfying, but it is basically counter-productive. In Aubrey's case, it led to the assumption that he was tougher than his boss,

William Paley, or than the president of CBS Inc., the brilliant Dr. Frank Stanton. By 1965, they moved to resume control and show the world that they and CBS could get along without Aubrey. After five years as president of CBS-TV, Aubrey was "through." In 1964 CBS's Nielsen rating lead was 22.5 to NBC's 18.8 and ABC's 17.6, while in 1965 they were at a dead heat. In his own terms, let alone Paley's, Aubrey's star had waned. "He who lives by the ratings," as they say, "dies by the ratings." Now he was even the subject of jokes. Referring to Aubrey's reputedly exciting private life, Goodman Ace remarked, "You have to get up pretty early in the morning to keep ahead of [Paley and Stanton], and Aubrey was always known to get in around four." Everybody wrote Aubrey off, except perhaps Jacqueline Susann, who said, "He could do anything for all I care, he was an exciting man," while her husband, Irving Mansfield, eulogized Aubrey on national television as "a dedicated public servant." The rest of the world was more of the opinion that like Icarus he had risen too high, fallen and drowned.

To connoisseurs of success, however, it should have come as no surprise that Aubrey surfaced shortly as president of the ailing movie giant, Metro-Goldwyn-Mayer, Inc. M-G-M had fallen on sad times since the days when it was "the home of the stars." It was losing $14 million a year on the record business, and $58 million a year on its movies. It had only just survived a bitter fight for ownership between Kirk Kerkorian (sometimes called "the Avis of Las Vegas" because his real estate holdings there were second only to those of Howard Hughes) and Edgar Bronfman, then president of Seagram & Sons. Kerkorian won control of M-G-M, allegedly with the help of Aristotle Onassis and Bernard Cornfeld, and by borrowing $72 million at an interest of 13 percent. Introduced to Aubrey by Gregson Bautzer, the jet-set Beverly Hills attorney, Kerkorian unhesitatingly chose Aubrey to take over M-G-M. As Hubbell Robinson, one of Aubrey's former subordinates at CBS, remarked, "I think they're going to have to teach Leo the Lion to hiss."

Aubrey waded in, announcing, "I have no nostalgic hang-ups." In a much-publicized auction, he sold off M-G-M's collection of props and costumes, including Jean Harlow's black lace gown, and the knee breeches worn by Marlon Brando in *Mutiny on the Bounty*. Forty percent of the personnel were axed, the 176-acre back lot at Culver City was sold off to a real estate developer, and much of the company's production schedule was canceled. Aubrey then set out to restore the toothless lion's fortunes with exploitation films like *Shaft in Africa* and *Skyjacked,* while systematically liquidating the company's remaining assets. In the *New York Times,* Vincent Canby wrote that his reign was "the realization of everyone's worst fears of what would happen to Hollywood when the money men take over."

Aubrey began cutting and reshaping M-G-M films, and announced that "My definition of a successful film is one that makes money," [23] thus exposing himself to hostility, both from critics, who wrongly resented his attitude, and from those who expected the new M-G-M films to make money. (It is always a mistake to expose yourself to criticism by making ambitious predictions or pronouncements.) In the meantime, Kerkorian had taken M-G-M into the hotel business, apparently seeking to beat Howard Hughes out as Number One in Las Vegas. At first, Aubrey was enthusiastic, and rejoiced over the forthcoming profits of the slot machines, a thousand of which were to be spotted throughout the facility. "The vigorish,"* he commented, "is going to be significantly profitable." [24] Alas, before this prediction could come true, Aubrey was out. Once again, he walked away to the comfort of his stock and termination pay, ready for the next call to duty. As Neil Hickey comments, it is surprising

---

* Underworld slang for a loan shark's exorbitant interest.

that he was not subsequently asked to head the Department of Defense.

You Can Never Be a Failure!

The stories of Culligan, Young and Aubrey illustrate an important point. Projects fail, plans fail, companies fail—*you* need not.

Furthermore, failure has its positive points:

• *Failure provides you with a pause in which to reassess your motives, your abilities and your opportunities.* A career of uninterrupted success would not only be dull, but would probably peak early, for want of any real opportunity for self-examination or self-criticism.

• *Failure can sometimes be made to seem more dramatic and exciting in some ways than success.* Very often, the best way of drawing attention to our abilities is to fail on a major scale.

• *Failure teaches you far more than success ever can,* if only because failure sharpens the survival instincts, and forces you to learn your business or profession in depth and detail. It is on the way down that we learn how things work. On the way up, we are enjoying the ride too much to pay attention.

• *Failure is the best school for success.* There is nothing like it for hardening the will and maturing the personality.

Therefore, do not be afraid to fail. You are joining a distinguished fellowship! The Duke of Wellington was so great a failure as a young man that his own mother described him as "no better than food for powder." He was packed off in disgust to the Army, where he became a national hero, a field-marshal and the victor of Waterloo. Einstein was a backward student and an unsuccessful mathematics teacher. Franklin Delano Roosevelt was judged a mediocrity and "a lightweight" by almost everybody who knew him, even after he was elected governor of New York State, and his own mother not only shared this disparaging opinion of her son's abilities but vocally expressed it to anyone who would listen. Napoleon languished for many years as an artillery officer of little promise. Dwight D. Eisenhower might have remained an unsuccessful major in a dusty Midwestern Army post for the rest of his life, a failure in everybody's eyes, had he not come to the attention of then Colonel George C. Marshall because he was "the best damned bridge player in the United States Army." Howard Hughes was a conspicuous failure at every school he was sent to, and was thought not worth sending to college.

Remember: Early promise seldom blooms, and success without the tempering effect of failure is seldom long-lasting.

"He Travels the Fastest Who Travels Alone . . ."

One of the paradoxical things about failure is that those who love you may unconsciously *want* you to fail. Failure is sometimes more comfortable, easier to live with, for your wife, mother, husband or children.

Most marriages can withstand failure, but success has a dangerous tendency to destroy the relationship quickly. In the case of a woman, failure in the business or professional world is not only less threatening to her husband and children, but may even be expected and rewarded. In the case of a man, he often finds that his wife will accept far more easily a pattern of failure, despite the financial disadvantages, than the changes that inevitably accompany success. We have all known marriages that endured years of poverty and broke up the moment the man succeeded: a woman spends years supporting her husband, but is often unprepared for the strain and tension that develop when he unexpectedly succeeds.

As one successful executive told me, discussing the collapse of his marriage, "Everything went fine so long as I was a failure. Jane never complained that we couldn't move to a larger apartment or buy a lot of the things we wanted. She felt safe because we formed, I guess, a small, enclosed world. Then suddenly I was making a lot of money, and I began to look outward and gain self-confidence. I needed her less, it's as simple as that, and every step up I took was against her pulling me back down. As a failure, she had control of me. As a success, she felt her control slipping, and it scared her. I was scared to stop, and she was scared to watch me go on, and finally I couldn't stand it any more and I left. Success gave me a new life, but it didn't improve the old one, and I could see it wasn't going to. Success in Jane's eyes was a kind of betrayal. I think if I gave up my job and went back to her, she'd be perfectly happy because she'd have me 100 percent again. But no way."

We must also beware of the fact that those who love us may conspire in our failure. This is an imperceptible but extremely destructive process. I once knew a couple, Mark and Helen, who had married young and were in everybody's eyes an "ideal" couple. He was a bright and ambitious young journalist, poor and Jewish, she was a journalist on a competing magazine, from a wealthy WASP background. For him, the marriage was a blessing—it gave him financial security, since her trust fund allowed them to live well above the standard of their joint salaries. Sharing a common profession, they were never bored with each other's work, and seemed perfectly mated.

Gradually, however, Helen began to sap Mark's will to succeed. He loved cooking, so she encouraged him to cook exotic and elaborate meals, to spend his time shopping and preparing food when he should have been working. She indulged his desire to collect antiques, and urged him to spend his weekends walking through antique shops and refinishing the things he found. By careful degrees, she tamed him, reduced him to the level where his work was no longer competitive with hers, and eliminated him as a threat to her own ego and ambitions. At no point did she ever attack Mark or openly undercut his masculinity. She simply made sure that he became too contented to be ambitious, until laziness and self-indulgence finally sapped his will to succeed. Now he was a gifted amateur chef, their home was full of beautifully restored furniture—but Mark's career faltered; he was soon out of a job, while Helen soared to the top management of her magazine.

If Mark had *wanted* to live this way, there would have been no cause for complaint. There is, after all, no good reason why the man in a marriage should not fulfill the domestic role. But Mark *hadn't* wanted to fail in his profession. Instead of getting the support he needed, he had been cleverly and deliberately undermined. When he realized this, as he eventually did, he moved out to the West Side YMCA and launched into his career again.

The lesson is that we must be careful to avoid settling into those comfortable roles of risk-free failure which the people who love us may well find it convenient for us to adopt, or may honestly think are best for us.

In some cases, married people share a *symbiotic* failure. A husband or wife who fears success for himself or herself will deliberately prevent the spouse from succeeding, as if failure were more bearable when shared equally. The operative sentiment in such cases is "Never mind what other people think, you're good enough for me!" This phrase, used by men and women, is a warning signal not to be ignored if you want to get ahead. It is dangerous to fall into the habit of failing in order to please others. Instead, you should learn how to drag those close to you *upward* toward success along with you!

There is a psychological truth here which must be

taken into account: the more you allow yourself to be thought of by other people as a failure, the more likely you are in the end to regard yourself as one. Therefore all the disparagements that are the small change of life are to be guarded against strongly. Do not *let* yourself be criticized, diminished, made fun of or "put down" by anyone near to you, however much you may love them. In order to succeed you must first persuade yourself that you are a success, and in order to do that, you need the support and backing of other people's belief in the possibility of your success.

It is, of course, possible to overcome other people's view of you as a failure, and as we have seen, many great men have done just that. But it requires a lot of will power to succeed against everyone's preconceived view of you as a natural failure. In most cases, *their* opinion (particularly if "they" are close to you) tends to become *your* opinion of yourself, and holds you back. It is hard enough to succeed in the first place, without having to fight your family to do so. You must begin by convincing those around you that you can succeed, you must encourage them at every opportunity to share your own belief and determination, and you must teach them to take a positive attitude toward each step you take on the road to success.

The popular notion that the family that fails together, stays together is not necessarily true. It is important to talk about your work and your ambitions, equally important not to complain and ask for sympathy because you work hard or have problems. Create a positive environment for yourself in which your success is shared, understood and enjoyed.

Many people—men especially—go out into the world every day to be dazzling, charming and successful, and return home every night to take out their fatigue, their irritations, their fears and their bad temper on their families. Under the circumstances, it is hardly surprising that they fail to find in their families any kind of real support for their further ambitions. There is nothing wrong with shoptalk—indeed, for many of us it is the only subject on which we are likely to be interesting, knowledgable and enthusiastic—but it should be positive and informative, not simply an account of the terrible things that happened to you during the course of the day.

As women are forever saying to their husbands— and not a few husbands are learning to say to their wives—"If you hate it so much, why do it?" It is a question bound to enrage, and in fact *designed* to, because if the point were pushed to its logical conclusion the answer would normally have to be "I'm doing it because I want to," in which case the complaints and demands for sympathy are unjustified and irrational. Do not become a martyr to success; nobody ever succeeded who didn't want to, and if it weren't worth the effort and the troubles, you wouldn't reach for it in the first place. Enjoy it!

And do not be afraid of failure, or ashamed of it. The road to success is a long one, and day-to-day judgments may be very deceptive. You have to be strong enough to believe in your own goal, whatever other people think of it, and to bear in mind that success lies in the final accomplishment of your hopes and dreams, and cannot be measured at any single point in a lifetime, but only at the end.

In the words of Martin Buber, "When we consider the history of Moses we see how much failure is mingled in the one great successful action, so much so that when we set the individual events which made up his history side by side, we see that his life consists of one failure after another, through which runs the thread of success. True, Moses brought the people out of Egypt; but each stage of this leadership is a failure. Whenever he comes to deal with the people, he is defeated by them, lets God ever so often interfere and punish them. And the real history of this leadership is not the history of the exodus, but the history of the wandering in the desert. The personal history of Moses' own life, too, does not point back to his youth, and to what grew out of it; it points beyond, to death, to the death of the unsuccessful man, whose work, it is true, survives him, but only in new defeats, new disappointments, and continual new failures—and yet his work survives also in a hope beyond all these failures."[25]

PART 3

The Meaning of Success

Your Right to Succeed

People do not lack strength; they lack will.
—Victor Hugo

SUCCESS: THE AMERICAN CREDO

In our culture success is a long journey, not a destination: training and enduring count. In other, older societies, it has sometimes been possible to achieve a certain measure of success, then stop, secure in one's own self-esteem and the recognition of one's peers. Most of the ancient orders of chivalry were created to reward success of one kind or another. And traditional honors and rewards still provide a useful and stable system for measuring achievement.

Americans may not realize the extent and care with which the governments of other countries reward their successful citizens. In France, for example, a civilian may be awarded any one of twenty-four major decorations, each of which has between three and five classes, ranging from the ultimate prestige of the Grand Cross of the Legion of Honor or the slightly less prestigious National Order of Merit (which was created by General De Gaulle because he felt that too many nobodies were getting the Legion of Honor) to a vast array of decorations for civic success, including the "Mérite Touristique"" (for hotel keepers) and the "Ordre du Mérite Postal" (three classes—Commander, Officer, and Knight of the Order of Postal Merit—with a five-pointed gold star bearing allegorical images representing post, telephone and telegraph services, and a ribbon with two black border stripes symbolizing telephone wires). No French achiever need feel left out: awards exist for sports, labor, commerce, teaching, the arts, public health, maternity, and almost everything else, not to speak of such exotica as the Order of Nichan-el-Anouar (colonial service) and the Order of the Black Star (for Africans). The small ribbon on a Frenchman's buttonhole represents a visible step upward in a recognized hierarchy.

Human nature being what it is, Americans have substituted a variety of private rewards systems for those that might otherwise be created by the government. These involve a number of special arrangements, privileges and status symbols, but the common denominator of American society is simply money. Success can usually be measured by the amount a person has made or will make at a given point in a career. Money is in any case a particularly effective status system in a democratic, egalitarian society, since it transcends class distinctions, educational differences and all questions of style, charm and appearance.

"Religion Demands Success"

Money and success constitute, after all, the American Way—our national myth, like fair play for the English or military glory for the French. It is the dream of success, in the sense of "making it," and making it in as big a way as possible, that motivates most Americans, and has been a major force in American history. It was not so much freedom that drew our ancestors here as the desire to succeed.

Our national success myth is derived from the Puritans, and to a lesser degree the Quakers. Ostensibly they fled to America in search of religious freedom (as one descendant put it, "the Puritans came to the New World to practice their religion freely and to prevent others from doing the same"), and were determined to remain here. Like Moses leading the Jews to the Promised Land, they had no intention of returning to the fleshpots of the Old World, where they had already aroused the hatred of their neighbors. Pious, quarrelsome and eminently practical, the Puritans brought to the shores of New England a traditional English view of justice and society with a very radical approach to ethics and profit. The Mayflower settlers demonstrated their sturdy English heritage by their first act on American soil—they hanged one of their number who had murdered a woman during the crossing, thus establishing the continuity of the British approach to crime and punishment on both sides of the Atlantic. In this, they were traditionalists; in other respects, they believed in what then amounted to an extremist Protestant ideal—the sanctity of works.

Until the seventeenth century, the Roman Catholic Church had generally adhered to the ancient Christian belief that it is easier for a camel to pass through the eye of a needle than for a rich man to enter the Kingdom of Heaven. Needless to say, this belief did not prevent the rich from controlling the Church nor deter Churchmen from the desire to become rich themselves. Nobody expected the entrance requirements of the Kingdom of Heaven, whatever they might be, to be applied to the Vatican or the See of Canterbury. Still, in theory, the Church was bound up in the mystique of poverty, and there was a general consensus that comfort, success and honors in this world would have to paid for in the next. What is more, entry to the Kingdom of Heaven was assured by ritual—no matter how great the sin, confession and absolution were sufficient to assure salvation; no matter how virtuous the life, the rites must still be observed.

Protestantism shattered this comforting edifice by leaving man to deal with his own conscience and his own Maker. If a man prospered, it must be with God's blessing, and his prosperity must therefore be pleasing in the eyes of God. Successful labor was the sign of God's approval, from which it was swiftly con-

cluded that successful labor was the best way of
pleasing God, and the more successful one was, the
more He would be pleased.

Even John Wesley, the dour founder of Methodism,
remarked that "It is man's duty to make all the money
he can and keep all he can . . ." [1] He subsequently
advised giving as much of it as possible away, but the
basic religious exhortation to become rich was heard
with more attention than the cautionary warning attached to it.

Wesley had succeeded in creating a credo peculiarly
suited to the needs of the time, when a vast increase
in wealth was about to make possible the rise of the
common man. Henceforth, material success and religious virtue were to be inextricably intertwined in the
Protestant consciousness. A hundred years later,
echoes of Wesley's revolutionary statement were still
reverberating in the ears of American congregations.
William Makepeace Thayer, who eventually abandoned his Congregationalist pulpit to preach the gospel of success in books and pamphlets, exhorted the
Christians of late nineteenth-century America to remember that "Religion requires the following very
reasonable things in secular affairs, namely that man
should make the most of himself possible . . . *Indeed,
religion demands success.*"[2] (Italics added.)

To be sure, Protestants of all sects deemed it necessary for a Christian to be virtuous as well as prosperous, but it did not take long before the belief set
in that prosperity and virtue were synonymous, especially in England, where a rising middle class was
cut off from the rewards and honors lavished on the
aristocracy. Protestants in general have shown a
marked respect for worldly goods, together with a
noteworthy lack of enthusiasm for all those bedraggled
and eccentric saints who demonstrated their piety by
extreme poverty and self-deprivation. In their attempt
to destroy the "heathen idolatry" of Catholicism—
the stained glass windows, the incense, the robes and
the ritual—the Puritans also turned away from the

traditional Christian fascination with beggars, lepers, cripples and madmen. They had no desire to wash the feet of the poor or to talk to the birds and animals, like St. Francis of Assisi. The poor and miserable were no longer blessed but merely shiftless.

The Fear of Enjoyment

If the Puritans were clearly in favor of making money, they were ambivalent on the subject of spending it. Success might be proof of godliness and virtue, but it was important in their eyes not to enjoy or flaunt it, as if the basic fear of Puritanism was that "someone, somewhere, may be happy."[3] Prudence, virtue and thrift were joined to hard work, industry and ambition. Displaying good fortune was almost as bad as poverty, since it carried with it the risk of offending the Almighty. Indeed, the Puritans were very conscious that what God gave He might take away, and this pervading fear gave them all the more reason to accumulate worldly goods in anticipation of some Divine change of mind.

These beliefs etched themselves deeply into the American consciousness, in part because the Puritans were successful, and therefore influential, in part because a new nation requires a new credo. Europeans, particularly Catholics and Anglicans, had always been tolerant of failure and poverty, a position that was all the more easy to justify as long as one believed that the poor were particularly beloved by God. In the New World, poverty and failure were less easily accepted, both because of the unyielding belief that those who failed deserved nothing better and because the country itself was so big, so rich, so untapped that failure seemed proof of weakness and sloth.

From Cape Cod to the unknown West, the land waited to be cleared and plowed. In Europe or England, a man might fail honorably or be born to failure, for the rigid social hierarchies and divisions of wealth ensured that most people would live and die in poverty—in England, the urban poor were doomed to disease and drunken despair, in France the peasant was held in servitude by feudal laws and taxes, in Poland, where there was no primogeniture, small holdings of land were divided from generation to generation between the sons until a man might find himself forced to eke a living out of a plot no bigger than a kitchen garden, with fields so widely separated that over 30 percent of the arable land consisted of roads and paths.[4]

In the New World, no such constrictions existed—there was land aplenty for everyone, and for those who did not choose to clear and tame the wilderness, the opportunities for trading and commerce were almost as good. Under the circumstances, failure was difficult to excuse or explain. After all, it was a man's duty to make use of his opportunities, and the opportunities were limitless, so if he failed, the fault must be his own. In what other country could a man grow rich so quickly? And in what other country could a clergyman preach, as did Russell Conwell in his sermon entitled "Acres of Diamonds" (delivered over 6,000 times to millions of listeners), "While we should sympathize with God's poor—that is, those who cannot help themselves—let us remember that there is not a poor person in the United States who was not made poor by his own shortcomings, or by the shortcomings of someone else—it is all wrong to be poor, anyhow."[5]

Puritan idealism had glossed over the inherent materialism of a society committed to rugged individualism and personal profit by arguing that success was a form of prayer. As the strength of that idealism waned, materialism became respectable in its own right—it was no longer something that had to be justified or apologized for, or supported by Scripture. The national character of the United States was set at an early stage for that enormous increase in prosperity, industry, wealth and nervous tension that is so recognizably the heart of The American Way of Life, and which was perfectly described by Andrew Carnegie: "The old nations of the earth creep on at a snail's pace; the Republic thunders past with the rush of the express. The United States . . . is destined soon to outstrip all others in the race." [6]

For Americans, almost from the beginning, life was a race—competitive, demanding, exhilarating. Nobody wanted to miss the express. In other cultures, success and failure might be thought of as a game of chance, cruel perhaps, dishonest in that some players were manifestly favored over others, but essentially arbitrary and predetermined. Here, success was a duty and an overwhelming concern, as if the sheer size of the country were a challenge to conquer. Americans threw themselves with passion and intensity into the pursuit of "the bitch-goddess" on a scale never seen before in the history of mankind, confident that success would not only be rewarded here below, but above.

As the settlers moved Westward, new waves of immigrants followed in their wake, fortunes were made in cotton, California gold, whiskey, land. But the Puritan orthodoxy survived, a genetic strain in the American bloodstream. No matter how great the success, it could never be great enough, and it must never be enjoyed for its own sake. Success was to be taken seriously, and the will to succeed was firmly established as a religious duty, not to be confused for a moment with pleasure. The Puritans thus prepared the way for the modern corporate executive who works sixty hours or more a week and lives for his work.

The "Log Cabin" Myth

In America, success has always been easy to measure. It is the distance between one's origins and one's final achievement that matters, the extreme example being symbolized in the old political slogan "From log cabin to the White House." Americans believed, with some justification, that the land offered an equal opportunity to everyone, and that everyone owed it to himself to "get ahead" in it. In other countries, men inflated the nobility and wealth of their ancestors as they made their way up; in America, the reverse was true. Successful men exaggerated the poverty and hardships of their childhoods, for a man's achievements were greater if he had begun the journey in circumstances of deprivation and misery.

Even in our own day, politicians are instinctively drawn to this aspect of the national myth. Richard M. Nixon laced his speeches with references to how poor his childhood was; in fact he seems to have come from a typically comfortable middle-class American household. Lyndon B. Johnson went so far as to create a whole popular image of himself as a kind of Texas young Abe Lincoln, walking barefoot to school from a humble cabin. In fact, his parents were comparatively well-to-do and well-connected. Hubert Humphrey orated about his youth as if he had grown up in the wilderness and studied by candlelight, which seems doubtful in the case of a relatively prosperous Minneapolis druggist's son. Where it is impossible to fabricate a humble and impoverished childhood, as in the case of John F. Kennedy, the hardships of a stern and demanding upbringing are substituted. The legends about old Joe Kennedy's harsh attitude toward his sons derive from a need to show that Jack Kennedy, though born into a rich and powerful family and educated at Choate and Harvard, had suffered, had "paid his dues." Nothing did more harm to the presidential aspirations of Thomas E. Dewey or Nelson Rockefeller than the fact that they were unable to connect themselves in any way to the national rags-to-riches myth. Few remarks can have done as much political damage as Harold Ickes' famous description of Wendell Wilkie as "the barefoot boy from Wall Street."

This characteristic of American life has scarcely diminished with time and social change. Successful businessmen today will reminisce happily about their poverty-striken childhoods, when they played stickball under the Third Avenue El, went hungry and earned their pocket money by delivering groceries. In a great many cases, a careful examination will reveal that they were in fact the children of prosperous parents, and were probably taken past the Third Avenue El, if at all, by their nannies. They have simply manufactured a background that makes their success that much more dramatic and "inspiring."

The first person to hit upon this peculiarly American device of downward self-promotion was Benjamin Franklin, who succeeded in convincing his audience that Poor Richard and Franklin were one and the same person. Franklin consistently exaggerated the poverty and obscurity of his youth, just as he went to great efforts to conceal the shrewd, manipulative and ambitious side of his character in favor of that bogus figure the pious Quaker. At the same time, Franklin's writings strongly emphasized the value of material success. The maxims of Poor Richard preach a *morality of purpose,* in which industry, temperance, frugality and order are valuable not so much in themselves, or because they might be pleasing to God, as simply because they will make the reader prosperous. It was not for nothing that the first collection of Poor Richard's maxims was called *The Way to Wealth*—Franklin had given his countrymen a code of behavior whose end was profit. Just as Cotton Mather had provided a rationale for worshiping God, by making him a kind of cosmic business partner, Franklin provided a rationale for civic virtue, self-restraint and self-improvement, as the necessary ingredients for the successful accumulation of wealth.

The religious justification of success was now supported by a secular ethic—it was not only one's duty to God to strive for wealth (one Baptist divine told his flock, "I say that you ought to get rich, and it is your duty to get rich . . .") but also a *civic* duty and a duty toward oneself. To be *born* poor was a blessing, provided one availed oneself of the opportunities and rose from rags to riches; to *die* poor was the ultimate curse, the final expression of the failure to maintain or launch one's upward journey.

The upward journey became the central American myth, the very purpose of American life, symbolized by the success of Horatio Alger's novels, which were bought in the millions, and served as inspirational guides to several generations of American youth. Newer immigrant groups, the Jews and the Italians, were trapped by the desperate desire to hold on to their own children, to preserve their identity and the family unit in a strange and hostile world, but the success ethic demanded that each generation should rise as far as it could from its origins, and, like the Pied Piper, drew children away from their parents. To stay at home was to fail, and the decisive measure of a man's success was how much distance he could put between himself and his parents.

Nor was extreme youth an impediment to learning the virtues of success. Between 1836 and 1900 over 122,000,000 copies of William Holmes McGuffey's *Eclectic Reader* were sold, through which children learned the success ethic along with their ABCs. In them the message was clear: "The road to wealth, to honor, to usefulness . . . is open to all, and all who will, may enter upon it with the almost certain prospect of success." The desire to succeed was encouraged and nurtured, the justification for getting rich was spelled out precisely: "God gives a great deal of money to some persons, in order that they may assist those who are poor."

American education, like American religion, was committed to the idea of success—to succeed was to take advantage of the American Dream, and to fulfill one's duty toward God and Country, and each new wave of immigration brought with it a renewed commitment to the success ethic, for after all, the immigrants came here to succeed, or at the very least to make possible their children's success. To travel thousands of miles and fail in the land of golden opportunity would be—and, of course, was for many—the ultimate defeat, and if anything could be said to unite the disparate people who came here to become Americans it was the belief in upward mobility.

What is more, each wave of immigration increased the intensity of the struggle for those who were already here. As a newly arrived ethnic group struggled to rise and become prosperous, it competed with those who had already begun to move upward. The Irish fought their way up out of the slums of New York and Boston at the expense of the least successful Protestants, annexing the police departments and the political machinery of the great cities, until they in turn were threatened by the Jews and then the Italians. The rise of each ethnic group increased the competition for those who had already "made it," however marginally, for even in the United States there were only so many jobs, civil service appointments and business opportunities to go around.

Inevitably, the rise of a new ethnic group drove out the weakest members of the group above it, leaving them isolated in urban or rural poverty, so that success was, in effect, a mandate for survival. In a country without a common religion, the determination to get ahead served very well as the national creed— and getting ahead was usually defined as working hard and making money.

Vulgar Money

Making money has always been one of mankind's more powerful and universal desires, perhaps second only to sexual satisfaction. And like sex it has always been camouflaged with a certain amount of hypocrisy. In most cultures, the process of making money was usually regarded as somewhat vulgar. *Having* money was perfectly respectable everywhere, but the business of acquiring it, like child-birth in Victorian times, was best kept hidden.

There were many reasons for this. In medieval times, the Christian prohibition against usury made most business dealings seem morally suspect, and the ambition to rise from one social class to another was regarded by most right-thinking people as an offense against God and the King, and a threat to established order. The French Revolution and England's Industrial Revolution unleashed ambition on a large scale, and indeed one of Bonaparte's promises was to maintain the revolutionary ideal of "Every career open to talent," a natural enough sentiment in a man whose own career was to provide the nineteenth century with the most stunning example of just how far a self-made man could go. Nevertheless, making money still remained a somewhat sordid idea to most people, however emancipated they were politically. When Napoleon talked about opening careers to talent he meant the Army, the Navy and the professions—in effect, the removal of the class barriers that had made promotion within the State hierarchy an aristocratic monopoly for centuries. But even though Napoleon and his relatives acquired prodigious wealth, most of it from the spoils of the Emperor's campaigns, he had nothing but contempt for money-gathering as such. His dismissal of the English as "a nation of shopkeepers" is typical of the eighteenth-century attitude toward trade and the mechanics of acquiring wealth.

In England, the attitude toward shopkeepers differed little from Napoleon's. Gentlemen were born with money, the poor lived only for drink and violence, and both groups regarded the pious aspirations and the commitment to hard work of the emerging middle class with contempt and hatred. And indeed there *is* something ridiculous about those solid, bourgeois figures of the early nineteenth century, serious, self-important men who worked hard (and worked their employees even harder), saved money and paid their debts. Gentlemen seldom felt obliged to pay their creditors, and both King George IV and King William IV of England died hundreds of thousands of pounds in debt, after lifetimes of unpaid bills and protracted bankruptcies. Well into the twentieth century, English gentlefolk thought it a mark of breeding not to pay tradesmen; a middle-class banker paid his tailor's bill, but a marquess would never have dreamed of paying promptly, if at all—it was a crucial social difference in the age before credit buying.

Prudery about money was something of an English national characteristic, and people went to extraordinary lengths to disguise the fact that they, or their ancestors, had worked to acquire it. Two generations removed from "trade" were thought the minimum necessary to render a fortune "respectable" in society's eyes. Much of Victorian literature revolves around the alarming discovery that behind some respectable middle-class fortune there lurks the sinister memory of the man who actually acquired it. Young Pip's horror of the convict Magwitch, his anonymous benefactor in Charles Dickens' *Great Expectations,* is fairly typical of the genteel attitude toward making money, and is echoed in the literature and the life of the time.

In Shaw's *Major Barbara,* young Stephen Undershaft expresses the "respectable" attitude toward money very accurately when he tells his father, the millionaire arms manufacturer, with a nice blend of moral superiority and priggishness, "You are very properly proud of having been industrious enough to make money, and it is greatly to your credit that you have made so much of it . . . It is natural enough for you to think that money governs England, but you must allow me to think I know better."[7]

The Gospel of Wealth

America was the first country in which making money was *respectable*. "Here," said one French visitor, "there is no hypocrisy about money, and little interest in anything else." Most people agreed that the particular excitement of America, what William James called "the bottled-lightning" character of the American personality, came from this consuming interest in the hectic business of getting—and staying—ahead.

The gospel of wealth was peculiarly American, but it also exerted a potent fascination on foreigners as well. As early as 1858, an audience of over 3,000 Englishmen packed St. James Hall in London to hear Phineas T. Barnum lecture on "The Art of Money-Getting." His performance was preceded by a massed band playing "Yankee Doodle," and he was to deliver this lecture over a hundred times in England, to wildly enthusiastic audiences. He was defining the American credo, preaching about material gain as if it constituted a religion, and drawing the parallel between Christianity and success.

In a country where self-made men were treated with contempt, Barnum's gospel of success created a vivid sensation, and did much to establish the belief among Englishmen that Americans were "go-getters." Barnum, with shrewd instinct and a showman's flair, had not only picked the right subject to lecture on, but also understood that it was something about which Americans were presumed to have a special expertise. Over a century has passed, but the world still feels very much the same about America and what it has to offer: Americans may think they have a right, possibly an obligation to teach the world about democracy, justice or morality, but in most countries the natives merely want to learn how to become as rich as Americans. On the subject of success Americans are universally listened to with a respect that is denied to them in other areas.

It is thus scarcely surprising to find that Dale Carnegie's *How to Win Friends and Influence People* (of which nearly 10,000,000 copies have been sold in the United States since it was published in 1936) has been published in thirty languages, and is read with avid interest by Turks, Burmese and the blind.[8] The gospel of success is the voice of America, whether it is interpreted by Carnegie, Smiley Blanton, the Reverend Norman Vincent Peale or Bruce Barton. Barton took the American tradition of combining religion and success to its ultimate form in his famous best seller, *The Man Nobody Knows,* when he wrote: "[Jesus] was the most popular dinner guest in Jerusalem! A failure! He picked up twelve men from the bottom ranks of business and forged them into an organization that conquered the world."

The description of Jesus as the successful president of a large corporation (of which His Father, presumably, is the absentee chairman of the board) is interesting enough as an example of the Protestant belief in the success ethic carried to its logical extreme. But more interesting is Barton's angry dismissal of the notion that Jesus might be considered by some to be a "failure." Barton recognized that the conventional portrait of Jesus as a sacrificial victim would have little appeal to those who believed in dynamic success, and therefore set out to prove that Jesus was in fact what every American wanted to be—a winner. Not only was secular success pleasing to God, but the Son of God was shown to have come down to earth to compete with other men, working as the world's greatest salesman: "Surely no one will consider us lacking in reverence if we say that every one of the principles of modern salesmanship, on which businessmen so much pride themselves, are brilliantly exemplified in Jesus' talk and work," putting together Christianity in his role as the world's most successful executive, and becoming "Jerusalem's most popular dinner guest in his leisure time . . ."

Dedicated Employees?

What one psychiatrist calls "the central urge to master life"[9] is present in each of us, reinforced and sometimes exaggerated by the nature of our society. In no other country is this "central urge" so relentlessly pursued; in many countries it is not even *understood*. The Japanese, despite the fact that they have taken a wild and unexpected lunge into the modern urban-industrial world, remain rigid believers in hierarchy. Even when they claim to be formulating their own version of the American success gospel, they somehow miss the point. A recent announcement from the Matsushita Electric Company (with sales in 1975 of $4.6 billion) sounds at first glance like the standard American corporate exhortation to succeed, but in fact reflects a very different message.

Matsushita people don't work just to enlarge a bookkeeping entry. They work to enrich society by developing themselves . . . Konosuke Matsushita has done this by emphasizing *personal* growth, of workers and executives alike. By urging people to make the most of themselves, he has created an environment in which a person's job becomes a primary source of self-development and self-esteem. The result is 82,000 dedicated employees.

Most Americans would agree that "self-development and self-esteem" are important qualities, and in no country is "personal growth" pursued with the energy it is here, whether through the Dale Carnegie Course in Effective Speaking and Human Relations, Werner Erhardt's EST, the Maharishi Mahesh Yogi's Transcendental Meditation movement, or the Alexander Hamilton Institute ("Once you feel that vital inspiration to get ahead . . ."). We may get the message from Dr. Peale's sermons at New York's Marble Collegiate Church ("Never entertain a failure thought") or from the back of matchbooks ("YOU *can* succeed!"), but nobody can argue that Americans do not believe in self-development and personal growth—indeed the problem of our society may be that we believe in nothing else. However, most of us would not assume that the purpose of personal growth is to make us "dedicated employees."

The whole point of succeeding and "growing" in America is to become independent, to rise from one's origins to some far-away personal dream of wealth and success, to mold the world around us to our desires, rather than to be placed in a predesigned slot by someone else. Our American aim is to remake the world in our own image, not to fit into someone else's scheme of how it should be.

"Now You Won't Get a Toy"

Americans find it harder than most people to think of themselves in collective terms. The old dream of independence—of being one's own man, or woman—dies hard, even in an age of corporations, labor unions and civil service bureaucracies. "The reaffirmation of our competitive spirit" is so highly valued that former President Richard M. Nixon used it as the somewhat inappropriate theme of his Labor Day address in 1971, drawing a special contrast between the collective approach of other countries and certain American "special-interest groups," (presumably labor unions) and "the morality of individual self-reliance."

This competitive spirit is bred into us at a very early age. In a recent study of the difference in competitive spirit between Anglo-American and Mexican-American children in Los Angeles, it emerged that while Mexican children cooperated with each other and with Anglo children in the experiments, Anglo-American children were, by comparison, "systematically irrational," and displayed a competitive spirit that would have given President Nixon great satisfaction.

Ten-year-old Anglo-American children repeatedly failed to get rewards for which they were striving because they competed in games that required co-operation. In other situations these children worked hard and even sacrificed their own rewards in order to reduce the rewards of their peers . . . Anglo-American children defended their possession of toys . . . and never submitted to having their toys taken away. Anglo-American children are not only irrationally competitive, they are almost sadistically rivalrous. Given a choice, Anglo-American children took toys away from their peers on 7 percent of the trials even when they could not keep the toys for themselves. Observing the success of their actions, some of the children gloated "Ha! Ha! Now you won't get a toy!" . . . Mexican mothers tend to reinforce their children noncontingently, rewarding them whether they succeed or fail, whereas Anglo-American mothers tend to reinforce their children as a rigid function of the child's achievement.[10]

The Germ of Greatness

Disagreeable as these children may sound, they are recognizably our own (and ourselves). Ours is a society that requires and rewards a high level of competitive spirit, and values it far above cooperation and team-playing.

Winning is more natural. We don't have to produce the desire to succeed, it is born into us, a product of our infancy. In a fascinating study of *Jesus Christ Superstar,* Stephen A. Appelbaum, Senior Staff Psychologist of the Menninger Foundation, writes: "The germ of greatness exists in every man. It is instilled in his early years when he feels he is the center of the universe, when his needs are gratified by others, when the environment seems controlled by him, and when his standard achievements of growing up are hailed as if they were unique."[11]

It is natural to nurture this "germ of greatness," to cultivate its fullest growth. Success is not an aberration, it is the healthy norm, the only way in which an adult can make a significant impact on society and retain, in a pleasurable and productive way, the primal satisfaction of childhood. Yet for some, the drive to succeed is destroyed at an early age. The American system demands success, and in order to succeed we must first believe that we *can*. Yet our society, with its intolerance of failure and poverty, traps millions of people in positions where any kind of success seems impossible to contemplate, and in which failure itself is a kind of passive rebellion against their own misery and the social system which created it in the first place.

To succeed it is necessary to accept the world as it is and rise above it. For many people—and not just those who live in the urban ghettos, or the rural slums —the world as it is seems too harsh, ruthless, and dangerous to accept, and the possibility of rising above it appears almost inconceivable. Several studies of lower-middle-class attitudes have confirmed that a very high percentage of what are generally referred to as blue-collar workers believe that "women on relief and men on welfare [get] more than they deserve,"[12] and are basically shiftless and lazy; but in truth, one of the few nonviolent ways of rebelling against society is to abandon hope and sink into failure. Every American child is taught that this is the land of equal opportunity. Advertising, television and the motion pictures portray the rewards of success, at an early age we ensure that everyone understands the system. The only way of defeating the system without fighting it is to fail.

Failure is an escape, and frees us from the responsibility of succeeding—but at enormous cost. Our culture discriminates against failure far more harshly than it does against race, and ensures that failure is a progressive downward spiral. It is very hard indeed to fail and remain in place—the tendency is to sink to the bottom.

Clearly, the will to fail occurs most often among the

very poor, for whom success seems improbably difficult and who have every reason to rebel against a system which is clearly rigged against them. The Puritan belief in individual merit and hard work was not designed with a modern industrial society or a nation of 250,-000,000 people in mind, and Horatio Alger would doubtless have been dismayed by the South Bronx or Watts. The fact that we reward those who escape from poverty and rise to success is not a valid excuse for turning our backs on the real social problems of modern America.

But it is not just the poor who fail. People who are well educated, ambitious, prepared for success and *anxious* to succeed fail every day, fail primarily because they have never been taught how easy it is to succeed. They choose the wrong job, make the wrong decisions, turn away from the main chance instead of taking it, set the wrong priorities for themselves, ensure in a hundred small and large ways that they will fail. Most people can briefly summon up what Andrew Carnegie called "That persistent and concentrated energy upon which depends success," but very few people can maintain it over the long haul, or direct it toward a realistic goal. The particular combination of self-confidence, self-knowledge, energy and optimism that produces success simply eludes them. It is necessary to know when, where and how to apply the energy that each of us has within us, and to direct it very precisely where it will do the most good.

Our Puritan heritage, our restless desire to achieve, the demanding nature of our social system, the risks of sailing alone on the uncharted sea that is our own life—these are real and a part of our heritage. We must learn to accept them, and to develop that inner spark that demands the highest of us, that tells every one of us that it is better to succeed then to fail, that we are responsible for using our strengths and resources to the utmost, and that life on any other terms is a waste. A society which is built around the notion of success for the individual may be cruel, as ours often is, but it is at least free, in the sense that we are responsible for ourselves and our own choices, for everyone has the right and the *need* to succeed. In the words of one psychiatrist: "Every human being obviously wants to succeed—to realize the best of his potentials. And yet many of us clearly defeat ourselves in life."[13]

TAKE THE FIRST STEP
TO SUCCESS TODAY

If this book has taught you that the will to succeed is natural, and that success is more pleasurable than failure, you will already have taken the first step toward becoming a success. You have to want to get it, and you have to realize that if others can, so can you.

In a pessimistic age, the success-oriented person is unfashionable, an optimist, for to succeed is to believe in the future, or at least to believe in the possibility of a better one. Cities are crumbling and going into bankruptcy, the world's survival seems to hang on the whims of the Arabs, taxes are higher than ever, and poverty seemingly ineradicable—all this is true. But you can still succeed. Remember: There has *never* been any time in history when things were not more likely to promote pessimism in the thoughtful than the reverse.

For those who rely on statistics, it may be of some comfort to learn that there are over 180,000 millionaires in the United States, and two billionaires, since the deaths of Howard Hughes and J. Paul Getty. One is John D. MacArthur, who runs his insurance empire from his apartment in Singer Island, Florida, or from the coffee shop of the local hotel (which he owns and in which the waitresses act as his receptionist-secretaries). The other is Daniel K. Ludwig, who parlayed a failing tugboat fleet into a vast shipping enterprise. At the age of eighty, he is in the process of building up an agricultural empire in the Amazonian jungles, where he owns over three million acres. Among his holdings: a 175,000-acre attempt to reforest the Amazon with a tree called *Gmelina arborea* (which grows ten times faster than most trees used for pulp and lumber), a $22-million rice plantation, a town of his own, a kaolin mine and a livestock operation.[14]

The upper brackets are expanding, whatever the other problems of the country and the economy, and you owe it to yourself to move upward, if only because the rate of inflation is likely to ensure that those who don't rise, in fact fall.

You have to make your time valuable, both to yourself and to the people you work for. After all, from a corporation's point of view, your time is expensive, even if you feel you're underpaid. A recent corporate study computed the cost of maintaining its executives at various salary levels by the hour and the minute, and the results were startling:[15]

YEAR	HOUR	MINUTE
$10,000	$12.36	$0.21
$20,000	24.73	.41
$30,000	37.10	.62
$40,000	49.47	.82
$50,000	61.84	1.03

At 20,000 a year, your work time is worth $24.73 an hour—good reason not to waste it, or underrate your importance. At $50,000 a year, the time it takes to make a short telephone call costs your company over $1.00. You cannot expect to get ahead if you are not, therefore, bringing in more than a dollar's worth of business every minute. At these prices, you have to succeed if you're going to stay even, let alone rise.

The techniques of success are available, and can be mastered by most people. What is difficult to achieve is the conviction that you can and will succeed, the power to turn the daydream into reality. If you are lucky, motivation will be provided for you, as it was for me.

When I first went to work, as an assistant editor in a publishing house at $85 a week, I saw no reason why my position or salary should ever increase. I had never expected to be in the book business, and had merely taken the job becuse it was all I could find. It seemed like a reasonable occupation for a well-read Oxford B.A., whose previous "experience" included an R.A.F. service career, waiting on tables in an expresso coffee bar, free-lance TV script writing and a short stint as a water-skiing instructor. Having just married, I needed a real job, and my choices were working as a receptionist or becoming the assistant to a book publisher.

In practice, I spent my days sitting in a tiny cubbyhole which I shared with my boss's secretary, reading an endless pile of hopeless manuscripts ("the sludge pile," as it was called), and doing the menial errands that the secretary found beneath her dignity to perform. I read prodigiously—a publishing house receives at least 2,000 "unsolicited" manuscripts a year, so there was always plenty to read—and wrote long detailed reports on each manuscript. I was not yet aware that these reports were read by nobody, and that it was considered quite sufficient to write "garbage," "junk" or "poetry" on the reader's report, attach a form letter and send the manuscript back. I even got into long impassioned correspondence with the authors, thereby wasting my time and cruelly raising their hopes, or arousing their psychopathic instincts in some cases.

Nobody could deny that I was working, but I felt not the slightest connection to the company I was working for. Every morning at nine, the mailroom boy would bring me a pile of manuscripts; at nine-thirty my boss would arrive, nod to me, and closet himself with his secretary to answer his mail. At five-thirty he would nod to me on the way out, sometimes with a look of surprise, as if he had forgotten who I was or why I was there. His secretary at first resented my presence, then grew indifferent to it, since I clearly posed no threat to her.

Day by day, I sat at my desk and read. I was smart enough to see that I might enjoy publishing if I could ever get into it, but it all seemed to be taking place elsewhere, and my boss had made it clear that he did not want me wandering around the office. He expected me to stay put. And I could see that there was a lot more activity in the other parts of the office, where things seemed to be *happening,* as opposed to the humdrum monotony of my little corner. I became depressed, and took to reading the "Help Wanted" section of the *New York Times* on my lunch hour.

One morning a young man about my age walked into my corner and sat down on my desk. He picked up a report I had just written, read it and smiled. "That's not bad," he said, "but it's a waste of time. Nobody's ever going to publish any of this," he said, waving at the formidable wall of manuscripts that separated me from the secretary. "And nobody is ever going to find you here. In fact, it took me two weeks to realize that you were here, or what your name is. By the way, mine's Bob Gottlieb."

Today Bob Gottlieb is the president of Alfred A. Knopf, Inc., one of the most successful editor-publishers in the United States, as well as a board member of the New York City Ballet Company. At the time, he was a thin bedraggled-looking young man, with a fringe of hair over his forehead, thick-glassed and with a face rather like Woody Allen's, at first glance. He was smart, shrewd, energetic, didactic, but above all enormously concerned and sympathetic. You couldn't help liking him or trusting him, and though we were of roughly the same age, he seemed years older and more experienced. He was the first person who had actually *noticed* me, and I was enormously grateful.

I pointed out I found the job somewhat dreary, but not all that difficult. He sighed theatrically, and combed his fingers through his hair, making it even more disheveled.

"Don't I know it," he said. "I used to sell greeting cards at Macy's, and I thought I was doomed to that forever. Listen: I've read a lot of your reports. I read them at night when you're gone. You're good at writing reports, and you seem to know what's wrong with a book. That's good, but it's more important to know what's *right* with it. Anyway, we're going to find out. You're going to read the books we're *publishing,* and write some catalog copy, and we'll see what happens. In the meantime, *get out from behind that desk!* Get out into the office, ask questions, make friends, make a nuisance of yourself, make waves, *do* something, *learn* something. These are like the greeting cards at Macy's, they're a dead end!" With a sweeping gesture, he waved to the pile of manuscripts, as if willing them to vanish, accidentally knocking them down, to reveal the secretary on the other side, carefully polishing her nails.

"The only trouble is that I'm supposed to stay here," I said.

Bob shook his head and leaned closer to me. "You've got to make your own way," he said. "If you don't, you'd be better off having my old job at Macy's. For a start, people have got to be able to find you, to see you. Your desk faces in, so nobody can see anything but your back. I'm the first person here who has ever seen your face. You're like the Man in the Iron Mask. Pick up your end."

Together we turned my desk around to face out toward the corridor so that everybody could see me, dropping several more manuscripts on the floor in the process. When he was satisfied, Bob kicked them out of the way, glowing with the satisfaction of a man who has done a good deed. "You can be a success here," he said, "you have to believe that. If you can be a success anywhere, you can do it here. *I did,* so can you. So get cracking."

He turned and ran down the hall, eager to get back to whatever it was editors did, and which I would obviously have to learn. But he had performed the magic service of indicating to me that success was *possible,* not as a daydream, but here, now, in this place. And nothing was ever the same again.

Not everybody can be motivated and challenged by a stranger, but it lies within everybody's power to learn the art of *self*-motivation. *Will* yourself to succeed, to step out of the ranks, to make yourself over. Dare to excel, to try, to take risks, to grow. Master the techniques in this book, but apply them with enthusiasm and joy, for the road up to success, however long and hard, will lead nowhere if it isn't exciting and challenging every inch of the way. To succeed is to change, to grow, to *live.* Start living *today,* and begin by taking the first courageous step that Bob Gottlieb urged on me, twenty years ago, that Ray Kroc took when he saw his first MacDonald's hamburger, that every person who has risen has had to take—the step of deciding today, *now,* that *you too can be a success!*

In the words of St. Francis de Sales, "Do not lose courage in considering your own imperfections, but instantly set about remedying them."

Acknowledgments

I am most grateful to Vincent Virga for his brilliant help in researching the material for this book, to Lawrence P. Ashmead, John Astarita, Ronald Busch, Carlos Castaneda, Jason Epstein, Joni Evans, Paul Gitlin, Morton Janklow, Cordelia Jason, Mildred Marmur, Lynn Nesbit, Joan Sanger, Anthony M. Schulte, George T. Serban, M.D., Mortimer F. Shapiro, M.D., James H. Silberman, Nan Talese, George Walsh, Jay S. Watnick and James Wilcox for their suggestions, support and enthusiasm—and especially to Margaret Glinn, with love.

Notes

Chapter One

1 William James, *Talks to Teachers on Psychology, and to Students on Some of Life's Ideals*, 1895.

2 *New York Times*, March 2, 1974.

3 *Fortune*, May, 1976.

4 *Psychology Today*, January, 1975.

5 This traditional division has been brilliantly expanded by Michael Maccoby (in *The Gamesman*, New York, 1976), into a veritable zoo of types, but for practical purposes the analogy of lions and foxes is sufficient to describe the successful. The unsuccessful can be seen as either beasts of prey, on whom the predators feed by strength or by stealth, or carrion eaters, like the vulture and the jackal, who live off the pickings of the stronger predators. After one successful executive fulfilled a lifelong ambition by going to Africa on a camera safari, he was asked what his impressions were of the great Kenya wildlife reserves, where one can watch the lions silently hunting down the zebra and the gazelles, and the giant rhinos and elephants, like elderly chairmen of the board, crashing their way through obstacles. "It's a lot like life at ITT," he replied.

6 Max Boas and Steve Chain, *Big Mac*, New York, and Linda Young, *Time* magazine.

7 Max Boas and Steve Chain, *ibid*.

8 *New York Times*, February 22, 1976.

9 *New York Times, ibid*.

10 *New York Times, ibid*.

11 *Fortune*, May, 1976.

12 *Fortune, ibid*.

13 *New York Times*, October 1, 1975.

14 *Fortune*, October, 1976.

15 *Success* magazine.

16 *New York Times*, March 7, 1976.

17 *New York Times*, March 9, 1976.

18 *Fortune*, August, 1976.

The portraits in this chapter are either based upon personal interviews or published material from *Fortune*, the *New York Times* and *Success* magazine.

Chapter Two

1 *New York Times*, April 26, 1976.

2 *New York Times*, ibid.

3 "Executive Perquisites," *Amacom*, May, 1975.

4 Discussion draft of proposed IRS regulations on Employee Fringe Benefits, September, 1975, Treasurer's Office of Assistant Secretary for Tax Policy, 26CFR, Part I.

5 *New York Times*, June 15, 1975.

6 "Executive Perquisites," *ibid*.

7 "Relocation Policies & Practices in Major U.S. Companies," Paul R. Ray & Co., Inc., Fort Worth, Texas, October 1975.

8 *New York Times*, November 5, 1975.

9 *New York Times*, September 19, 1975.

10 *Statistical Bulletin*, Metropolitan Life, Vol. 55, February, 1974.

11 *Ibid*. Vol. 49, August, 1968.

12 *New York Times*, January 2, 1974.

Chapter Three

1 Everett Mattlin, *New York Times*, June 5, 1974.

2 Henry O. Golightly, "Success Depends on Character," *EAL* magazine.

3 Marvin R. Godfried and Michael Merbaum, "How to Control Yourself," *Psychology Today*, November, 1973.

4 Niccolò di Bernardo Machiavelli, *The Prince* (XVII).

5 Richard Christie, "The Machiavellians Among Us," *Psychology Today*, November, 1970.

6 *Ibid*.

7 Jerome L. Singer, "Fantasy," *Psychology Today*, July, 1976.

8 *Ibid*.

9 Gordon H. Bowes, "How to . . . Uh . . . Remember," *Psychology Today*, October, 1973.

10 Herbert H. Clark, "The Power of Positive Speaking," *Psychology Today*, September, 1974.

11 Philip Zimbardo, Robert M. Norwood, Paul A. Pilkonis, *Psychology Today*, May, 1975.

12 *Wall Street Journal*, March 7, 1975.

13 This theory of passing is based on a discussion with Dr. David Viscott, author of *Risking*, New York, 1977.

Chapter Five

1 *Business Week*, June 21, 1976.
2 *Ibid.*
3 *Psychology Today*, November, 1969.
4 *Business Week*, August 16, 1976.
5 *Glamour*, June, 1976.
6 *Psychology Today*, May, 1976.
7 *Ibid.*
8 *New York* magazine, May 17, 1976.

Chapter Six

1 Morton Fricdman, M.D., "Success Phobia and Retarded Ejaculation," *American Journal of Psychotherapy*, Vol. 26, no. 1, January, 1973.

2 George L. Engel, M.D., "Guilt, Pain and Success," *Psychosomatic Medicine*, Vol. xxiv, no. 1, 1962.

3 Samuel J. Warner, *Self-realization and Self-defeat*, New York, 1966.

4 Sigmund Freud, *Some Character Types Met with in Psychoanalytic Work, Collected Papers*, Vol. IV, pp. 318-344, Hogarth, London, 1949.

5 Otto Fenichel, *The Psychoanalytical Theory of Neurosis*, New York, 1945.

6 Lionel Ovesey, "Fear of Vocational Success," *Articles of General Psychiatry*, Vol. 7, no. 2, August, 1972.

7 Mark Brewer, *Psychology Today*, August, 1975.

8 I am greatly indebted to Neil Hickey for his masterly analysis of "Upward Failure" (first published in *Penthouse*), which is a classic of its kind, and deserves greater recognition.

9 Michael H. Monney, *Atlantic Monthly*, November, 1969.

10 *Harper's* magazine, December, 1957.

11 *Time,* July 20, 1962.

12 *Time,* July 20, 1962.

13 *Newsweek,* November 19, 1962.

14 *Atlantic Monthly,* November, 1969.

15 *Time,* March 12, 1965.

16 *Newsweek,* January 31, 1966.

17 Pete Martin, *Esquire,* March, 1963.

18 Pete Martin, *ibid.*

19 *Advertising Age,* October 29, 1973.

20 Murray Kempton, "The Fall of a TV Czar," *New Republic,* April 3, 1965.

21 *Time,* March 12, 1965.

22 *Business Week,* April 25, 1964.

23 Murray Kempton, *ibid.*

24 *Dun's,* January, 1973.

25 Martin Buber, *The Way of Response: Selections from His Writings,* ed. by Nahum N. Glatzer, New York, 1966, reprinted by permission.

Chapter Seven

For the background to this chapter, I am indebted to the work of Richard M. Huber, whose scholarly analysis of the history of the American success ethic, in *The American Idea of Success* (New York, 1971), is unique in its completeness, and should be read by every upward striver.

1 John Wesley, *Causes of the Inefficacy of Christianity* (Sermon CXX).

2 W. M. Thayer, *Ethics of Success,* Boston, 1881.

3 H. L. Mencken, as quoted in R. Flesch, *The Book of Unusual Quotations,* London, 1959.

4 Richard M. Watt, unpublished manuscript.

5 Russell Conwell, "Acres of Diamonds," New York, 1887.

6 Andrew Carnegie, *Triumphant Democracy,* New York, 1885.

7 George Bernard Shaw, *Major Barbara,* Act III.

8 I am indebted to Leon Shimkin, chairman of the board of Simon & Schuster, Inc., for these figures.

9 Samuel J. Warner, *Self-realization and Self-defeat,* New York, 1966.

10 Linden L. Nelson and Spencer Kagan, "Competition

—The Star Spangled Scramble," *Psychology Today*, September, 1972.

11 Stephen A. Appelbaum, "Jesus Christ Superstar," *Bulletin of the Menninger Clinic*, Vol. 36, no. 3, 1972.

12 *Fortune*, June, 1976.

13 Samuel J. Warner, *ibid.*

14 *Fortune*, November, 1976.

15 Richard R. Conarroe, "You're Working Too Hard!" *The American Way.*

About the Author

MICHAEL KORDA is the author of *Power! How to Get It, How to Use It* and *Male Chauvinism! How It Works*. He has written for several years for many national magazines, including *Glamour, New York,* and *Vogue.*